THE COUNTRY THAT DOES NOT EXIST

GÉRARD PRUNIER

The Country That Does Not Exist

A History of Somaliland

HURST & COMPANY, LONDON

First published in the United Kingdom in 2021 by
C. Hurst & Co. (Publishers) Ltd.,
41 Great Russell Street, London, WC1B 3PL
This new and updated paperback edition first published in 2026 by
C. Hurst & Co. (Publishers) Ltd.,
New Wing, Somerset House, Strand, London, WC2R 1LA
© Gérard Prunier, 2026
All rights reserved.

Printed in the United Kingdom

The right of Gérard Prunier to be identified as the author of
this publication is asserted by him in accordance with the
Copyright, Designs and Patents Act, 1988.

A Cataloguing-in-Publication data record for this book
is available from the British Library.

ISBN: 9781805264422

EU GPSR Authorised Representative
Easy Access System Europe Oü, 16879218
Address: Mustamäe tee 50, 10621, Tallinn, Estonia
Contact Details: gpsr.requests@easproject.com, +358 40 500 3575

This book is printed using paper from registered sustainable
and managed sources.

www.hurstpublishers.com

CONTENTS

PREFACE TO THE HARDBACK EDITION

A recent article on Somalia presented the country as 'the most failed state in the world', giving its subtitle as 'twenty-five years of chaos in the Horn of Africa'.[1] As a kind of polite aside, the author of the article admitted to the existence of

> 'Somali statelets operating more or less independently. Some, such as Puntland in the north, are fairly well organized. Others are little more than warlords' fiefs ... But the real prize—a Somalia with a functioning government and safe streets—seems as distant as ever.'

And yet four months before this piece had been published, I had been sitting at a café in a safe Somali street, watching the school children, the civil servants and the soldiers of a functioning Somali government all parading in celebration of the proclamation of their independence twenty-five years before. But that independence was not the independence of 'Somalia'— which took place in 1960—it was the independence of a sub-unit of that 'country' which had broken away thirty-one years later from the deadly embrace of its brothers. It had achieved peace, stability and a fair amount of democratic governance. Its press was free, it had periodic free elections, and its streets were probably the safest you could find anywhere in Africa. Although 99 per cent Muslim, it had not given birth to any radical Islamist movement, preferring to collect the garbage and balance the budget as its most serious endeavours. This 'country' is called Somaliland and, by the world's legal standards, it does not exist.

Of course, it does exist 'for real' (as children would say) and its years of struggle and sacrifice have led to the birth of a perfectly normal and rational state. But since it was born as an exception to the sacrosanct principle of 'national determination' enshrined by the Treaty of Westphalia in European diplomatic practice since 1648 and reaffirmed worldwide by the creation of the United Nations in 1945, 'Somaliland' has never been recognised as a 'real country'. Never mind that it has achieved civil peace, built up democratic institutions practically without any outside help, and then lived up to its ideals, it has remained 'a country that did not exist'.[2] Peace, stability, democracy and human rights notwithstanding, it remained ignored by the rest of the world, which was meanwhile channelling diplomatic attention, military support and a fair amount of economic aid to the rest of 'Somalia', that 'most failed state' existing in permanent chaos.

This book is about trying to understand this bizarre paradox, its cultural and historical origins, its twisted development, its dead ends and its upturns. Let's try also to understand the frustration and shame of being shunned after so many efforts and so much suffering. 'Somaliland' was born in blood and fire, and it sacrificed much to exist. Later it succeeded in avoiding the clanic civil war that mangled its surviving relatives down south, in what is today called 'Somalia'. It also avoided developing the radical Islam which is today a hall of mirrors for many unhappy Muslim communities. Its southern cousins fell headlong into radical Islam and are still battling with it today. Somaliland was both typically Somali and the odd man out as well. To say that it is a mystery would be an exaggeration but to label it an enigma is fair. It shares a religion, language, social structure, prejudices and large parts of history with the rest of Somalia. But large parts only and not all history. And this is where the answer to the paradox might lie.

But the future is threatening. The past has been violent and bloody and the danger today is that an arrested development has resulted in paralysis and could end in decomposition. The majority of human beings who exist in that land and who are, willy-nilly, 'Somalilanders' are less than twenty years old. They live in the frozen dream of their parents and, without international recognition, they now have only three options: keep stagnating; join the confused anarchy of Southern Somalia, at the 'most failed state' level; or else jump into the boiling pot of the jihadist ideology. The world has a choice, and it could help Somaliland help itself. But does the world even know that Somaliland exists? This book is about trying to retrace its birth, explain its hard choices and doubts, understand from the inside what has made it. And then it tries to chart its pattern of survival since its painful beginnings, in the hope that, once all this has been said and done, it will enhance its powers of survival.

PREFACE TO THE PAPERBACK EDITION

The hardback edition of this book was published in 2021 and since then Somaliland has still not been recognised, nor has it disappeared. It simply has done just what we hoped it would at the end of the first preface: enhance its powers of survival. Meanwhile, the US has been sniffing around Somaliland and hesitating between a friendly bark or another period of continued neglect. Rumours abound but they do not figure as a main topic in the media. While everybody knows where Kyiv is, Hargeisa has yet to surface in world news. But something did happen on the ground: on 6 February 2023, a group of armed men attacked the town of Laas Anod.

Laas Anod had a population of about 300,000. The Somaliland Army took this first organised challenge to its physical integrity very seriously and retaliated by shelling the town with heavy artillery, killing about one hundred people. By 10 February, 180,000 refugees had crossed the 'border' into the federal region of Puntland, which although legally 'part of Somalia', was in fact a quasi-independent state. But what did Puntland and Laas Anod have in common? That old nemesis of Somali culture: clans.

To make matters clear, we must restate that Somali culture does not have tribes but is subdivided into clans. They share the same language, same culture, same religion but are fiercely separate segments. The invaders—the exact numbers of which are unknown but are said to be several thousand—were mostly Dolbahante of the Majerteen clan federation. And so was the population of Laas Anod, which meant that there was a big cleavage with much of the Somaliland population that belongs to the Issaq family of clans. Again, we face the recurrent problem of clannism which turns the existence of genealogy into a permanent problem. 'Give me an enemy, I'll be your friend to fight him. If you remain my friend for too long, your next misstep will turn you into my enemy.' This exaggeration, in reality, was aimed at creating a tenth Somali state.[1] The difficulty goes back to the situation during the civil war. The Dolbahante are part of the Majerteen, i.e. a segment of the Super Clans which Somalis see themselves as being part of, while the massive Darood clan comprises about 70% of the whole Somali population.

The problem was that the dictator Siad Barre was a Darood, and so were the Dolbahante/Majerteen. But the Issaq, who were the vertebrae of Somaliland's spine, were not. Therefore, during the Civil War, the government side—ethnically-speaking—were predominantly Daroods. However, when the victorious SNM decided to draw a border, the weight of the colonial tradition carried the day. But was that so strange? I surmise not. The Somali, as a people, were a constellation of clans whose common cultural identity did not prevent a fierce genealogical particularism. Contrary to the Centralist Italians (the Roman conceptual inheritance), the British, rooted in a multicephalous tribal culture, adapted much better to Somaliness, judging it well and governing it very little once the Mad Mullah insurgency ended in 1920. Post-1918 Somalia was a Mussolinian construct[2] and Somaliland was the exact opposite. Short of a model, the SNM—long accused of being pro-Soviet when seen through its Cold War lens—reached into the British basket of tricks for a usable state model. There was no 'socialist' influence in the newborn 'Somaliland' state but a quick grab at a Somali-oriented colonial model. After all, this was the one and only practically usable state the Somali had ever known.[3]

The SNM used tried and tested patterns, including the arbitrary border with Italy that the British had chosen in 1920. Whether this adaptation of the democratic model (with its shortcomings) will eventually work is impossible to know, but the 6 February 2023 attack was simply the product of the British looking at the clan-based map of the north of the Horn of Africa at a time when colonialism was seen as the white man's burden, and a long-term horizon for the future of civilised societies, backpacking the lesser breeds towards future progress. Laughable as this picture of African societies may be to a twenty-first-century reader, one has to make an effort to reframe oneself into an archaic picture of the world which then cared very much about whether the 'British-administered' Dolbahante were Darood or another clan, once the problem with Italian partition had been solved.

The Majerteen/Dolbahante attack impacted the myth that Somaliland was—by default—a neutral democratic constitutional state. It showed itself to be an aspiring democratic state that checked several of the boxes but could no longer hide its clan-based Issaq spine. This did not make it 'bad' but did make it lopsided; the Darood attack made this state with democratic aspirations just one of many, even if it was the best. On 25 August 2023, the SSC forces occupied the Gooja'ade Somaliland Army military base.[4] Its soldiers were mostly Dolbahante and to many Somalis this looked like the beginning of the end for Somaliland.

On 25 September 2023, Yoweri Museveni, ever the standard-bearer of a tinfoil version of African democracy, offered his services as a mediator between Hargeisa and Mogadishu in a bid for reunification. Even the *Shebab*[5] started approaching various important clans, apparently thinking that the time for their brand of (re)unification of Somalia had come. Hargeisa politely turned down the Museveni offer and the *Shebab* got nowhere with their efforts. ATMIS, the African Union force which was supposed to bolster reunification or, failing that, at least to achieve some kind of peace, withdrew. Some western clans, Issa and Gaddabursi, made noises about separation and floated the idea of leaving Somaliland and rejoining a united Somalia. But when they realised the degree of confusion as well as clannic, regional and personal quarrels at play in and around Mogadishu, this testing of the political waters was short-lived. Somaliland did not look like the best option but was not the worst. Despite being a stilted democratic state, this was definitely better than the total absence of democracy elsewhere. The UN silently agreed, and on 13 November 2023, negotiated with the African Union for a renewal of ATMIS. On 1 January 2024, Ethiopian Prime Minister Abiy Ahmed offered Somaliland international recognition of its legal status as an independent state in exchange for the cession of an Ethiopian commercial-harbour-cum-military-base around Berbera.

Since then, everything has been suspended in motion: Hargeisa agreed to the deal; Mogadishu denounced it as a violation of Somalian sovereignty; and Abiy Ahmed, without renouncing the deal, made sabre-rattling noises towards the old Ethiopian harbour of Assab, now part of Eritrea. The international community, as is frequent in such cases, kept silent. The US looked on and sent a trading mission from Africa Command with a few tidbit offers. Somaliland, the country that does not exist, continues to exist in silence, just trying to enhance its powers of survival.

21 September 2025

1

A NATION IN SEARCH OF A STATE

THE SOMALI MYSTIQUE OF UNITY

Trying to understand 'the Somali' means reverting to 19th-century political philosophy. Many words—nation, country, state, people, tribe, territory, borders, sovereignty—which were later used more and more contradictorily were defined in their modern sense between 1789 and 1871, by Europeans.[1] But after Europe progressively took over the world between 1885 and 1914, it exported its legal and geopolitical definitions worldwide, in the knapsacks of its soldiers. Later, after 1945, when the triumphant Europeans were pushed aside politically by their former subjects who regained a relative autonomy,[2] this abstract vocabulary became the building blocks for the new world order set up with the creation of the United Nations. The post-1945 model, into which all colonised people would soon be inserted, was that of the post-Renaissance European model, systematised in 1648 after the first great European civil war.[3]

But of the new states emerging from the 'decolonisation process', how many could readily fit into the proposed model? Many, but not all. And the degree of adaptability of these new entities to the Procrustean bed offered them would vary from quite high (the native states such as Morocco or Thailand that predated the European conquest) to moderate, for some culturally homogeneous territories in Africa or the Arab world. Some were highly problematic for political reasons, like Spanish Sahara, South Yemen or Eritrea. Colonies of the Soviet Union (USSR) were not eligible for nationhood as they were supposed to be part of a new form of supra-national political entity, a Union of Socialist Republics. Most of the others were arbitrary pieces of territory delimited by half-forgotten colonial arrangements. Finally there was the absolute square peg in the round hole, the Somali world. The Somali nation or people, which had had a long and strongly defined existence, were probably the human group that could be considered the most inimical to defining itself in terms of the raw material of an emerging nation-state. Why was this?

The Somali social organisation

The natural environment of the Somali people is probably one of the harshest existing anywhere on Earth and over the centuries it had fostered a very original form of social organisation, the clan system. Most books about Somalia start with an introductory chapter on that topic, which varies from interesting to superficial. There is no reason to repeat another one here, especially as we have the work of I.M. Lewis as a basic guideline.[4] Lewis was challenged on points of detail by other anthropologists but his vision remains canonical to this day. What he described—and showed operating—was a gigantic puzzle of imbricated, interpenetrating and overlapping social units (*tol*, translated for lack of a better term as 'clan'; but there are others such as *qabila*, *jilib*, all with slightly different connotations and no agreed meaning), making a huge human mosaic that anthropologists define as 'a system of agnatic[5] kinship'. The Somali, who tend to have a preference for strong individualism, often discuss the name or nature of the sub-units composing the mosaic. But they seldom discuss the relevance of the whole.[6] In this case, the meaning of the word 'clan' has to be taken in a strong sense. It is not some kind of loose grouping of people with like-minded interests. Nor is it the grouping of animist cults of people who are supposed to be descended from a mythical animal ancestor (the fish clan or the locust clan). It is a fantasised form of genealogy whereby a mythical human common ancestor—and his subsequent descendants—have created a 'total lineage' system binding strands of human beings into forms of agnatic solidarity that compete with each other.

This 'clanic' system is very different from tribalism. Tribes ('ethnic groups', if we defer to the proper, politically correct vocabulary of the early 21st century) are in fact small nations. They have many of the characteristics of nations, such as a common language, a historical memory, at times forms of positive and negative racism, a shared territory, often strongly defined cultural traits that set them apart from their neighbours; and before the introduction of monotheistic religions, they had tribal cults (called 'animism' in older ethnological books) that defined a specific religious view of the world. But none of that is true of clans. Clans are social sub-units that are not cultural, linguistic or religious. All Somali have the same culture, the same language and the same religion, both originally before Islam came and later within the boundaries of the Muslim worldview. Clans are the segmentary sub-units of a broader unified culture. In common speech (and this is particularly the case in Djibouti where the French language has had a strong invasive impact on the local Somali culture), the Somali themselves speak of their clans as 'tribes' and talk of 'tribalism' instead of clanism. This is incorrect but still commonly used in ordinary speech.

But why did this very peculiar social structure develop initially within a broad human group? We can only guess. In a large ethnic group such as the Somali the problems of priority, sharing (or grabbing) limited resources, fighting or cooperating were primordial. Pasture, wells, women and cattle were essential factors in group survival. Rules had to be developed to define how to deal with them—and with the violence that went with the conflicts they bred. The vast Somali nation chose to parse the ties of solidarity or dislike along the lines of a fantasised genealogy. In an environment where year-round drought tended to scale all nomadic human contacts either up into cooperation or down into conflict, belonging to a clan was a guarantee of support, a pooling of resources, an alliance against enemies and a reference point to deal with the consequences. It was the nomad's marker, his identity badge, his insurance policy.[7] Clans intermarried, traded with each other, fought, stole each other's camels, wrongfully occupied their neighbours' water holes, evacuated them when circumstances drove them out, and, in all cases, behaved as a solidarity group, for better or for worse. This was the framework of their world.

In such a world the state was not only something irrelevant, it was an annoyance and, at worst, an instrument for obstruction and oppression. It was something for sedentary peasants (such as the Abyssinians) or trading city-dwellers (such as the Turks). In any case it was something only fit for inferior people who were the subjects of a ruler. The Somali were not subjects and they had no rulers. They were free and their clans were the physical embodiments of that freedom. The Somali bush was like the sea and the camel herders were its sailors. In the pre-colonial world, their fellow nomads were the Nilotic Africans, the Sahelian Tuareg, the pre-Islamic Arabs or, very far away, the Mongols and the Plains Indians of North America. None had a state and none wanted one. When a state came, it was foreign and it was immediately perceived as an imposition. On the coast of the Indian Ocean, the inclusion of the Somali harbours in the Swahili long-distance trade between Africa and Asia gave birth to maritime 'Somali' city-states. In fact these trading cities were multicultural and the Somali were only one segment of the population. The rest were mostly Swahili and Arabs, with black Africans, Egyptians, Persians and probably a smattering of Europeans (Byzantines) and Asians (Indians, Malays) as subjects. Their 'rulers' were a cross between traders and soldiers of fortune and were called by the Arabic title 'Sultan'. But these were not really 'states' since their territory barely spread twenty miles inland. Some sultanates later took root locally and became more 'Somali' in the 19th century, but their territorial influence never spread very far from the coast.[8]

Why was there such incompatibility between the clan system and the state? First of all, the basic Somali culture was nomadic, i.e. a culture of movement where the accumulation of economic surplus value was unlikely. 'Wealth' meant a lot of camels and since camels eat grass, only a limited number could be kept at any given place at the same time without reaching a dangerous level of overgrazing. Settled people were foreigners, or at least their mode of living was foreign, and even Somali who were city-dwellers lived like foreigners and were seen as foreigners. The clan was adapted to camel nomadism but it was dysfunctional for settled commercial living. It was designed to give a man support in his herder's life, to guarantee that he would never be alone and to provide him with automatic allies. In order to root this genealogical network into flesh-and-blood people, children started to learn their family tree as soon as they could talk and began to memorise it at around the age of three. They learned it from their mothers, by heart.[9] Within that sphere, every man was just as good as any other, there were no born leaders and there were no born servants. It was rough and hard to master, but it was also fiercely egalitarian and democratic, almost to the point of anarchy. In many ways, it divided the world into friends and (potential) foes. But it was a poor predisposition for the hierarchy, organisation, specialisation and authority of a state structure. As a result the Somali never developed one in the full sense of the word, and this at a time when Europe was bristling with increasingly imperialistic states. The face-to-face encounter was going to be unfortunate.

The Somali and the outside world:

An unhappy misfit

Nobody wanted to colonise the Somali-populated areas, which had almost nothing to offer that could be looted or exploited. As a result, the reasons which led to foreign occupation were exogenous. The first European power to enter the Horn was France when, after the 1859 murder in Tadjourah of one of its citizens, the merchant Henri Lambert, Paris dispatched a small mission. Actually, the real motivation of that power encroachment had little to do with the Somali region and everything to do with the occupation of the harbour of Aden, at the tip of Arabia, by British forces in 1839. Aden had practically no local food supplies and the British began crossing the Red Sea to purchase sheep on the Somali shore. During the first half of the 19th century, a French presence had been dominant in Egypt and Napoleon III had recently agreed to support the French diplomat and engineer Ferdinand de Lesseps, who started working on the Suez Canal in that same year, 1859. But France had no territorial presence in Eastern Africa and, given the weak state of the Egyptian monarchy,[10] it had to engage in an increasingly tight power struggle around the canal. The future of an independent Egypt looked increasingly doubtful and Paris wanted to check British expansion in the Red Sea. All the more so since Italy, the youngest of the European nation-states, wanted to acquire what was at the time a badge of membership in the Great Powers club, a colonial empire. It had already begun by annexing the northernmost region of Ethiopia, Eritrea. From there its ambitions were growing apace along the Red Sea shores. The motivations and expansion scenarios of the other powers were equally varied. Between 1884 and 1889, the north-east African colonial race evolved thus:

- France occupied a small colonial outpost at Obock on the northern shore of the Gulf of Tadjourah.
- The British started buying shares in the Suez Canal Company after the defeat of the French Army in the war with Prussia in 1871 destroyed French imperial ambitions in Egypt.
- The Ethiopians, who feared that the European expansion might be aimed at colonising them, occupied the Somali-populated Ogaden region in 1887 to prevent either the British or the Italians from doing so.
- The British started to occupy the Somali shore across from Aden in 1888 to feed their Aden colony.
- The Italians occupied the Red Sea shore southwards from Massawa, with British encouragement. By reaching southern Dankalia, the Italians blocked the French expansion northwards, catching French Somaliland in a vice between their colony of Eritrea and British Somaliland.
- By 1889, the whole of Somali territory was in European or Abyssinian hands. The 'statist' societies had crushed the non-state one.

Did it mean that those foreigners had 'occupied Somalia'? Definitely not, since such a country did not exist and had never existed. But did it mean that they had colonised the Somali people? Of course yes, and the Somali felt it keenly. And this is the origin of the present paradox we are beginning to examine. As discussed earlier, the Somali social model is clanic, i.e. non-hierarchical, non-state-oriented and democratic to the point of verging on anarchy. But it is also highly conscious of itself, highly conscious of its specificity and of its cultural unity; it is proud and easily offended. After a decade of growing occupation, it began to realise that an ironclad network of culturally foreign invaders, who looked at the Somali mostly as a nuisance, had locked the space and its uses in ways that were basically inimical to it. Worse, those foreigners were so deeply involved in their own statist power games that they devoted much more time undercutting each other's strategies than being nasty to those they had colonised. This was the ultimate insult. The Somali began being conscious of themselves as having been dismembered without even having the time to state their existence in the new 'modern' paradigms that the foreigners had brought along with them to define the conditions of a legitimate international existence. The Somali non-state had been surgically erased because it had no territoriality or forms of identifiable governance; it only had a culture, at a time when that word had not yet acquired the high status it has today and at a time when 'native cultures' were seen as quaint and barbaric. 'Culture' of the lower races had a low status and could not be considered as a political base for a state. So the Somali non-state had lost the territory that belonged to it but that it never 'controlled', and had seen it pass into the hands of those who now controlled it without ever having owned it.

In any case, what was that territory? By 1889 it was cut into five different pieces belonging to four different foreign powers. None of the pieces was geographically coherent. None was clanically solid. But they were each a part of something that had no name although it had a strong presence. This was the heart of the matter: could the consciousness of existing be enough even if this existence was labelled with the wrong stamp? Was the unity stamp more important than the variegated realities it covered? Being culturally Somali was real even if this reality was wrapped up in the wrong package. But then, what should the package be? Hence the reason for the greatest living Somali writer, Nuruddin Farah, to call his most famous novel *Maps*.[11] The interplay between culture, state governance and geography has been at the heart of the Somali tragedy from the day that the people came into contact with statist societies. But since Somali are fast learners, they quickly developed a reactive form of protection by creating and fostering their own nationalism.[12] As we will see, this complicated the problem rather than contributing to solving it.

But 'nationalism' was a trendy catchword; and when it developed during the late colonial period, since it had no history, tradition or past state existence, it had to play to the hilt the one trump that nobody could deny: its cultural homogeneity. As a result, this cultural homogeneity began to grow into a kind of quasi-mystical political view, the bonding and unification of the various separated Somali-populated territories, called pan-Somalism and embodied in the Greater Somalia concept, becoming almost an article of faith. There was a Côte Française des Somalis, a British Somaliland, an Ogaden province which was fictitiously considered to be 'an integral part of Ethiopia',[13] a Somalia Italiana which the 1941 defeat of Fascist Italy turned into a UN trusteeship that was leased back to the former colonial master in 1950 and, finally, a piece of Somali territory added to the Kenya Colony in 1926 after negotiations with Mussolini which went under the name of the Northern Frontier District (NFD). All this was supposed to be 'Greater Somalia', thrust into existence by a culture which was fantasised as a monolith but which splintered before it was even born due to clanic division. This resulted in a kind of cultural schizophrenia in which unconditional unity was raised to the level of a supreme ideology while everyday life remained, as it had always been, driven and organised by splintered clan behaviour. When Ali Jimale Ahmed dared call an analytical book *The Invention of Somalia*, he breached the new modern taboo,[14] which could be articulated thus:

- There was, and there had long been, a coherent nationalism in Somalia.
- The Somali were a separate race.
- Somali were not 'negroes' but 'Arabs with a tan'.[15] Ali Jimale had the courage to note that the common use of a word like *jareer* (kinky hair) to talk about black Africans pointed to a native racism, which had developed independently of the Europeans.[16]
- Mohamed Abdulle Hassan, the anti-foreign leader of the late 19th century, had been a proto-nationalist.[17]
- Prior to the arrival of the Europeans, there was a national oral literature[18] which was the linguistic underpinning of nationalism.

Jimale's challenge to that dominant historical and cultural creed was launched prior to the 1991 disintegration of Somalia, but when the disintegration did happen, it brought a strong reinforcement to his maverick approach. The problem was what Basil Davidson aptly called 'the curse of the nation-state',[19] and its application to a (too) clever culture which was more than willing to bend over backwards in order to fit the European Procrustean bed. The Somali not only invented their nationalism but they inflated it, calling for the 'reunification of all Somali territories' (which had never been unified) and the ultimate creation of a 'Greater Somalia'. The problem was that this 'Greater Somalia' would have to be cobbled together from various external sources in its freedom drive and then kept together with its clanically fragmented common ground lest it exploded. This was why, of all the existing African states, Somalia was the only one to refuse to sign the Organisation of African Unity (OAU) Charter in May 1963. The reason was article 4b, which enshrined respect for the borders resulting from the colonial division of the continent; this was unacceptable to the Somali, who, at the time, were in the process of uniting two of the five pieces of their mystical 'Greater Somalia', British Somaliland and Somalia Italiana. For Somali nationalists, the three other pieces all had to come together in due course.

The hazardous road towards Greater Somalia

From Côte Française des Somalis to the Djibouti Republic

The four colonial powers had very varied policies and attitudes towards their Somali dominions. The French were, in a way, the most straightforward because, after they built the Suez Canal and then lost the race for controlling it, they largely gave up interest.[20] Even during the two world wars, their 'fortress' and 'impregnable maritime base' played no role at all. It was only during the French war in Indochina (1946–54) that it briefly acquired some use as a transshipment and refuelling harbour. Strangely enough, France was to be the last European power to release its piece of Somalia. The reasons were not geopolitical, but sentimental and financial. Sentimentally, Djibouti was one of those romantic places in the French colonies, the kind of 'Beau Geste' territory with French Foreign Legion outposts ready for filming a Jean Gabin or Gary Cooper movie.[21] Practically all French writers who dealt with the colonies went through Djibouti and wrote something about it. At the other end of the spectrum, Djibouti was also a juicy plum for the posting of French Army personnel.[22] Ever since France lost the war in 1940, it had a problem with its army: the split between Vichy and de Gaulle leading to an undeclared French civil war, then later the Dien Bien Phu defeat (1954) and finally the Algerian crucible. This saw a coup overthrowing the Paris government and the return of de Gaulle to power on the back of an army that later mutinied against him and tried to kill him when he decided to leave Algeria anyway. Djibouti was a safety valve for the French Army, a place to play, to bask in romantic memories and to make money. The special bonuses given to the officers and men were comfortable and, added to a bit of 'creative' procurement or real estate manipulation, could considerably improve retirement conditions.

As a result Paris, which did not want to aggravate its army, stayed on in Djibouti till 1977, more than fifteen years after it had left its other African colonies. The belated decolonisation process was a kind of stop-go process, with tame elections and polite political debates alternating with periods of terrorist attacks, riots, kidnappings of children, and the probable assassination of the main pro-independence leader, Mahmood Harbi.[23] This led to the independence of a half-Somali, half-Afar territory on 27 June 1977 and the setting up of a one-party state on the African model prevailing at the time The new state was an extreme example of the 'Françafrique' model and remained for years overly militarised as a French Army base, even earning in French politics the nickname of 'the Khaki State'. Apart from that niche situation in post-colonial politics, the Djibouti Republic disappeared from the political record and became a place that figured only in maritime statistics.[24]

British Somaliland

British Somaliland was the most uncomplicated and peaceful of the Somali territories, even though it did not start that way. As discussed, the British presence in Somaliland was an offshoot of the occupation of Aden on the other side of the Red Sea. London first occupied the African shore purely to obtain meat—the famed *berberawi* fat-tailed sheep—and then later, when 'east of Suez' became the byword for Empire, it turned into a (minor) link in the imperial chain connecting India to the metropolis. The occupation was at first difficult since some of the local clans—mostly Ogadeni and Dhulbahante—supported a religious *fiki* (preacher), *Sayyid* Mohamed Abdulle Hassan, nicknamed 'the Mad Mullah'. But the British relied on the support of the Issaq clan family, which was strongly opposed to the Ogadeni and the Dhulbahante. The war started in 1899 and lasted till the Sayyid eventually died of the Spanish flu in 1920.[25]

After such a stormy beginning, it is remarkable that the further history of the Protectorate was of such dullness that its history was not written as a coherent chronicle till very recently.[26] The author, very sensibly, decided to start his account in 1920, when the Darwish war had come to an end. And the next forty years, with the brief interlude of the Italian occupation (1940–1), saw the deployment of an original colonial policy. It was original but simple: do as little as you can and do not stray far from what seem to be the most logical decisions given the local conditions. Therefore, the British in Somalia, contrary to the French, the Italians and even the Ethiopians, never tried to improve the Somali or even get them to conform to any preconceived notion that would be foreign to them and their culture. The writer Gerald Hanley, who had served in the King's African Rifles during the Somalia Italiana 1941 campaign, reports a remark from his native adjutant whom he asked what would be his ideal political condition after the war: 'I want to be well-governed ... and to be left alone.'[27] In British Somaliland during the colonial years, the British almost achieved that prodigious policy paradox.

How did the British achieve that near-perfect handling of the difficult Somali? Mostly by harmonising their concept of British common law with the Somali customary law called *Xeer*. The British Somaliland administration was the Cinderella of the British Empire, with the lowest pay scale of any territory for its employees. But its minimalist administration was conducted in line with the most essential element of Somali culture, its clanic laws. They were *tol wa tolaane*, the tie that binds, the very stuff of Somali social cohesion, a form of harmony that came from conflicts squarely faced and from justice well administered. So it is not surprising that the first Somali political party, the Somali Youth League (SYL), although created in Mogadishu, was born in 1943, during the period of British occupation and of British political influence. Four of the five clan families were represented among the members of the initial party directorate and they duly refused to disclose their clan memberships. In a way this was a triumph for British political universalism locally applied but it was short-lived. Since the SYL was largely 'southern', it created a British Somaliland branch called the Somali National League (SNL) in Hargeisa. Within a year, SNL and SYL were at daggers drawn because SNL was essentially Issaq while SYL had a majority membership made up of Darood and Hawiye. They were already far from the initial anti-clanic impulse of the first SYL.

Ex-Somalia Italiana

Italy had to undertake a complex procedure of indirectly decolonising its part of the Somali territories. This was because it lost them militarily as early as 1941 and because it was embroiled in the incredibly complicated process of trying to deal with the colonial empire of a country which had started the war as an Axis partner and finished it as a second-tier member of the victorious Allies.[28] Italy had been officially eliminated immediately after its 1941 military defeat. But it returned through the back door in April 1950 when, as a result of a UN resolution, the former Italian colony was handed back to its former masters under the name of Amministrazione Fiduciaria Italiana della Somalia (AFIS). Like those concerning Libya and Eritrea, this UN decision was a mistake. Colonialism had played a very different role for Italy from that of the French or the British. In the years between its birth and the beginning of the First World War, Italy felt weak and newborn in a world dominated by older and stronger European powers. Italy did not so much want to benefit from its domination but wanted first and foremost to feel it was respected. Colonisation, contrary to what it meant in Paris or London, was needed in Rome for existential reasons.[29] This resulted in Italian colonialism being economically illogical (it was driven by prestige, not profitability), culturally self-centred and too militarily conscious. This unstable state of affairs was not improved by the advent of Fascism in 1922. A quick survey of Rome's three colonies showed that, apart from Eritrea, *la colonia primogenita* (the first-born colony), the two others were colonies in name only. A pre-1922 survey showed that barely half of Somalia Italiana's theoretical territory was actually controlled by Italian military power.[30]

Mussolini decided to retake full control of the whole territory, and the man he chose for this task was the extremely brutal Cesare Maria de Vecchi, a founding member of the Fascist Party and a leader of the March on Rome. He was Governor from 1923 to 1928 and launched the (re)conquest of the northern protectorates of Obbia and the Migiurtina, where he tried to develop 'a truly Fascist colonization system'. His policies still have consequences today inasmuch as he eradicated the elders (Garad, Nabadoon), who were the peace agents, because they stood in the way of direct, vertical, authoritarian administration. Since the Somali had been perennially at war, they had a long experience in peacemaking, even if Somali peace was, by definition, something temporary. But De Vecchi annihilated the men who were the potential peacemakers because all he wanted was a victorious war. And, even worse, he disenfranchised them even in the areas that were outside the zones of military operations.[31] In the end, even Mussolini got tired of his violence and brought him back to Italy, commenting: '*Questo uomo ha una fama di macellaio*' (This man has the reputation of a butcher).

This is one of the reasons why bringing back the men who had been associated with such a 'colonial' regime was, to say the least, imprudent for the UN after 1950. Even if they had not been personally responsible for violent excesses, such men shared the same values and the same worldview. They were used to operating in the Somali world against the Somali and they dispensed with everything the Somali had developed over the centuries that enabled them to deal with the most difficult and questionable aspects of their culture, such as war and clanism. Right up to the end of the period in 1960, AFIS officials kept dealing in an obsolete rhetoric which sounded like something carried over from the 1920s into the contemporary world. It was one of the main features that differentiated the southern Italian territories from British Somaliland and that later helped to explain both the failure of unity in 1960 and the rebirth of Somaliland in 1991.[32]

Kenya's Northern Frontier District

This territory was a by-product of a late colonial readjustment. In 1926, in order to please Benito Mussolini and reward Italy for siding with the Allies in 1915, the British government decided to assign a part of the north-eastern region of Kenya to Italy. What remained on the British side became the so-called Northern Frontier District (NFD) of Kenya and, in 1960, when Great Britain was about to grant independence to British Somaliland, London made an official declaration calling for the unification of all Somali-speaking territories.[33] The 1960 declaration was the hurried expression of an intention to fulfil the promise of 1946. But in the meantime the situation of Britain had changed considerably, from that of a 'great power' emerging victorious from the Second World War, to that of an exhausted imperial power now in global retreat all over its former Empire. This meant that decisions taken did not belong exclusively to the British themselves but had now to be shared with the emerging 'native' governments. And these soon displayed imperialisms of their own, which neatly fitted into those of the departing colonialists, 'African unity' notwithstanding. During the Lancaster House conference of 1962, Jomo Kenyatta gave strict instructions to the Kenyan delegation not to agree to any partition of territory and any cession to the newborn Somali state. But the British organised a referendum anyway and the NFD 'split from Kenya' came way ahead of the 'stay in Kenya' option in the referendum results. Since it was too late to include the results of the referendum in the Lancaster House debates,[34] Kenya became independent with its 1926 boundary. An insurrection immediately broke out. Called the Shifta[35] War, it was to last till 1967 and cause great violence in north-eastern Kenya, where thousands of civilians were murdered by the Kenyan Army under the guise of counterinsurgency operations. This was the situation denounced by the British anti-colonial author Lord Lytton.[36]

The Ethiopian Ogaden province

This last colonised part of the Somali territory was special in that its coloniser was not European. The conquest of the Ogaden started after the battle of Chelenqo (6 January 1887) in which the Kingdom of Shoa occupied the Sultanate of Harar. This occupation was peculiar in that the occupying power was not 'Ethiopia' but one of its sub-states. Shoa, under King Menelik, was a feudal vassal state of Abyssinia, which was ruled at the time by *Negus Negussie* Yohannes IV, King of Tigray. Why did Menelik pursue an independent military conquest of a neighbouring Muslim statelet? The reason was that Egypt, the regional hegemonic power which had occupied Harar for the previous ten years, was in a crisis and had been compelled to abandon it. Egypt was a sub-unit of the Ottoman Empire and, since the conquest of the Sudan in 1821, had built a large African empire of its own, independent from Istanbul. This colonised territory broke out in rebellion in 1880 and Egypt, which had over-spent its imperial resources in accelerated modernisation,[37] found itself sandwiched between an exploding military budget and an overstretched debt crisis. It was forced to shrink and abandoned many occupied territories, among them Harar and its Somali hinterland. Given that this was taking place shortly after the Berlin Conference, at a time when European imperialism was rabidly on the rise, the Egyptian withdrawal had to be replaced by somebody else's expansion. There were plenty of potential takers: Great Britain, France and Italy in the first rank, followed by less likely outsiders such as the Ottoman Empire, Germany and Russia. Abyssinia, which was first at risk, was unable to react because its political core, Tigray, was threatened from Eritrea by the Italians and from Sudan by the Mahdists. Emperor Yohannes thus had his hands full. But not so Menelik, the King of Shoa, who let Yohannes take the brunt of other threats and kept a large, well-equipped standing army of 20,000 men for his own use.

Menelik invaded the Harar Sultanate in order to prevent a European (or Ottoman) move from the Red Sea coast. He was extremely lucky in having a remarkable general, Ras Makonnen, who took part in the conquest and then was made Governor of the new territory. Almost immediately (1888), Makonnen started to push southwards and eastwards, to expand Shoan and later Ethiopian rule.[38] Harar, and its loose vassal of the Ogaden territory, had no clear boundaries. Makonnen knew that his main task was to control at least superficially the area but, even more, to push Ethiopian domination as far away from the Abyssinian Highlands as it was possible, so as to keep the European imperialists at bay. The French were not much of a problem—they had no real ambitions away from the Red Sea coast and preferred commerce[39]—but both Italy and Great Britain were the main dangers. Given their lack of central political structure, the Somali were seen as relatively easy to control. The Ogaden was used as a buffer territory giving strategic depth for the protection of what was truly Ethiopian: the Highlands. Consequently, what mattered for Addis Ababa was not 'colonisation' but securitisation. There was nothing to exploit in Ethiopian Somalia; it was only a protective space. The Italians eventually invaded it in 1935, but after Ethiopia had been freed from Mussolini's armies by the British in 1941, it had a difficult time freeing itself from its liberators when they almost started colonising what they had just liberated. In order to do that, they used the Somali territory as a hinge to close a door on the east, staying for thirteen years after the war, till their evacuation of the Hawd in 1954.[40] Twice again—in 1964 and 1977—Ogaden became a battlefield, but this time the 'invaders' (liberators?) were Somali. In all these years, Ethiopia never looked at the Ogaden for itself and in itself, but always considered it as some kind of prosthesis strapped to its side, enabling it to extend its protective reach far away from its 'real' borders.

* * *

What did all this mean for the Somali world at the end of the colonisation period? Actually, a great deal of confusion. 'The Somali world' was an existential experience, not a nation-state ready to spring up as soon as the colonisers withdrew. It was a living experience but a very strong one indeed. Its problem—and its resulting myth-making—was its division between five separate locales. This splintering was quite real and its reality became an obsession among its subjects. Given the deep feeling of cultural unity between all Somalis and the massive alienation caused by colonial rule, it was that manipulation by the colonisers which in itself was seen as the major problem of the Somali world. Let us unite and the land of milk and honey will open its wonderful vistas to our eyes. 'Unity' was not seen as a target with its difficulties and its doubts, its imprecise hopes and foggy horizons. Unity was all good, it was the magical antidote to colonial humiliation, the shining star at the end of the road. The disunity factors, be they clanic politics, regional differences or the impact of many years of dissimilar foreign administrations, were all neglected in the enthusiastic road towards the national ideal.

The year of reckoning was 1960. In its first piece about Somalia, the future *Africa Confidential* rhapsodised: 'On July 1st Somalia will join the ranks of the newly independent African nations, much better prepared and equipped for independence than most of them ... No internal tensions, no foreign influences ... intertribal [*sic*] clashes which used to result in hundreds killed, are a thing of the past.'[41] In hindsight, this upbeat diagnosis is easy to criticise. But we need to keep the then unseen heart of the problem clearly in sight: the contradiction between the territory and the state, the cleavage between the clans and the nation. Foreigners implicitly agreed with the Somali themselves in regarding the name 'Somali' as a kind of magical unity-maker, the 'natural' root of a nation-state. The only problem seemed to be how to disentangle the overlapping foreign imperial markers. The *Africa Confidential* article stated: 'At the Somaliland Conference taking place in London this week, the Secretary of State has a difficult problem ... concerning the amalgamation [of Somalia and Somaliland].' Fifty-eight years and hundreds of thousands of dead bodies later, a series of conferences have not yet managed to solve the 'difficult problem'. But they are still trying, albeit with much diminished enthusiasm.

2

UNITED WE FALL

SOMALIA FROM INDEPENDENCE TO CIVIL WAR

The first phase of Somalia's unification

The Somali 'question', or rather the Somali 'dispute', was at the heart of the Somali decolonisation process.[1] Given the fact that almost none of the African borders were the product of native state-building processes[2] and that almost all had been engineered and discussed over the heads of their populations, the limited number of territorial quarrels among the newly decolonised states was remarkable. The Somali world was by far the biggest exception and the Somali Republic was the only state on the continent that refused to sign the OAU Charter when that pan-African organisation was created in 1963 at the behest of Emperor Haile Selassie.[3]

In a way, the main challengers of the colonial status quo were, paradoxically, the British themselves. Due to the unpredictability of war, by 1945 the British armies had found themselves in de facto control of almost 98 per cent of the territories that made up the Somali world (except French Somaliland). At the same time, in spite of Winston Churchill's glorious wartime performance, the Conservatives lost the July 1945 general election and the new Labour government under Clement Attlee gave the Foreign Office to Ernest Bevin. Bevin was extremely pragmatic,[4] and he thought that colonial problems were at the forefront of his responsibilities (he was the promoter of

17

independence for Ceylon, Burma and the Indian Raj). Looking at the nature of the Somali world, he tried to leverage Britain's military control into a process of national unification, which he proposed to the British parliament on 4 June 1946. His effort seemed supported when, on 15 December 1950, the new United Nations voted in favour of putting Somalia under UN trusteeship as a first step towards that end. But this was too hopeful a view, one which did not seriously take into account the variety of conflicting regional interests which would eventually lead to 'the betrayal of the Somalis'.[5] The first breach in Bevin's Somali unity plan came on 29 November 1954 when the British government led by Anthony Eden renegotiated the 1944 Agreement between the British Military Administration and Emperor Haile Selassie, replacing British military control with 'full and exclusive sovereignty of Ethiopia over the Hawd and Reserved Area'.[6] In the short run, this placed Ethiopia not only in the position of an equal partner but also in that of an arbiter of the 'Somali question'. When the question of the independence of Somalia was raised while trying to apply the 29 November Agreement, the Emperor declared with a poker face: 'As to rumours of a Greater Somalia, we consider that all the Somali peoples are economically linked with all Ethiopia and, therefore we do not believe that such a state can be viable standing alone, separated from Ethiopia.'[7] This was a bold claim indeed: from being only one of the actors in the spatial division of the Somali world, the Ethiopian monarch claimed that its only possible independent existence—if one could say that—lay in being annexed by Ethiopia.

The pronouncement was bold but massively counterproductive, as Somali political consciousness was spurred by this daring statement into a brusque intensification of unitary demands. These had been championed so far by an organisation sponsored by the British Military Administration in the south in 1943. This organisation—the Somali Youth Club, soon renamed the Somali Youth League (SYL)—had initially been encouraged by the British, who saw it as an anti-Italian element. But it soon emancipated itself from its British sponsors and grew into a broad nationalist movement. It was multiclanic but its main membership was Darood and Hawiye and, in spite of its common nationalist or unitarian outlook, in the north it developed into a separate movement, the Somali National League (SNL), with a distinct Issaq clanic base. Both SNL and SYL had the unity of the Somali world as the main political target, but in the meantime they could not cohabit the same political organisation, which was typical of Somali culture and a portent of things to come.

Many of the Greater Somalia 'ideals' were reactive—independence from colonialism, keeping Ethiopian imperialism at arm's length—or transcendental: strive towards modernity, bask in the lyrical warmth of shared cultural values, assert Somali uniqueness. But there was no reflection on administrative or constitutional principles, no suggestion of how to deal with the clanic threat to the state, no clear views of the Cold War conundrum which split the region,[8] and, perhaps worst of all, no idea of how to breach the gap created over the years by contradictory forms of introduction to Western modernity, depending on the colony. In line with the idealised idea of a homogeneous unitary culture as a base for the future state, the SYL favoured a strongly centralised form of administration. The notion that some form of decentralisation or federalism might accommodate the future state better was often dismissed out of hand. This deepened the gap between the 'great' clan families—Hawiye, Darood, Majerteen and Issaq, who were all camel nomads—and the 'marginal' Digil-Mirifle clan family[9] and its surrounding Bantu bondsmen, who were agriculturists. The Digil-Mirifle, uneasy with the Hawiye–Darood domination, had regrouped in a distinct party, the so-called Hizbia Dastur Mustaqil Somali (Somali Independent Constitutional Party, or HDMS). But the demographic weight, political prestige and organisation of SYL gave it a wide electoral victory in 1959. This resulted in a groundswell that went beyond victory, as many HDMS MPs immediately abandoned their party to join the SYL ranks. The final tally gave an almost single-party coloration to the parliament. This led to the contradictions that would have normally existed between government and opposition being transposed within the government itself, making it rather difficult to operate as a single coherent unit.

But as this developed in the south, the northern British Somaliland Protectorate rushed headlong into the unification programme that had been proffered as a popular goal by the SNL. On 6 April 1960 the Legislative Council, with the unanimous support of all its elected members, passed a resolution calling for immediate independence and union with Somalia; the motion requested that the date of independence and unification 'must be July 1st 1960, the date when Somalia will attain its full freedom'. The Protectorate administration, which had hoped to gain time for further developments and preparation, was left to make the necessary precipitate arrangements. British Somaliland became independent on 26 June 1960 and on 1 July Somalia followed suit, the two territories uniting forthwith as a single Republic. This four-day passage into total independence is today the basis for Somaliland's claim to full sovereign status, arguing that what one government freely decided can later be freely undone by another government. In addition, the Atto di Unione drafted in Mogadishu was never confirmed in Hargeisa, and the Somalia and Somaliland Unity Law was never voted by the southern parliament.[10]

During his 1998 trip to France, I took the opportunity to ask Mohamed Ibrahim Egal, then President of 'independent' Somaliland who had been head of the unity delegation to Mogadishu on 1 July 1960, how he felt when he signed the merger document: 'Happy and enthusiastic. That was the stupidest thing I had ever done in my life, but I was sure at that moment that it was the best and most progressive thing that I should do. I had years later to regret it. Now could we please talk about something else?' This is interesting because three years after this conversation, Somaliland nationalist leader Abdirahman Awale would venture exactly the opposite opinion about Egal: 'When he says he is for independence, it is for local consumption only. He tells the people here one thing but in his speeches elsewhere he has clearly declared that Somalia will unite one day ... He says one thing to the public and a different thing to the international community.'[11] What did Egal really think? Perhaps none of the above. Contradictions are the perfect expression of a Somali statesman's thought. The merger between the British and Italian colonies had been mostly an ideological and emotional thing, while the practicalities had been seen as secondary, a very Somali way of looking at politics. Unfortunately, reality is made of sterner stuff.

Two into one hardly go; five into one don't go at all

Right from the beginning, the merging of the two separate colonies created major problems. First, there were large structural discrepancies that had never been addressed: from 1950 onwards, AFIS had planned a course towards independence within ten years, as recommended by the UN resolution. But not so in the north where the British, whose government seemed to support a union of all Somali territories, were at the same time quite negligent in preparing their own Protectorate for any kind of independence, unitary or separate. AFIS accelerated the training of civil servants in the south while very little was done in the north. Given the fact that the demographic balance was extremely uneven (the north had barely a quarter of the total Somali population),[12] this difference in training levels gave a massive advantage to southerners.

In parliament, nobody paid attention to the fact that since we had had different administrations and that those of the Italian part were pledged ten years before we got independence, their people were trained and they had diplomas in political science; in contrast, our people were not even prepared to learn the protocols, the public service and even basic governance ... Mohamed Haji Ibrahim Egal was almost the only one who had a full university education, he had enrolled as a student in 1943, been sent to England and taken a diploma in business administration. Most MPs were just people, 50 or 60 years old, running little businesses such as shops or garages, with no literacy; there were also three seamen who had seen some of the world but they could not read and write well, even if they identified themselves as civilised.[13]

But when SYL leader Abdirizak Haji Hussein became Prime Minister in 1963, 'he transferred many officials from the north to Mogadishu. Hence many senior officials, especially the accountants and auditors, were from the north.'[14] But these appointments were technical rather than political and, in addition, the cadres who were transferred southwards were not replaced, leaving gaps in the administration of the north. Politically the southern dominance was overwhelming.

Everything had been carried out in haste and even the basic legalities had been neglected. The Somaliland legislature passed a roughly drafted text of union with the south on 27 June 1960, the day following northern independence. Strangely enough, the representative from Mogadishu who was present that day in Hargeisa abstained and did not sign the document.[15] And then on 1 July, the very day of independence of the south, the local authorities in Mogadishu brought forward an Atto di Unione (Act of Unification), written in Italian, which was the equivalent of the 27 June Hargeisa declaration. But neither was this one signed by the representatives of the other side. So, even though nobody had refused any unification document, nobody had signed one either (or either of the two prepared), leaving the merging of the two colonies as a de facto move, without international or constitutional basis. But united they were, somehow. And within a year, the dysfunctionalities were there in plain sight, for everyone to see.

On 20 June 1961 a draft constitution was submitted to a referendum. The results were 91 per cent in favour and only 9 per cent against. But these 'significant' results were deceptive. First of all, the south had perhaps three times the population of the former British colony; and then, on top of that disparity, only about 100,000 of the registered voters had cast their ballots in the north, and even among that limited number, there was a 63 per cent rejection rate. The overall result showed one firm contradiction: the north, whose SNL had been even more sanguine than the southern SYL in promoting unification, had rejected it within a year of its proclamation. Within six months, on 10 December 1961, a group of northern officers attempted to carry out a coup, with the hope of seceding from the newborn unitary state. The coup was led by an Issaq major, Hassan Kayd. But among the coup leaders were one Gaddabursi (from the Dir clan family) and four Dhulbahante, who are Darood. This showed that even if its main body of support was clanic, the attempted coup was broadly regional.[16]

The coup—and the trial which followed it—was more farcical than tragic. In March 1963, Mr Justice Hazelwood, a British former colonial judge whose court sat in Mogadishu, dismissed the case arguing that there had been no proper act of unification and that therefore the southern authorities had no jurisdiction to enter a charge of high treason against northern officers who were not technically part of the 'national' army. Surprisingly, the 'national' government in Mogadishu accepted the legal argument and freed the detainees forthwith.

But this did not stop the regime from trying to carry out its 'Greater Somalia' policy. With the approaching independence of Kenya, the Northern Frontier District (NFD), populated by Somali, was next in line for diplomatic action. On 27 July 1962, Mohamed Ibrahim Egal, who was both a northerner (Issaq) and the Minister of Defence of the mostly Hawiye–Majerteen southern regime, met Jomo Kenyatta in Mogadishu, telling him that 'a desire for unity[17] must be matched by a willingness to sacrifice a measure of sovereignty … This Republic [Somalia as it then existed] has made a unique practical contribution to African unity by merging two independent African states into one.'[18] Kenyatta, who had observed the process of 'unification' between Hargeisa and Mogadishu over the previous two years, retorted that 'it will not be enough merely to have an organisation coordinating the operation of a few selected services. This would entail going further and lead to the creation of a new Federal State of Eastern Africa.' This was something he had no intention of doing, as he declared in August 1962: 'we regard NFD as part of Kenya … and any discussion with the Somalis in NFD is a domestic affair of Kenya.'[19] It could not be clearer.

The British government was caught in a quandary, having to satisfy both this Kenyan nationalist requirement and its own acceptance of the previous fusion between British Somaliland and Somalia Italiana. In October 1962, London reluctantly organised, through the Commonwealth, a referendum in the NFD. The results were clear, as roughly 80 per cent of the voters supported seceding from Kenya and joining the new Republic of Somalia. Fearing a Kenyan backlash at the time of independence, London left the referendum unfinished,[20] and, when popular demonstrations developed, it collaborated with the native Kenyan security forces in repressing them violently. Even before independence was proclaimed (December 1963), the whole NFD was prey to war—the so-called Shifta War—a conflict which would eventually last till 1967. The common struggle of Kenya, trying to keep the NFD from becoming part of Somalia, and of Ethiopia, to keep the Ogaden in the same way, brought the two countries closer together as soon as Kenya became independent.

But what about the Côte Française des Somalis, or French Somaliland? Its situation was different owing to two factors. One was the French reluctance to abandon what they considered to be an essential strategic position.[21] The other was the fact that the majority of the population was not Somali but Afar, and the Afar had no desire to belong to either Somalia or Ethiopia, even if both countries pretended to have claims on the French colony. In fact, even though the main Somali party, Ligue Populaire Africaine pour l'Indépendance (LPAI), officially advocated union with Somalia, this was far from being a widespread sentiment, even within the Issa, the majority Somali clan (a Dir clan family) among the Djibouti Somalis.[22] So though the LPAI kept an official pro-Somalia position, the aim was largely to put pressure on Paris and to get money from Mogadishu.[23] This was almost the absolute opposite of the NFD Somali choice. There were two reasons for this. First of all, the main problem in TFAI was not pan-Somalism but rather the Afar–Issa politics; and secondly, the clan relationships formed another dimension. The Issa were used to dealing with Gaddabursi and with Issaq—for them the southern clans were probably more 'foreign' than even the Afar—while, in the case of the NFD, the main clans like the Ogadeni or the Ajuran belonged to the Darood or Hawiye families. The Greater Somalia mystique became diluted in geographical distance and, later, in the perceived experience of the 1960 Union. Reality was reasserting itself and it did not fit the mythical scenario.

Vanishing democracy, rising dictatorship

The experience of democracy in unified Somalia roughly covered the 1960s (July 1960 to October 1969). It was a period when a grand illusion replaced practical analysis, when a political dream permanently parasitised real politics, and when undercurrents of non-state governance, largely clanic, were allowed to develop, fester and eventually undercut the attempt at building a democratic regime in the wake of withdrawing colonialism. Up to the October 1969 coup, democratic functioning had been unsatisfactory but had existed. In clanic terms, politics were dominated by members of the Majerteen clan family and, among those, by Abdirizak Haji Hussein and Abdirashid Ali Shermarke. Both were Majerteen and alternated as Prime Minister and President throughout the 1960s. Abdirizak was the more moderate of the two on the question of Greater Somalia. Of course he supported the Dream— every politician had to—but he did so reasonably, moderately, and without a time frame requiring immediate action. But he also introduced the practice of systematic vote rigging, something which in the short run was useful since it favoured reasonable candidates but which also undermined the democratic process itself, turning elections into a mockery. The army was the only coherent body which operated more or less as a nationwide unit, at least until the coup. Given the corruption and the nepotism of civilian politics and the increasing ineffectiveness of the support for the Dream, there was a certain restlessness and desire to intervene on the part of the army.

Part of the problem was the Somali approach to the Cold War. Since 'the Dream' was considered a strategic goal, it could only be realised in opposition to the West because both Kenya and Ethiopia were strong US allies while Djibouti was still in French colonial hands. In the Arab world, support for Somalia's unification had come from Egypt, Libya, Syria and Iraq, countries that were at the time all pro-USSR.[24] On 15 October 1969, President Ali Shermarke was shot and killed by one of his own bodyguards. The motivation for the killing seemed mostly personal but there was a sub-plot which seemed to link the assassination with some elements of the armed forces. In any case, whether army men had abetted this killing or whether they thought it opened a window of opportunity, a group of officers led by General Siad Barre took power a week later in a bloodless coup, created the so-called Supreme Revolutionary Council (SRC) and soon took it in a 'socialist' direction. This trend of 'military socialism', which had started regionally with Egypt's Gamal Abdel Nasser, was then dominant and led directly to Moscow.[25] But in the case of Somalia, the logic of alliances steering the Cold War had already brought Mogadishu to sign a military aid pact with the USSR in 1963. The root cause of this move was not any ideological sympathy for the 'atheist' Soviet regime but simply a strategic choice since both Kenya and Ethiopia were close allies of the United States, and being a friend of their enemy seemed like a wise choice. As a result, the new SRC orientation was not a radical change but simply an intensification of an already existing policy direction.

What was more important (but was not noticed in the international climate of the time) was the role of clanism. The Majerteen elite which had ruled Somalia since the AFIS days was relatively moderate in its use of clan solidarities. But this was not the case with the new regime, where the personality of Siad Barre himself started to impose a growing clanic weight. Siad was half Marehan (on his father's side, the culturally more important one) and half Ogaden, i.e. wholly Darood. In clanic terms, the Darood were the silent majority of post-colonial Somalia, and they had every intention of recovering what they considered to be their birthright. So Siad Barre joined the military regimes all heading for Moscow, following a doubly legitimate diplomatic path by reinforcing the pan-Somali camp both inside and outside the newly amalgamated 'country'. But how much of a country was it?

Somalia's post-independence forced birth

We have already seen that the December 1961 Hassan Kayd military coup, while abortive, had been a significant sign of a deep malaise in the brotherly union of north and south. 'All the institutions that were important and supported by foreign funders were moved away from the north. The SIBA Institute in Mogadishu was the copy of the one in Hargeisa, the CTC Institute was relocated, the Police Academy was a copy of the Madera Police Academy of the north, the Livestock Breeding Project in Afgooye was a replica of the same institution in Geed Debleh, the Agricultural Extension Project in the south was a copy of the Abuuriin one in the north. Many boarding schools in the north were closed and many of the good teachers were transferred to Mogadishu, leaving the bad ones for Hargeisa. The GCE examinations from London were suspended. And after the 1977 war [with Ethiopia], over forty schools were closed in the north so they could be taken over as barracks for the military. It was started in Wajaale, Dararweyne was next, Allaybaday was next, Bali Cabane was next, and then Baligubadle and Oodweyne and Dacarbudhug, and I can't count the rest. There was constant fighting in the Ministry of Education. Many people agreed to stand up to stop this policy in the North but they failed. There were many high-level politicians, not only Issaq but even Majerteen, Dhulbahante and Hawiye, famous people such as Omar Arteh, Ismail Ali Abokor, Omar Haji Masale or Ahmed Jaamjaam Gileh who held a conference and concluded that if Siad Barre was allowed to continue this way, the country would end up in a civil war ... But then, apart from Omar Arteh, who was very well known, and from Dr Mohamed Aden, who was from Marehan by clan but who was with them, all others were arrested, tried and condemned to death.'[26]

In spite of this increasingly gaping administrative chasm between north and south, the 63 per cent rejection of the union by those northern voters who did vote in the 1961 referendum had not been taken as a warning by the southern political elite (and this was years before Siad Barre took over). The Dream reigned supreme, largely through ignorance.

> Ordinary people in Somaliland were mostly nomadic pastoralists who were not familiar with the possible consequences of unification without conditions, and they used to think that if there was unification with other Somali there would be universal prosperity. They were not well informed by the opposition political parties ... It was only NUF that was against unification without conditions and asked for negotiations and a previous agreement ... But when the military junta took over the country, Mohamed Siad Barre and his family and his clan were prioritised and we became even more dissatisfied with the system. But our lack of experience at that time was almost complete.[27]

The event that turned that dissatisfaction into open hostility was the 1974–5 Dabadheer drought.[28]

> During that drought a lot of people lost their livestock and many people from Somaliland, especially those from the east,[29] became refugees in the south. The government did not set up refugee camps in the north but they set up temporary camps at places like Beer, Caynaba or Taleex, and the people were later transferred to places in the south, mostly around Marca. Then they were told to farm and were given land, but these people were pastoralists and did not have any idea about farming. So they started migrating to the Gulf countries, mainly to Saudi Arabia, in search of work.[30]

There were other disrupting consequences of the drought. Not everybody could go to the Gulf, and over 200,000 internally displaced people were sedentarised and resettled. The programme, presented as an effort of trans-clanic nationalist social transformation, was not very efficient and in fact created further clanic problems. Another consequence of the drought was the establishment by the USSR of a programme for the non-maritime Somalis to learn to fish. In spite of their long coastline, the Somali had remained landlubbers and, apart from members of the Warsangeli clan on the Red Sea, had only dabbled in sailing. Under Russian supervision, apprentice fishermen of various Majerteen sub-clans took to the Indian Ocean.[31] This was not really popular either. Since the drought situation improved only very slowly in the north, most of the emigrants stayed in the Arab countries and did not come back to Somalia, making the Dabadheer drought a kind of watershed.

The Somalilanders realised that the Dream of national unity, whether popular or not, had little weight in the eyes of their southern brethren. This was particularly painful since one of the points that had led many northerners to support the military-socialist coup was the fact that the officers reacted strongly against the foreign policy of the last prime minister, Mohamed Ibrahim Egal. Egal, a smooth diplomat who had come to realise that pan-Somalism was very unpopular internationally, started to tone down irredentist Somali claims. But the Dream was still popular and his moderation looked like cowardice in the eyes of the population. So Siad Barre's first public speech after the coup strongly reaffirmed the pan-Somali ideals that had led to the hurried 1960 merger.[32] To see these ideals, still theoretically held, being so poorly practised in reality undermined further the already strained north–south relations. But worse than the Dabadheer drought, the real, massive and final breaking point in the north–south marriage would be war, the war with Ethiopia, which, in the ideal pan-Somali scenario, should have been the next step in realising the dream of Somali unity.

The impact of war with Ethiopia on Somalia

Why a war with Ethiopia rather than a war with other governments controlling parts of the Somali world? The reasons were a mix of diplomatic, political and clanic causes, with some practicalities thrown in. The first round of military efforts at uniting the Somali territories had been, as we saw earlier, a move against Kenya's Northern Frontier District, resulting in the 1963–7 Shifta War. This was before the socialist-military coup of 1969 and before Egal tried to heal the relationship with Kenya. But the Shifta War was a kind of secondary theatre of operations. Kenya had no desire to push the quarrel further, whereas Ethiopian policies were designed to be aggressively integrationist. And this fitted in a very tight way with the clanic political landscape of Somalia. Siad Barre himself came on his mother's side from the Makahil sub-clan of the Ogadeni, one that was deeply embedded in southern Ogaden. In early 1976 the Ogadeni launched an irredentist armed movement in the Ethiopian province, the Western Somali Liberation Front (WSLF), led by Abdullahi Hassan Muhammad. This movement had a 'sister' organisation, the Somali Abbo Liberation Front (SALF), led by the veteran Oromo rebel, Wako Gutu. Wako Gutu had been a nationalistic Oromo peasant leader ennobled by Emperor Haile Selassie but he later rebelled, was arrested and sentenced to a jail term. The beginnings of the Ethiopian Revolution set him free and he went back to his rebellion. For Siad Barre to associate support for the genuinely Somali WSLF with the same backing for SALF, which was a wholly Ethiopian movement, was a deliberate bomb thrown in the Ethiopian backyard. It linked Somali nationalism with support for an ethnic group that dreamt of dismantling the Ethiopian Empire and actually destroying Ethiopia as a state. And this happened at a time when the revolution had deposed the Emperor and undermined from within Ethiopia the traditional legitimacy of the nation.[33] Together, WSLF and SALF were deadly projectiles aimed not only at bringing about the secession of Ethiopia's Somali population (through the WSLF) but even at dismantling the Ethiopian core territory completely (by way of SALF)[34] and wiping the whole country off the map.

Why would Siad Barre want to fire such deadly missiles at his Ethiopian neighbour? Basically, he had run out of governing devices in an increasingly difficult situation, and not because he had failed to try other means. As we saw, the one basic problem of governing the Somali was clanism, a form of social organisation which is more efficient in competing with and sidetracking state authority than even the more commonplace tribalism of African societies.[35] In his simple military way, Siad tried to 'reform' Somali society and assert the authority of the state over a society that not only had never had any state but had even actively resisted obeying one. He started by introducing the notion of individual responsibility in the legal code to try to marginalise clanic responsibility, which made the whole clan accountable for the offences committed by one of its members. The state de facto 'nationalised' grazing areas and water wells, guaranteeing free access to these assets to any 'citizen', no matter what his clan was. This was a courageous move but also a foolish one because, firstly, geographical ties to certain regions were strong among particular clans and could hardly be freely altered by representatives of the state; and, secondly, those very representatives of the state were themselves not free of clan attachments and therefore could not be considered neutral. In despair, the regime even organised communist-style 'agitprop' public events, with militants of the SRSP[36] marching along carrying fake coffins, supposedly burying 'clanism'. The only segment of Somali society which refused to obey or even give lip service to the anti-clanic directives were the Muslim Brothers, who rejected the 'atheist regime', including its use of the Latin alphabet to write the Somali language.[37] In 1975 Siad arrested ten of the most vociferous Ulama and shot them, causing a serious setback to the expansion of the Muslim Brothers' network in Somalia.

For a military leader who had based his leadership on the Supreme Revolutionary Council (SRC) and then proceeded to transform the SRC into a one-man dictatorship, the situation after five or six years in power was extremely problematic. The deeper meaning of the coup was considerably simplified by observers at the time, who could write:

> No really stunning changes in the political stance of Somalia, either at home or in external policy, can be expected. Siad Barre is very much an establishment man, an elder who has shown considerable ability in maintaining tranquillity in the Army which always had suffered from the divisive influence of the rival clans ... If he shows a similar ability to balance the clans in the new regime which is to rule Somalia, he will have done much to ensure his success ... Siad is certainly not a political self-seeker.[38]

Resurrecting such a quote is not intended to make the reader laugh. It is mentioned because it is typical of the common assessment of Siad Barre's coup at the time.[39] But it was inadequate even then. The anti-clanic policy never really took off, and it failed notoriously when the new master of Somalia felt forced to arrest and execute General Mohamed Aynanshe, Colonel Salaad Gabeyre and Colonel Abdulkadir Dheel, who were leaders of dissident clanic strands within the army. The ideological overhaul which was supposed to marginalise both clanism and Islam through the use of Marxism-Leninism had failed. The executions of the Ulama had riled Muslim consciousness. And the Soviet alliance had led to the development of a command economy with stagnant results. At this point Ethiopia suddenly came undone through revolution, offering an unexpected opportunity for a possible military 'solution' that was too tempting for the champion of a hyper-nationalist movement and army to resist. Pan-Somalism had been a key legitimising factor for the coup in October 1969, and now this was its best opportunity since independence.

The army, having expanded massively, now felt ready to move. It had had only 2,000 men at the time of independence and 4,000 in 1968, a year before the coup. But by 1977 it had grown to 53,000 men, equipped by the Russians with 250 tanks (T-34, T-54 and T-55), over 300 armoured vehicles (BTR-40, BTR-152), and 66 combat aircraft (Mig-15, Mig-17 and a few Mig-21).[40] In addition, the Somali guerrillas of WSLF could bring a force of about 80,000 men, often poorly equipped but extremely resolute. In normal times, the Ethiopian Army would have had sufficient men and equipment to face a Somali Army attack. But since February 1974, it had been unravelling, along with the rest of Ethiopian state institutions. Ethiopia had a 50,000-strong, well-trained army, a reasonable fleet of somewhat ageing US battle tanks, and good combat aircraft, in particular 28 new Northrop F-5 fighters to supplement its Korean War-vintage F-86 Sabre. But this army was deeply involved in leading a revolution and, by then, owing to the revolution, both countries had become Soviet allies without Moscow knowing what to do about this fight between two of its protégés. The confusion was complete.[41]

In March 1977, as the danger of war was nearing, Fidel Castro flew to Aden to meet both Siad Barre and representatives of the Ethiopian Socialist Army Revolutionary Committee, or Derg, led by Mengistu Haile Mariam, who, a month before, had assumed all power in Addis Ababa through an internal coup, eliminating his army rivals. Castro put forward a grand design of creating a regional socialist federation that would bring together Ethiopia, Somalia and South Yemen, a hasty improvisation in such a tight framework at a tense moment. Siad threw the proposal out (and with it the prospect of continued Soviet support) and showed clearly that he intended to take over the Ogaden by military force. On 13 July the Somali forces crossed the Ethiopian border and attacked westwards, immediately scoring great successes against the dispirited Ethiopian troops. Within weeks the Somali Army and its WSLF auxiliaries had occupied three-quarters of the Ogaden and were besieging the main towns such as Harar and Jijiga. Taking advantage of the Somali attack, the Eritrean guerrillas went on the offensive and occupied most of the province while the conservative pro-monarchist guerrillas of EDU did the same thing in Tigray. The Derg feared imminent collapse and military defeat. But Mengistu took things strongly in hand and Brezhnev rose to the challenge, deploying a massive Soviet aerial logistical capacity to bring in heavy equipment, especially heavy artillery, and allied troops from Cuba and South Yemen. With these reinforcements the Ethiopians and their allies could counter-attack[42] and push the Somali forces out of the Ogaden. By 8 March 1978, their last units had withdrawn.

The nation is thrown backwards

The Ogaden War was a typical illustration of the Clausewitzian notion of war as extending politics by other means. But it failed. And that failure boomeranged, soon starting to challenge the peaceful 1960 union. Part of this was due to the methods Siad Barre had used to try to grab territory. In order to be successful and use the moral and social support of the local population, he deployed more WSLF militias—80,000 of them—than regular troops (50,000). In addition he also used an unknown number of 'irregulars', either Ethiopian SALF Oromos or armed nomads operating outside the frame of any formal command. Many were recruited in the former British Protectorate or in the Hawd, and when defeat came, these men started to ask the regime to fulfil its promises. But this came later.

In the very short term, the main threat to the military regime was an attempt by the Majerteen to regain what they felt they had lost in October 1969, i.e. the upper hand in Somali politics. By the end of March 1978, Siad Barre had arrested many officers and shot 90 of them. Over one million refugees had come over the border in the wake of the retreating Somali forces. The confusion was tremendous and humanitarian aid, quickly improvised, could hardly cope and keep people alive. On 9 April 1978, almost exactly a month after the defeat, a group of mostly Majerteen officers tried to overthrow the government in a coup and failed. Many were arrested, and 17 were tried and shot the following October. A major part of the problem was that many armed men were drifting along in the flow of refugees. These men could call upon the government to honour its previous promises. Siad Barre belonged to the broader Darood clan family, as did the Ogadeni refugees. Many had long-standing grievances which the regime had exploited to acquire their loyalty. But now pay-off time had come, at a moment when the state was broke and Siad Barre wanted somebody else to pay the bill.

So, many of the refugees and vanquished militiamen were steered northwards, away from the Darood lands. There these newcomers met with other clanically and politically disenchanted segments of the population, those 'irregulars' who had been drafted into the campaign. Some of the outstanding demographic and historical debts Siad Barre had used to try to buy clanic support were quite old, as in the case of the Mahmood Garaad sub-clan of the Dhulbahante, which had lost a good part of its traditional territories during the wars against the 'Mad Mullah' between 1900 and 1920,[43] or some of the Ogadeni clans who had been pushed aside at the same time.[44] Together with the retreating WSLF forces, these irregulars had every intention of getting what they felt had been owed to them for over half a century. As for the refugees, they would settle for anything they could grab. Weapons were distributed freely to all those who supported the government and were ready to fight against any attempt at overthrowing it.[45] By late 1978, the estimate was that there were 220,000 men under arms while there had been only 168,000 at the height of the offensive in Ethiopia.[46] The 50,000 extra gunslingers were all highly irregular (even when they called themselves WSLF) and they all moved northwards, to the former Somaliland. They were armed, vanquished, frustrated, half starving, and they felt the government was behind them. It meant their intentions were definitely not friendly and the local civilian population began to pay the price.

This period was extremely ambiguous. The Issaq, like most of the Somali population and in spite of their doubts about the unification, had joined wholeheartedly in the war effort.[47] But now, with the reflux of the army and the dumping of refugees in the former Somaliland, the ambiguity grew and a stiffening of anti-government reaction began to replace support for the nationalist dream. The security situation was extraordinarily contradictory and this contradiction was spectacularly embodied in what became known as the Afraad (the Fourth Battalion), popularly known as Watatir Mohamed Ali, Mohamed Ali's soldiers. Mohamed Ali's real name was Mohamed Farah Dalmar Yusuf. He had acquired his first military experience in the ranks of the Palestine Liberation Organization; later he had taken part in the Lebanese civil war, and when he eventually came back to Somalia with such a record of independent soldiering, he was a natural candidate for the recently created WSLF. He then became the military leader of the organisation and was at the forefront of the 1977 invasion in the Ogaden. But as an Issaq, he quickly realised that he was leading a military outfit which was on a collision course with his own clansmen. In 1979 he had been detached to head a special branch of the WSLF to which he gave the name Afraad and which Siad Barre used to fight the new Somali Salvation Front (SOSAF) rebels. He stayed in the same area of the Ogaden where he had fought the Ethiopian Army and switched to fighting the Majerteen rebels of Abdullahi Yusuf instead, as well as fighting the Ogadeni at the same time, even though they were WSLF themselves. Watatir Mohamed Ali's first loyalty was to their leader, and he was so popular that Afraad followed him blindly. So, in a way, he was the first armed fighter of the future Somaliland rebellion, even before the creation of the SNM rebel movement.

But there are limits to ambiguity and Mohamed Ali's high-wire act backfired in 1979 when he was arrested in Mogadishu. He had much to explain about his complicated loyalties, but he did not have to because he was saved at the last moment from facing a military court when he was rescued by one of his superiors, who was also a veteran comrade in arms from the Ogaden, Mohamed Hashi Deria, better known as 'Lixle'.[48] Lixle was a respected front-line commander and a war hero who enjoyed the full trust of his superiors. Given the total confusion in the months that followed the end of the war, he decided to brazen it out, put on his full uniform and spring his subordinate from jail. But when he got him out, he advised him to lie low. Mohamed Ali left Mogadishu and went farming in southern Somalia during most of 1979–80. After his brush with the government, he was reinstated in the WSLF in early 1981. But by then the WSLF had turned into an 'every tribe for itself' formation, and the fight with the Ethiopians had become 'a disguise or cover-up for getting weapons'.[49] 'The name of the various units (Kowaad, Labaad, Sadexaad) simply indicated their rankings in WSLF. Afraad just meant the Fourth Battalion. All the other units were engaged in robbing and killing the population. So the Fourth, led by Mohamed Ali and Cabdikareem Ali Buux, came out in order to protect the people, and while the other units remained on the Somali government side, the Fourth had to seek the help of the Ethiopian government. It thus became the initial nucleus of the SNM. Hostility between the clans was at its peak. There were many tribal units before SNM was formed, but Afraad went back to 1978.'[50] Now the high-wire act was in the hands of Lixle, and during these days when the future (and already active) rebels were still 'government', he was the one helping these units at the forefront of an armed movement in the making.

By 1979, was 'Somaliland' still part of Somalia or had it already started to drift away? The answer is 'both'. The Ogaden War had been a moment of romantic exaltation which had, for a while, made people forget the prejudices and incompetence that had marked the days following the 1960 'unification'. Victory might have enabled the reluctant joiners to share in the heroic dream of the movement. But it was the opposite that happened, not so much the defeat but rather the way in which it took place. All the pre-war shortcomings were back, with a vengeance. The Ogadeni refugees were integrated into the civil service in the north-west, keeping a facade of national unity but also bypassing local candidates for scarce jobs. The economic competition got fiercer and more ethnically slanted:

> There was a businessman who was a Marehan and a relative of President Siad Barre. He had livestock to export and he did not want to wait, especially as his name was at the end of the list. So he asked a Marehan colonel to help him in Berbera harbour and his clansman told the harbour authorities that as a Marehan his livestock should be allowed to go first on the ship. And there was even worse. When people brought vehicles from Saudi Arabia or Dubai, influential Marehan military people would come to the port and ask for the keys. If they liked a car which was beautiful, like a Land Cruiser, they would ask for the keys from the port manager or the customs, and they would drive out of the port without paying and nobody would dare to stop them.[51]

Increasingly the post-war situation in the north began to look like a free-for-all where members of the Darood clans, especially those labelled 'MOD'—Marehan-Ogadeni-Dhulbahante—behaved as if Somaliland had become their private property. In addition, all forms of economic benefit were ended, withdrawn or taken over by others. A key element was the cancellation of the *franco valuta* system, which had allowed businessmen to procure foreign currency for exports that did not fall within a government monopoly.[52] This system was quite beneficial for the Issaq, who made money by exporting livestock to Yemen and Saudi Arabia. Unlike the banana exports from the south, which occurred within a government monopoly system—the Somalfruit parastatal company—livestock exports were wholly private and the north raked in a fair amount of foreign currency. But in October 1981 the *franco valuta* system was abolished, depriving the Issaq of their main, if not only, source of foreign currency. The negative impact was considerable. At the same time, the looting of the economy reached extreme heights.

> The Marehan or other Darood, they would come to the harbour and take whatever they wanted from any importer, without paying, just like that ... If one of them wanted to organise a wedding, he would kidnap an Issaq and then ask money for his release. It got to the point that there were even agents that engaged with the government in negotiations for release ... In the rural areas, the camel herders were asked to pay money, particularly if they had a *berked* [dugout cistern for irrigation and watering cattle] ... In Jijiga there was a market where you could buy goods that had been stolen by the army or the police.[53]

At first, civil society reactions were limited because, in the absence of any anti-colonial movement, there was no tradition of politicisation.

> There was only one small movement, Waxdada, an Islamic group that drew ideologically from the Muslim Brotherhood Movement. It was not very political, contrary to Ansar ad-Din. But Ansar ad-Din was more active in the rest of the country ... Those that adhered to this ideology were mostly living around Bura'o.[54]

But what first challenged civil society's neglect was the catastrophic situation of Hargeisa hospital. There had been no health investment in the hospital since independence, including during the Ogaden War, when it had to treat a high number of military casualties. After the end of the war, the emergency facilities set up by UNHCR to help refugees were of a much better quality than the 'national' hospital in the northern capital.[55]

> Young intellectuals who had been educated abroad were shocked when they came back ... The gynaecological service was the worst, to the extent that the midwives had to fight off the cats to protect the newborn. One night it happened that a man had brought his pregnant wife to the service, but since there was no electricity and no generator, he was ordered to use the headlights of his

car to light up the delivery room ... Dr Adan Abokor was the hospital manager at the time, a recent graduate from Warsaw University, and he sent us an appeal to assist him with the hospital ... Some of the traditional leaders and some businessmen started to collect money to cover the medical supplies, and we brought in the German emergency doctors, who started helping. They were very courageous. I remember a German sewerage engineer who went and worked with his bare hands in the sewage. It motivated many people ... But it was not only the hospital, the need was everywhere ... The schools had no teachers because salaries were low and most of the time they were not even paid. Maths, biology or physics were not taught because no qualified teachers had been recruited.[56]

Given the dilapidated condition of most government services—and this within a command economy where the state was in theory supposed to run everything—the embryonic volunteer movement that had coalesced around the needs of the hospital started to grow. 'However, there was nothing organised and there was no intention of creating a big unrest or protest against the regime. Because the regime at that time was very powerful and no one dared to go against it.'[57]

This was the time when General Mohamed Hashi Gani became Governor of the north, replacing Salhan Mohamed Salhan, whom Siad Barre suspected of being too friendly with the Issaq population. The public atmosphere changed immediately. 'Within two months of his nomination, Hashi Gani had created an emergency military court which tried, condemned and shot Colonel Abdullahi Said, the military commander of Togdheer region.'[58] People were charged, pushed around or demoted on the slightest pretext. Facing growing popular dissatisfaction, General Hashi Gani hardened his attitude by resorting to arbitrary repression. Meanwhile, the voluntary service movement had been gaining ground and had completely renovated the hospital, 'even repainting the walls'. Drugs and basic equipment were bought with private funds and people volunteered to do unpaid work. The so-called Hargeisa Hospital Group acquired the nickname Uffo (the wind before the storm), which was quickly taken up in every *mabraz* of the city,[59] and it soon became a symbol both of self-help and of opposition to the government. In fact, Uffo remained an opinion, a state of mind and not a regular organisation. It did not have a formal structure, a membership list or any form of dues. It did publish a newsletter, for a while which it stopped issuing in October 1981 when it realised that it angered the government without adding much to the task at hand.

But from the point of view of General Hashi Gani, things had already gone too far. Two months later the police started arresting Uffo sympathisers.[60]

Arrests were made on the basis of family connections, friendships or word of mouth, and spread like wildfire since even having been seen in the company of a 'suspect' was enough for a person to be arrested. On 20 February 1982 all the 'Uffo members' were taken to court and later sentenced to long jail terms on 6 March. The Uffo trial triggered massive street protests, remembered as 'the stone throwing' (*dhagax tur*) when ordinary civilians started to throw stones at the police guarding the tribunal and the police replied by opening fire.[61] The government admitted to 14 people being killed but the real tally was about 30. The punishments meted out to civil society volunteers for having worked for the common good were so absurdly inappropriate that disturbances occurred over the whole of former Somaliland, leading to further casualties. The wave of arrests that accompanied the Uffo repression, and then the approaching trial, triggered the start of an emigration of armed insurgents to Ethiopia as early as December 1981.[62] Uffo and its *dhagax tur* conclusion were the warning winds from which the future tempest would come. And this was because, unknown to most of the people demonstrating, a group of men had met in far-away London and quietly begun to set up an organisation that would give the furious crowds of the former British Protectorate a political voice and a military dimension.

3

FOUNDING AND FOSTERING THE SOMALI NATIONAL MOVEMENT (SNM)

A broader theoretical overview

When one tries to conceptualise what the 'Somaliland' phenomenon represents—the recycling of a former colonial space as the framework of a new nationalist movement—one must realise that this was in complete contradiction to what had so far been the heart of the movement towards decolonisation. Returning to a colonial boundary (which meant adapting to a colonial boundary) was diametrically opposed to the pan-Somali ideology, built entirely on the idea that cultural identity equalled citizenship (which meant trying to destroy the colonial boundaries). For most African countries struggling towards anti-colonial nationhood, the equation was radically different. Their problem was how to build a nation to support an abstract state sitting on top of the tribal diversity they had inherited. Borders for them were secondary. The problem of the Somali was the exact opposite: the nation was a given but it was split into five separate state entities. And in between, like a succession of bridges to nowhere, lay the broken lines of the clans. Borders (which ones?) were at the heart of the Somali conundrum.[1] Pan-Somalism was—and remains today, in so far as it still exists—an act of faith. Pan-Somalism was the hope, dream or delusion that the myth of the state would be powerful enough to cut through the swathe of the clans. Therefore all clans and all territories had to be brought together, as leaving any outside the sanctity of the Holy Fatherland would irreparably damage the very existence of the whole.

Clanic rivalries, often mistakenly compared to tribal differences, are the complete opposite. Clans are all similar, which is why they cannot live together under one state. This derives from the fact that Somali culture, being radically democratic, will use the clans to challenge, refuse and disobey the state because no full-fledged, free-born Somali will ever willingly agree to bend the knee to another man's authority. Since clans are designed to help and support any and all of their members in a hostile environment—whether the hostility is from nature or from other people is irrelevant—the clan means brotherhood and entails solidarity against any risk or danger. The clan will support its members against the state if the state does not support the clan. This is why building a state on an architecture of clans is akin to trying to fit square pegs into round holes. The clan is not an enemy of the state; it is its competitor. All the attributes of the state are already present in the clan: security, support, authority, identity, economic help, territory. The clan is a small state, with the added advantages of kinship, warmth and humanity. The state, with its abstraction and cold-bloodedness, is a poor second to the cozy niche of the clan.

This was all good and well back in the days when the clanic arrangements of Somali society were functional, given the prevailing technological level (low), information level (low), natural dangers (high) and foreign entanglements (low). Colonisation, with its well-armed armies of (mostly) white barbarians suddenly bursting upon the Somali world as an irresistible horde, put an end to that period. This was not akin to keeping the Ottomans at bay, skirmishing with the Arabs or hoping to conquer the lands of the Abyssinians, who were all peripheral. This was survival. The Europeans were absolutely destructive. They played by radically different rules, their resolve for war was equal to that of the Somali themselves and they had vastly superior weapons to achieve victory. Their culture was attractive and therefore corrosive. The only way to stem the flow was to build what made the Europeans powerful: a state. Never mind that it was something the Somali were culturally very poorly equipped to achieve. Therefore, in a burst of hopeful pride, the Somali resolved to build the biggest state they could possibly imagine, the state of all the Somali, hoping that size and trans-clanic relations would trump the kinship obstacle. But they were wrong. The clanic sand was so present, so penetrating, so intimate, that it gripped the state machinery even before it was created.

This was not for want of trying. As we saw in the first chapter, the Somali Youth League was *the* finely shaped theoretical tool to cut through the clanic complexities. Its problem was that it was too theoretical. There was only one part of the Somali space where the seeds of a possible transformation already existed: Somaliland. Was it because it had been administered in a more progressive and more efficient manner than the other parts of the colonised Somali nation? Not in the least. In the only in-depth analysis of colonial Somaliland,[2] a colonial administrator is quoted as saying in a report of 1920: 'transforming activities [what we would call today "development"] are not necessary because the Administration is only popular with the natives insofar as it is confined to settling disputes and preserving order.' The Somali particularly resented education and in May 1939 they rioted against school attendance. 'Indirect rule was a non-starter because there simply were no native authorities to associate with the task.'[3] The picture of pre-war British Somaliland that comes out of these pages is paradoxical but coherent in Somali terms, and it corresponds to a clear-cut assessment made at the time by another man who knew the Somali well. In the 1993 reprint of his book,[4] Gerald Hanley quotes the remark an old Somali made to him in 1941, after he had been 'liberated' from the Italians: 'I want to be well-governed and to be left alone.' This was the gist, the hard core of the Somali concept of good governance. Millman sums it up in another quote, this time from a British administrator: 'The Empire is in the business of enforcing *her*.' What is 'her'?[5] *Xeer* is the system of (unwritten) legal obligations and punishments observed by each clan. This 'traditional law', far from being 'primitive' or 'embryonic', is, on the contrary, extraordinarily precise and detailed in respect of those elements that pertain to traditional Somali life. Its adaptation to all aspects of Somali life is such that it has always trumped Shari'ah law, even after the Somali became Muslims. And *Xeer* was conceived without any reference to an overall state which would be a law-giver and law-enforcer. *Xeer* went with the clan, it did not go with any (theoretical) state.[6]

So what was good governance for a traditional Somali? It was a system that would respect *Xeer*, provide an impartial interpretation of the law and, in case of need, act as a referee that would make sure the *Xeer* customary legal decisions would be carried out. But at the same time it was a system which would not tell the Somali what he should or should not do outside the judicial areas of his life. This is exactly what the Protectorate authorities provided. Their courts blended *Xeer* clanic law with British common law (for the 'modern' aspects of life), with *Xeer* being prevalent and with an impartial (i.e. non-clanic) arbitration provided, both in court and later outside. The authority to carry out judicial decisions was given to the Illalo police units, made up of

Somali soldiers commanded by British Camel Corps officers. They patrolled the arid territory and took care of wrongdoers. Apart from that, they had nothing to enforce since the Protectorate did nothing apart from supervising respect for native law. Was this system a kind of Western-enforced formalisation of the 'noble savage' vision? Yes, in a way, but not just that. Here the Somali were neither 'developed' nor 'oppressed'; in Hanley's words, they were 'well-governed and left alone'. Conditions were primitive, including for the British administrators. Salaries were close to bare survival, distractions were non-existent, utilities scarce, the administration skeletal,[7] and the economy Spartan.[8] But something essential was present: a constructed, practical-ideological framework which neither denied nor bowed to clanic legal and civil practice. 'Development' was absent but Somaliland was 'well governed and left alone'. For Western observers, this was completely counterintuitive,[9] even if it was the first step in crossing the incredible obstacle course of the clanic field. Of course, the British administrators had no inkling of the fact that they were setting up the first foundations of a modern state that could be acceptable to the requirements of Somali culture. In their view it was 'minimum Empire', in the same way we talk about 'minimum wages'. But it fitted Somali reality, something that more ambitious 'development plans' did not.

In particular it was the exact opposite of the Italian colonial perspective on the Somali world, which combined extraordinary political (and social) authoritarianism with exaggerated notions of economic development. In Somalia Italiana (as in the Côte Française des Somalis) the combination of high-handedness and Romanic law provided a very poor counterpart to the light political touch of the British administration and its common law accompaniment, which composed the first structure the Somali could tolerate in any transition to a trans-clanic state. This should not be taken as a blanket endorsement of British colonial policies. Neighbouring South Sudan is a showcase of the results of catastrophic British neglect. But given the fact that there was never one British colonial policy but rather as many policies as there were colonial territories, some were better suited to their object than others. Moreover, the British treatment of the Somali was, through a mixture of chance and cultural coincidence, a menu the Somali could swallow. It was bad luck that in the hurry of trying to implement the pan-Somali dream, British Somaliland fell into the hands of possibly the worst-colonised segment of the Somali region, the Italian one.

But resuscitating 'Somaliland' in any shape or form was such an abomination for true dyed-in-the-wool pan-Somali nationalists that in their eyes it could only be the result of a plot. The alleged 'plotters' were never clearly defined but they tended to be darkly hinted at, their identity being, of course, 'anti-Somali' (and 'anti-Islamic' for the radical Muslim groups who were later to emerge at the political forefront). Given the support provided to the SNM by Ethiopia during the war, the enemy could be conveniently labelled as 'Western' since 'Christian Ethiopia' (a pleonastic formulation for many Somali) was the hereditary enemy and the natural military arm of 'the West' in the region. Never mind that at the time Ethiopia was a communist state and therefore not the ideal flag-bearer of 'the West'. But for most of those who were to establish it, the self-asserting Somaliland 'splinter' did not amount to an 'anti-Somalia' decision, but was rather another positive vision of the same thing, i.e. another way to give shape and substance to their social hopes, not through submission to any colonial nostalgia but through self-assertion in a different form. 'Somalia', in the mind of its pan-Somali supporters, meant 'freedom', not only freedom from foreign domination but freedom as an absolute human right, in the sense the French had used *liberté* as one of the three guiding principles of their 1789 revolution. So it was freedom from any domination, including Somali domination. This is where the experience of the Issaq Somali diverged widely from that of their southern brethren.

The point where things went wrong was when the new 'Somali' authorities, far from offering a path to freedom, turned into a path towards more oppression. The situation had been tolerable between 1960 and 1969, and then far from ideal but still tolerable between 1969 and 1978. The Siad Barre regime had staked all its future on making the pan-Somali dream come true. But after 1978 and the defeat at the hands of the Ethiopian Army and its communist allies, that dream turned into a nightmare. And it was not any kind of nightmare, but a typically Somali kind of nightmare, a clanic nightmare. In other words, the pan-Somali ideology which had justified the October 1969 coup, and later the July 1977 war with Ethiopia, finally crashed on the rocks of reality and destroyed its own worshippers. However, the people who were scapegoated and made to pay the price for that defeat were not the members of a political party or the supporters of a certain ideology, but the members of a clan family, the Issaq.

Why the Issaq? In all cases of social discrimination in ethnically (and religiously) homogeneous societies, the victims are perceived as separate, strange or unduly prosperous. This was the case with the Issaq, both because they had prospered in commerce—for example, as we saw earlier with the cancelling of the *franco valuta* financial system—and because they had been a military enemy in the past. In a society which is very historically conscious, it was shocking that during the war the image of Mohamed Abdulle Hassan, the 'Mad Mullah' who had fought the British in Somaliland during the early 1900s, was so angrily resented.[10] Mohamed Abdulle Hassan, who was seen in the south as the first Somali nationalist and whose statue graced a central 'piazza' in the national capital, was commonly called 'a Darood murderer' in the north and regarded as a forerunner of the present violence. The Issaq, even though they had no visible differences with other clan families in Somalia, were subtly perceived as being 'different'. And this perceived difference seemed enough for Siad Barre to resuscitate the old prejudices of the 1910s, giving a typical clanic answer to a trans-clanic national contradiction. The Issaq did not start rebelling for the sake of secession and they did not start either with an armed movement, Mohamed Ali and his Afraad being the exception rather than the rule. But the consequences were inescapable: if the problem was clanic, then so did the solution, turning the targeted identity into an existential shelter.

The militant committees

The committees that would eventually join together and create the first network of the Somali National Movement (SNM) rebellion were the end product of quite a long process, which had started before the war but which the war with Ethiopia and the 1978 defeat would eventually bring to a final conclusion. It all began in an ambiguous atmosphere in which a form of revolutionary nationalism was unexpectedly mixed with traditional clanic feelings and confused dreams of socialist transformation. The year was 1970, the place was the People's Democratic Republic of Yemen (PDRY), then a communist state, and the man who made it all happen was the confused idealist and revolutionary soldier of fortune Mohamed Farah Dalmar aka Mohamed Ali.[11] He went to Aden with an Adari friend only known as Ramadan[12] and opened 'an office'. It was an office of subversion but with imprecise subversive views. The new Supreme Revolutionary Council (SRC), which had just taken power in Mogadishu, was an unknown quantity for many, and in the complicated Cold War atmosphere of the 1970s its ultimate aims were not yet clear. Several actors, particularly among the 'socialist' movements that wanted to maintain a measure of independence from Moscow, felt that keeping options open was preferable. The SRC asked the Aden authorities for the closure of Mohamed Ali's office but the PDRY refused, saying 'it could not close it because it had been opened at the request of the Iraqi government, the people who were running the office had Syrian passports, and they were known to be Eritreans'.

This was an odd answer. But in fact the whole construct was a kind of common Arab revolutionary venture in which two national branches of the Baath party seem to have collaborated in creating a common 'Eritrean' structure with the complicity of the PDRY. The result was a big bowl of political soup where several different spoons seemed to be plunged in a commonly funded mix.[13] Everyone for himself and Marx for all. But all members had their reasons for being there and their own causes. 'When I discussed with Mohamed Ali,' said Mohamed Dacar, 'he told me that Somalia had just been taken over by a new Mohamed Abdulle Hassan,[14] and that our mission was to stop him before he became too strong.' This was a typically 'Issaq nationalist' argument[15] and had nothing to do with either Eritrea or revolutionary Marxism.

> Mohamed Ali and his colleague started recruiting Somalis in Yemen, 36 of them. Then they requested the Yemeni government to provide them with expert trainers to train these recruits in the arts of guerrilla warfare, and the Yemeni government provided them with six trainers ... After some time the Ambassador, who had good relations with Mohamed Ali, was replaced with Abdi Osman 'al-Habashi', who had been a leader of the failed coup of Hassan Kayd in December 1961.

True to his personality, Mohamed Ali and his 36 men crossed by boat from Aden to a point equidistant from Zeyla and Lughaya, on a quixotic 'national liberation' mission of uncertain ideological character. They had been betrayed by a double agent and Somali National Army soldiers were waiting. There was a short exchange of fire. Ramadan and four of the men in the commando were killed and the rest were arrested. Mohamed Ali would later be released in 1975 and would play a key role in preparing the invasion of Ethiopia. After his release from jail, he fought in the war and became one of the main leaders of the WSLF, as we saw in the previous chapter. But he remained under a pall of suspicion as several security officers had realised that he was not an Eritrean,[16] and suspected he could be organising a secret Issaq fighting force. His close ties with men such as Ambassador Abdi Osman in Aden and, later, Colonel Mohamed Hashi ('Lixle') kept him in an ambiguous position where his military talents were highly valued but his political loyalty was felt to be questionable. So the first 'maximalist' tendency, which had tried to jumpstart an armed insurrection, ended up in failure, more because of ideological haste and confusion than because of its accompanying lack of military preparation.

Meanwhile, in the late 1970s, two unarmed proto-rebel groups had begun to develop, one in Jeddah and one in Riyadh, while a third one grew out of the intellectual diaspora in the UK. Many of those in Saudi Arabia were Issaq civil servants—about sixty of them—who had all been thrown out of the civil service in 1970 in a 'socialist' purge. The man who brought all of them together was Engineer (later Colonel) Mohamed Hashi. Although he had the ability to act with sudden bold-faced courage—as he did to free Mohamed Ali from direct arrest by Siad Barre personally—Lixle was not an adventurer, as his comrade was. Even if he accepted the need at times for action, he had no personal fascination with the means of violence. And he fully realised that the Somali had a tendency to neglect planning and to let things fall into place on their own.

Mohamed Hashi had gathered a number of Issaq around himself in Jeddah and, unlike Mohamed Ali, he did not think that armed activity was the main priority for the political action which he felt was needed. He did not move in the same circles of soldiers of fortune which were Mohamed Ali's natural milieu but rather among workers, technicians and small traders, the rank and file of the working Somali emigrants to the Arab countries. He had gone back several times to Somaliland since the end of the war and gained a sense of the terrible deterioration of political and economic conditions, which had damaged the social environment of the former British colony. He knew that the situation was heading for a violent upheaval and he wanted to prepare for it.

When he went to London, he asked the diaspora there why it was not publishing any kind of newspaper or bulletin which could be used to disseminate information about home, provide a chronicle of violent events, and add a measure of propaganda encouraging the people to revolt. Although his correspondents agreed with him about the seriousness of the situation, they were taken aback since they had no organised group, no idea about how to publish any kind of broadsheet, and they totally lacked funds. Upon returning to Jeddah, he started to reorganise his contacts and steer them towards fundraising. Soon they had $20,000, which they channelled towards England where the intellectual community was in a better position to publish something. Lixle insisted that it was better to publish in England to avoid irritating the Saudi authorities, who were likely to be nervous about a political insurgent group operating out of their own territory, even if they had no sympathy for the Siad Barre regime, which they perceived as too 'leftist'. Saudi Arabia was a polity both viscerally conservative and built on a fragile tribal support network. It instinctively disliked any popular, democratic type of political action and so the money was forwarded to London.[17] This transfer of funds and the new tasks undertaken by the diaspora in England helped to bolster the importance of what had been so far a rather politically passive intellectual group. The work of the UK committee would, in the medium term, bridge the gap between the mostly reflective non-armed militants and those who, in the wake of Mohamed Ali, saw no other solution than armed insurrection.

SNM is (discreetly) born

By late 1980 the UK committee began to look like a possible beacon of unity for the various Issaq 'revolutionary committees' that had developed in Saudi and, to a lesser degree, in the United Arab Emirates. SOSAF, which was then itself only a guerrilla force in the making, sent a delegation to London and proposed a merger. But beyond the fact that the two possible partners were at the time still quite unsure of where they were going, the clanic feelings— Majerteen versus Issaq—were too much of an obstacle for the two fledgling groups to unite and the SOSAF offer was politely refused. But the Issaq actors felt the moment was ripe.

> We decided to form a transitional committee to give more people a chance to join. We did not stop because we did not want to lose the momentum. Then we decided to meet on 6 April 1981. There was no particular reason for that date but I remember it was on a weekend, a Saturday, which gave us a convenient time to meet in Connaught Hall. The event was well organised and had a good participation. I was chairing and there was a panel made up of Hassan Esse, Abdisalam Yassin, Hassan Adan Wadaadiid and Ismail Duqsi. I made the opening speech and stated the objectives of the movement.[18] The hall was full of people, more than we expected ... Most of the money to stage the event had been sent by the Somali community in the Gulf through Mohamed Hashi and Abdisalam Yassin. The event started around 10 o'clock and lasted about three hours. There were no foreign guests at the event. It was only us and our community. The most important media for us at the time was the BBC because our target audience were not the people in London or in the Gulf, it was the masses back home.[19] The people who attended were quite happy and they congratulated us. But there was fear also: everybody knew we had very little material capacity and we were in London, very far from home. But it was the only hope we had ...[20]

> There had been a radical shift over the last three years; our support for the Somali government and for the idea of Somalihood had shifted to a radical opposition, and the only thing we wanted now was for that regime to collapse ... We wanted to create a structure that would encompass all the Somali. We contacted most of the clans. We started with the Gaddabursi and at first we got some responses; but later the Gaddabursi leadership went to Djibouti and the

government convinced them not to join the SNM because it was not in the interest of Djibouti. We also approached the Dhulbahante but got no response. We did the same with the Hawiye but received no support. The Majerteen—those that were not yet with SOSAF—did not respond. After this complete failure to gain support from the non-Issaq clans, we asked ourselves: what shall we do? Our decision was to go on with the movement and to put the structure of the leadership on hold while we looked for other groups. We gave ourselves six months. After about five months without any sign from any other clan, we decided to finalise an independent structure to start working on relocating to Ethiopia. We assigned this task to Said Abdullahi Egal, who knew Amharic and had a contact with the Ethiopian Embassy in Sweden. At first the embassy did not give us a response. At the end of 1981 SSDF, which had organised in the meantime, contacted us. One of their envoys was an Issaq, the brother-in-law of Mustafa Hajji Nuur. But they were not convincing. Then in February 1982 four commanders we knew, Mohamed Kahin, Adan Shine, Adan Saleeban and Ahmed Dhagah, crossed the border from Awdal into Ethiopia and used our name, telling the Ethiopian authorities that they were SNM. They asked the authorities to contact us, and the Ethiopian Embassy in London got in touch with us. Then several Somali businessmen living in Ethiopia got into the act and provided us with personal contacts and financial help. At that point we began to ask ourselves: what are we going to do if we liberate the country from the regime and we come to realise that the whole Greater Somalia agenda has completely failed? Then what can we do? Could we not go back to our own Somaliland? However, we decided to move [to Ethiopia] and not mention anything about secession.[21]

By now the door to Ethiopia—and therefore to armed action—was (half) open. This was so because, first of all, the Ethiopian authorities were only partly welcoming. Mengistu and his Libyan ally, Colonel Gaddafi, wanted to convince—or even blackmail—the nascent SNM into accepting a merger with the newborn SSDF.[22] As we will see, SSDF was a strange concoction in which all the peculiar godfathers of the new organisation—Ethiopia, Libya and South Yemen—had a horse in the race. Behind them, Moscow was still hesitating about its final plans. In a way, all three communist-allied regimes (and their sponsor) were looking for a fourth partner in the alliance so as to beat their 'friends' to the draw in order to control the future of a country which, even after Siad Barre's ousting, would retain a key strategic position: with one huge coastline overlooking the Indian Ocean while the other stretched across the largest oil reserves in the Middle East. And the Ogaden War had shown how quickly the winds could change in global strategic terms. Washington, even though it had no appetite for the region, had had to be realistic and returned to the area in order to limit the collateral damage caused by the recent Soviet switch. On such a broad stage, the SNM was a folkloric addition to a complicated, exotic battle, with non-existent means, no friends and few business contacts. SSDF, on the other hand, was not really a big actor but its comparatively greater weight and its (theoretical) prospects were definitely more promising. When SNM meekly landed in Ethiopia in early 1982, the pressure on it to merge with SSDF was considerable and could have driven it into the deadly embrace of Abdullahi Yusuf. We will later return to the relations between the two groups when dealing with the early days of SNM operations; but the initial prudence of the Issaq movement, seen at first as unrealistic and immature political posturing, ended up saving the day when the SSDF's contradictions brought it to organisational shipwreck.

But beyond the problem of an eventual merger with SSDF, there was another obstacle: the complete confusion of the clanic military landscape in the northern part of the Somali region, both in the Hawd and in western Somaliland. The Ogaden War and its catastrophic ending had not only left a field of destruction but it had also exposed the social (and economic) relations between the clans to the manipulations of the Mogadishu regime, which was trying to retain some kind of control over the situation by pitting its possible allies against its visible enemies.

Somaliland's clanic geopolitics

There were a number of structural contradictions that lay at the root of what would become 'a neo-nationalist regional movement', if the reader is considerate enough to tolerate such a jaw-breaker. The contradictions can be listed as follows:

- The shapeless 'movement' that started to take shape in northern Somalia in the wake of the 1978 defeat was reactive rather than aggressive, i.e. it was a reaction against the growing persecution of the populations of the provinces of Sool, Sanaag, Togdheer, Woqooyi Galbeed and Awdal (all part of the former British Somaliland) by the political regime in Mogadishu.
- This persecution was mostly directed at the central and central-eastern parts of the former colony, populated by Issaq, leaving the western region (populated by the Dir clan family—Issa and Gaddabursi) relatively untouched. Similarly, the eastern part of Somaliland, populated by Warsangeli and Dhulbahante, both members of the very large Darood clan family, was not targeted by the anti-Issaq measures.

- There were several subsets in the geography of conflict. In the extreme west (Awdal) the Issa were not bothered but, incited by the Djibouti authorities, they started snapping at the heels of the southern regime, betting that its eventual collapse would allow the Djibouti Somali (who are also Issa) to unite with their cross-border cousins. In the east, the small Warsangeli clan tried to steer clear of the conflict and remain neutral. But the Dhulbahante, on the contrary, rallied to the support of the Siad Barre regime and provided the shock troops in the war with the Issaq when it finally came about.

- The core Issaq population was largely united in the face of the Darood assault;[23] but this did not mean that all Issaq sub-clans operated hand in hand; quite the contrary. Even if the SNM did try to project this image, it was far from the truth and the extreme prudence which two SNM regiments showed when meeting and dealing with each other (regiments were organised on a sub-clan basis) demonstrated that trust was limited by clanic definition.[24]

- But, overall, one should definitely not see the Somalilanders, regardless of clans, as a secessionist movement. On the contrary. The pan-Somali ideology was still dominant in the late 1970s when the first anti-Siad Barre movements started to take shape. The majority of Somalilanders were anti-Siad Barre and anti-government. But many were still in the grip of 'the Dream' and they had volunteered to fight Ethiopia in 1977 in the hope of freeing their fellow Ogadeni Somali from Ethiopian domination. As Issaq, they tended to be anti-Darood but made distinctions among the Darood. They were mostly anti-Marehan (Siad Barre's clan) and anti-Dhulbahante, the feeling being that, as fellow northerners, the Dhulbahante should have sided with the rebellion. But far from being persecuted by the regime, the Dhulbahante were courted by it (they provided most of the cannon fodder to fight the Issaq after the war heated up), so they had no interest in rebelling. As for the Ogadeni, Issaq attitudes were very divided. At first it was a matter of 'these are our brothers who suffer under Ethiopian domination'. But later, when they saw the Ogadeni refugees settle on their land and take advantage of government support to pillage the north, the feeling changed and the Ogadeni slowly turned into the Issaq's worst enemies.

- But the main question remained—in the aftermath of the Ogaden War, what should we do? The simple idea that the 1960 partial unification was a sufficient path towards a better future was gone. As we have seen by looking at the mood of the Issaq founders of SNM, secession was only a hazy possibility among a diverse range of possible solutions. Meanwhile, what should be done? This was the dilemma the SNM faced, practically, when it arrived in Ethiopia in early 1982.

Armed actors during the post-Ogaden War period

The coup attempt

The paradox is that, while former Somaliland was socially and politically the most problematic part of Somalia, it was not there that the first anti-government rebellion started. It started in Mogadishu through the coup attempt led by two Majerteen army colonels, Abdullahi Yusuf Ahmed and Muhammad Sheikh Usman. Given this, Siad Barre later had an easy time in presenting the coup as a 'Majerteen coup'. Of course this was not a ridiculous interpretation, in the light of the Majerteen dominance of the pre-Siad Barre democratic regime.[25] Moreover, given the fact that Siad Barre's coup had sidelined both the establishment figure of Haji Musa Boqor (scheduled to replace the dead President) and the only genuine opposition leader, Abdirizak Haji Hussein, who were Majeerteen, a revenge clanic coup was a possibility. But this is not the view of Daniel Compagnon, probably the best analyst of the Siad Barre regime,[26] who points out that, of the 17 officers shot in July 1978, four at least were not Majerteen (there was one Issaq and three Hawiye plus at least two more whose clanic identity was unclear). Compagnon attributes this 'Majerteen coloration' of the coup to four factors:

- The Majerteen had been the clan family that dominated the politics of the pre-1969 era.
- The Majerteen had the largest clan presence in the army.
- Siad Barre had marginalised the Majerteen in 1969 and as a result was wary of them.
- Abdullahi Yusuf Ahmed used his clanic connections to prepare the coup while capitalising on the overall discontent of the armed forces after the defeat. In other words, he spearheaded what he felt was a broader popular tendency. But his calculation was wrong: the discontent was there but the army was not at its forefront.

The coup attempt was easily crushed, but Abdullahi Yusuf did not give up. He fled to Kenya and later Ethiopia, starting to put together an operational armed rebel movement. From its beginnings, it was a completely different movement from what had developed among the 'Somalilanders'.

From the coup attempt to SSDF

When Abdullahi Yusuf fled abroad, he could connect with the first opposition movement which had been created back in 1977, the Somali Democratic Action Front (SODAF). Based in Rome, it was an organisation of notables that represented the elites displaced by the October 1969 coup. It was not planning to resort to armed action and had no particular clan identification. Its activities were mostly just propaganda, but it was composed of people with a broad range of political contacts. Things began to change for them when they joined the escaped leaders of the failed coup, moved to Ethiopia and started to contemplate the possibility of armed action. In February 1979 the organisation was renamed the Somali Salvation Front (SOSAF) and it started to make more threatening noises. But in spite of being based in Addis Ababa, it still tried to keep on the good side of the US State Department and the CIA by not criticising the retrocession of the former Soviet base in Berbera to the Americans (August 1980), in spite of the loud Ethiopian opposition to the switch. In January 1981 SOSAF travelled to Washington and tried to capitalise on continued US resentment against Siad Barre. But Jimmy Carter was about to leave the presidency, and this was not Ronald Reagan's fight.

SOSAF had come too late and, without any opening on its right, it started to explore what it could pick up on its left. The enormous strategic vacillation that accompanied the Ogaden War had left a number of convinced communists disoriented when their country started to fight another ally of the Soviet Union. The Somali Revolutionary Socialist Party (SRSP) had a (frustrated) left wing, which was divided into two groups. Exceptionally for Somali political groupings, they had no clanic differences. The first group was made up of (minority) members of the SRSP Central Committee and considered 21 October 1969 to have been a genuine revolution. But Siad Barre had been too moderate and had made alliances with 'reactionaries'. The solution was therefore to create a genuine Marxist-Leninist, Soviet-type communist party and take power. The main leader of that group was the Dhulbahante Abdirahman Aydid, who managed to slip out of Mogadishu in October 1980 and reach Addis Ababa where he created the Democratic Front for the Liberation of Somalia (DFLS), with Mengistu's full support. The second group was made up of what would be called at the time 'leftists' in the political vocabulary of Western countries, i.e. anti-Soviet communists.[27] They considered October 1969 to have been a mere military coup and did not think Siad Barre had any 'revolutionary' credentials. The leaders of that sub-group moved not to Ethiopia (where they feared being too tightly controlled by Mengistu and his Russian allies) but to Aden where the People's Democratic Republic of Yemen was both communist and more independent. In Aden, Said Jama Hussein, a Marxist Issaq intellectual, created the Somali Workers' Party (SWP) and made contact with the other dissidents. On 16 October 1981, after long and arduous negotiations, SOSAF, DFLS and the SWP signed a full-fledged merger agreement, taking the new name of the Somali Salvation Democratic Front (SSDF) and establishing their seat in Addis Ababa.

The new organisation was massively asymmetric: SOSAF was a military outfit, made up not only of Majerteen soldiers but also of Majerteen of the Omar Mahmood clan and even mostly (80 per cent) of men from the Rer Mahad sub-clan, that of Abdullahi Yusuf himself. Those who were not Rer Mahad were Rer Khalaf, a sub-clan which lived in Ogaden territory, out of easy reach of the Somali Army. There was also a smattering of non-Majerteen and almost no civilians. SOSAF had between 3,000 and 4,000 men under arms, with top-notch Russian equipment provided by Libya.[28] This made the new SSDF a real army, with armour, artillery, modern communications, generous supplies of cash and fuel, and a close relationship with the regular Ethiopian Army.

But to this prosperity the left-wing newcomers, DFLS and SWP, contributed very little in practical terms. They had only a few hundred members, no money, no weapons and no military training. What they had were political ideas and the complete works of Lenin in twenty volumes produced by Progress Publishers in Moscow. But this was also useful for Abdullahi Yusuf, who was not known for ever having read Lenin but who needed Russian and Derg support, particularly heavy weapons, which he wanted to use against the Somali Army in conventional battles.[29] In 1981, secure in its Ethiopian bases, SSDF stood alone on the armed opposition stage, even when seen from an Issaq perspective:

> The reason we wanted to join SSDF was simply because everyone wanted to join the Somali struggle against a brutal regime. But we did not know what was going on inside SSDF. The Majerteen did not only treat the Issaq badly, they did the same with the Hawiye or the Dhulbahante. The internal conflicts were very bad, even among the Majerteen themselves. We had not expected such treatment from them. But there was no alternative. The SNM was still in its infant stage and we believed we needed an established movement for the struggle. But when we realised what was happening within SSDF, we knew we had to move out. SSDF could not absorb anyone, they could not even absorb themselves. Abdullahi Yusuf was a notorious dictator and he could arrest anyone he wanted.

So I think I only spent eight months with SSDF, and as soon as I could I moved out to SNM.[30]

In Somalia, the support given by the Majerteen—and particularly by the Omar Mahmood clan—to the rebels carried a very heavy price. In Mudug, in northern Galguduud, in the easternmost part of the Ethiopian Ogaden, commandos of the military security (Hangash) and the National Secret Service would shoot civilians at random, rape women, blow up wells, and steal camels. SSDF retaliated by carrying out night raids, attacking Somali Army military outposts, laying mines and shooting up road transport. But for Gaddafi, who put a lot of money and equipment into supporting SSDF; for Mengistu, who had to suffer reprisal air bombings when the Somali counter-attacked after the cross-border raids; and for Abdullahi Yusuf, who had to face the complaints of the clan elders, something had to be done. In late June 1982, 15,000 regular Ethiopian Army troops and about 2,000 SSDF guerrillas attacked Somalia across the Mudug border, aiming for Galkayo in the north-east and Belet Weyn in the centre. The plan was to cut Somalia into two by driving troops all the way to the ocean, but the plan backfired. The main reason was that, in spite of exhaustion after defeat in 1978, the Somali Army had licked its wounds and regrouped. In addition, the open Ethiopian attack caused a massive upsurge of support for the regime and Siad Barre regained, at least partly, some of the legitimacy he had lost four years before. Volunteers rushed to join the army and civil society closed ranks in support of the nation.[31] In addition, the Russians, who did not want the Cold War to heat up again at this late point, collaborated with the Americans to stop the crisis. Moscow sent a serious warning to Mengistu, and Washington decided to finally deliver the arms it had been promising Mogadishu for the last three years. The Ethiopian and SSDF forces never reached Galkayo or Belet Weyn, stopping at the villages of Balambale and Goldogob. Abdullahi Yusuf and his SSDF had a hard time explaining to the suffering Majerteen civilians that this was all, that the great offensive to overthrow Siad Barre would come later.

Abdullahi Yusuf's interest and worth in the eyes of Mengistu then shrank, and the latter cast SSDF into a new role, considering it no longer as a first-line ally but rather as a poorly led and poorly organised auxiliary force. He then began to see its future role as being restricted to harassing the Somali regime by carrying out a series of limited hit-and-run raids, without any larger strategic view. Gaddafi also began losing faith in the possible success of SSDF and scaled down his weapons deliveries. By early 1983 he stopped them altogether.

As often happens among groups which are failing in what they attempt to do, the members of the rebel movement started to fight each other. The logical fault line dividing them—since most of them belonged to the same clan family—was their social inscription and their ideological orientations. Roughly speaking, it was the military leadership, with its narrow, traditional view of the role of the clan and with its conservative social views, pitted against revolutionary Marxist intellectuals. The former DFLS and SWP members were soon criticising Abdullahi Yusuf, accusing him of exactly the same sins as Siad Barre: of authoritarianism, clanic manipulation, ideological hypocrisy and theft of their collective funds. In the training camps and all the way to Balambale and Goldogob, partisans and enemies of the SSDF leader started to shoot each other. Abdullahi Yusuf had manipulated the last congress of the Front and stuffed its ruling hierarchy with his own Rer Mahad supporters, who now took their quarrels to the streets of Ethiopian cities[32] and even to their training camps. The Issaq, in the meantime, had created their own rebel movement, the SNM.[33] Long a poor second to the powerful SSDF, the SNM were now only too glad that they had obstinately refused the bribes in money and equipment taht the Ethiopians and the Libyans had long offered them to merge with the Majerteen Front. When Abdullahi Yusuf ended up having two members of his own Central Committee murdered by his nephew (in October 1984), the movement practically collapsed and Mengistu had him arrested.[34] For the SNM, another road had begun to open.

The WSLF in the clanic melee

Which side was the WSLF on? The probable answer to this rhetorical question is 'none' or more precisely 'its own'. The reason for the internal explosion was the arrival of the (very small) SNM forces. Not that they had been able to actually do anything: it was simply their presence which acted as a catalyst. In January 1981, the last elements of the Somali Regular Army still operating in the Ogaden had been brought home, leaving behind an abandoned WSLF and a worsening situation. The Ethiopian Army and its allied militias struck headlong at the Somali population of the Ogaden, in the midst of a particularly severe drought. Civilians began streaming eastwards to escape the violence of the repression and loose units of the WSLF floated on the surface of that sea of human misery. But for Siad Barre what mattered was not the hordes of refugees, but the SNM. Not that its arrival caused enthusiasm among the populations it was coming to liberate. 'There were frenzied discussions on where to locate the new SNM military bases because most people were afraid that the location of the bases would be a signal to attract Siad Barre's reactions against certain clans; therefore most of the people refused to host the SNM.'[35]

Siad called a large Darood clan family meeting to distribute the roles in the fighting: he gave orders for the Ogadeni WSLF militiamen to attack the Habr Yunis sub-clan of the Issaq from the Ethiopian side while the regular army would catch them in a pincer movement from the Somalia side.[36] But WSLF was in a state of upheaval and its members felt betrayed by Mogadishu. In January 1981, the old executive of the movement had been kicked out of its leadership position and the secretary-general, Abdullahi Hassan Mohamed, was replaced by Mohamed Diriye from the Rer Abdullah lineage, one openly hostile to Siad Barre's family.[37] As a result, the President's orders were followed tentatively, loosely and with little military efficacy. The SNM itself was not even attacked, but the Habr Yunis had their own militia and they fought against the Ogadeni, killing many.

Even if the SNM was identified as a future danger, at the time it did not amount to much. The men with guns were either the Habr Yunis clanic militia or the WSLF Fourth Battalion of Mohamed Ali. The SNM political leadership was in the hands of Ahmed Jimale, who had been elected chairman in the UK. But Jimale was not seen as a solid leader and many would have preferred Mohamed Hashi ('Lixle') as chair. Jimale was displaced as chairman by an internal coup but he refused to step down. So SNM came to Addis Ababa in a state of confusion and disarray and was not even taken seriously by the Ethiopians, who preferred to back the SSDF. The Movement's first congress was not a very impressive affair:

> We prepared for our first congress in Nazareth ... We requested the Ethiopians to facilitate our movements. But we were restricted to the major cities and therefore we needed a pass to participate in the SNM meeting. After we got a pass, we left for Jijiga.[38] There were not many of us. We stayed at the Havana Hotel, which had only about 20 rooms. This was all what SNM needed, 20 rooms was big enough for us. At the time our only real force was the Mohamed Ali army, which was in Durya.[39]

But while SNM was painfully trying to organise itself in Ethiopia, the voluntary service movement had been gaining ground in Hargeisa[40] and had by-passed the government to carry out civilian work and charitable programmes under the nickname Uffo.[41] As we saw in the previous chapter, a crackdown on Uffo supporters triggered widespread disturbances over the whole of former Somaliland and caused a movement of armed insurgents to Ethiopia where they usually joined Watatir Mohamed Ali, the Fourth Battalion of WSLF, which had much more visibility and organisation than the struggling SNM. By then the Fourth Battalion was fighting both the Somali National Army and the other WSLF battalions. Somewhat later, the 'Afraad' would merge with the original elements of SNM. Thus began the long uphill battle for the creation of a real revolutionary army. But in early 1982, this was still a very distant prospect.

4

SNM

THE SLOW GROWTH OF AN ODD GUERRILLA FORCE IN THE HARD-EDGED COLD WAR LANDSCAPE

The opening measures

Sheikh Yusuf Ali Sheikh Madar was elected as the new chairman of the SNM in January 1982. By putting him at the head of the recently created organisation, the SNM supporters chose an easy way forward. Sheikh Madar belonged to a prosperous and respected family of the Sa'ad Musa sub-clan of the Habr Awal Issaq. His great-grandfather was a Sufi saint who was reputed to have founded the city of Hargeisa, and his uncle had led a delegation of Issaq elders who attempted in March 1982 to open a dialogue with Siad Barre in order to ease the persecution of the clan family by the regime. Together with a number of other Issaq notables, he represented a moderate Islamist political trend and was accepted as such by the Ethiopians. In Mengistu's Marxist view, the SNM embodied the conservative religious wing of the rebellion, whose vanguard 'socialist' wing was supposed to be Abdullahi Yusuf's SSDF. Yusuf's 'socialism' was even more paper-thin than Mengistu's own, but in the highly ideologised political landscape of Eastern Africa in the early 1980s, this was good enough.

At that time, in terms of political effectiveness, the SNM looked highly unconvincing in comparison with its Majerteen rival. The SSDF had many more men, most of them former Somali National Army soldiers, it had the

57

support of both Mengistu's solid army logistics and of Gaddafi's well-publicised 'universal opposition' and, behind both, Soviet arms supplies. The SNM had none of that, and its 'Islamic image', back in the early 1980s, seemed quaint and faintly reactionary. In the ideologically charged outlook of the 1980s, the announcement of its birth from London had a slightly amusing, post-colonial whiff. In Cold War terms, SNM was the odd man out.

And then, brutally, in an unexpected thunderclap, an SNM commando unit infiltrated deeply into Somaliland from its makeshift Ethiopian base[1] and attacked the big Somali Army prison in Mandera (2 January 1983). The operation went without a hitch and 744 prisoners were freed by the commando unit. Actually the attackers were not even really SNM; they were Mohamed Ali's Afraad. But for the first time the name SNM was used in a military operation. Lixle's speech to the prisoners was absolutely typical of the mindset of the young and somewhat naive SNM:

> O prisoners, you are from everywhere.[2] Now we will release you. You have three options to choose from: (1) whoever wants to join the SNM, as we are fighting the regime, you can come and join the Jihad;[3] (2) whoever wants to go and join his family, we will help you get back home; (3) whoever wants to join the regime, you should know we pushed them back to Abdaal when we came; so go to them and we will not do anything to you until you reach them. But be careful: we might attack you later and then our bullets will hurt you. So choose one of these options'[4]

The effect of the speech was electric, and many among the Somali joined SNM (the foreign prisoners preferred the 'going home' option). It also had a huge impact outside the north, in media and propaganda terms. Another commando unit had come from Ethiopia, and on 5 February it fought a standing battle in Durosi, where 38 were killed. The National Security Sevice started to panic and in Hargeisa over 700 people were arrested on charges of complicity with the guerrillas. But even if there was broad public support for the action in the north, there was no existing underground SNM network and the accusations of complicity were imaginary. Indeed, the operation had been prepared and carried out in complete improvisation, something which had a later impact on the SNM's modus operandi.[5]

On 9 February Siad Barre himself flew in from Mogadishu, accompanied by two colonels, one Issaq and one Gaddabursi, so as to give himself some veneer of local support. The President was assured by the authorities in Hargeisa that this was an isolated incident and he released the 700 detainees on the spot and re-established some semblance of government control over the situation. However, three weeks later he prohibited the use of and trade in *qat*.[6] The *qat* merchants, particularly in the north, are a power unto themselves and a great deal of cash passes through their hands. In Somaliland they were suspected of having guerrilla sympathies, and prohibiting the use of and trade in *qat* was seen by the government as a way of drying up an important source of finance for the nascent rebel movement. The reality was more complex: *qat* traders had diverse political sympathies and clanic belongings, and they were not particularly pro-SNM. However, they had only one source of income: the drug. Overnight, they were all ruined by the ban and immediately switched over to the guerrilla side. This had a major military impact. Till then SNM was so poor that it had only one truck and one Land Rover, both stolen from inside Somalia. Overnight the *qat* vehicles—*qat* merchants all had fast cars that could cross the desert from Ethiopia at top speed to bring the freshly picked leaves swiftly to their customers—were given to the guerrilla group. Many of these four-wheel drives (most were Toyota Land Cruisers), which had been seized on foreign territory, were later sent to Djibouti and re-imported into Ethiopia by train. The SNM immediately got to work on them: they cut down the body, bolted machine guns, ZUG 23 mm automatic light cannons or recoilless rifles on the back[7] and added supplementary fuel tanks, turning these vehicles into improvised deadly weapons of desert fighting, locally known as 'technicals'.

These new military developments were not immediately turned into direct offensive operations against the Siad Barre regime. The situation was much too complicated. The war against Ethiopia and the resulting defeat had wide-ranging effects on Somali society. The Ethiopian–SSDF attack of July 1982 had ended in failure.[8] But in the Cold War context, it was seen in Washington as a 'communist' attack. The Russians, who disapproved of it, tried to explain it away and persuade the US that it was unintended. But they did not want to expose their disagreements with the Mengistu regime to too deep a probing look from the Americans, and their reservations were seen in Washington as ambiguous and unconvincing. For Siad Barre this was an opportunity. A previous visit to Washington by a Somali delegation in March 1982 had brought disappointing results; but a new one in August, after the Balambale–Goldogob battles, was much more fruitful, especially as it was backed up by the intervention of a Saudi delegation. The Americans went for a $60 million gift of military equipment[9] (APCs, TOW anti-tank missiles, M-16 rifles, 106 mm RCL light artillery) while the Saudis gave $150 million in cash and a year's supply (360,000 tons) of fuel.

In fact, most of the new money and equipment was not used directly against the SNM (or even the SSDF) but in the clanic war between the Issaq and the Ogadeni. This fighting was not explicitly linked with the SNM, even if there was a lot of overlap in terms of combatants. The Ogadeni were a mixture of refugees from the Ethiopian Ogaden province, former WSLF guerrillas, and rogue Somali National Army soldiers or deserters. Their Issaq adversaries were mostly the powerful Habr Yunis militia (which had not fought against the Ogadeni but at their side four years before when they both battled the Ethiopian Army and the Cubans) and Lixle's Afraad, who were themselves former WSLF. This mishmash was not immediately clear to US analysts, and so, when seen from Washington, the situation was easier to explain in terms of a communist versus anti-communist duality. The genuine SNM (then quite small) was lost in the confusion.

Meanwhile, back in Mogadishu, Siad Barre, who had a much clearer grasp of the situation, had to parry both the military blows and their political consequences. For a certain segment of the SRSP,[10] things had gone too far and the defeat had deeply upset not only the regime but also the entire hold of the 'Greater Somalia' ideology on Somali minds and therefore the capacity of the regime to keep ruling in its present form. Siad Barre had to go before it was too late, some kind of a nation-wide *shir*[11] had to be convened, and a new regime had to be set up. In June 1982, seven high-ranking SRSP leaders who shared these views were arrested. They belonged to a variety of clans (Hawiye, Issaq) and their leader was General Omar Haji Mohamed, a Marehan (Siad Barre's clan), who was Minister of Defence. The men arrested really represented a cross-section of the highest ranks of the SRSP. Their ideological preferences were also quite eclectic, ranging from Mohamed Adan Sheikh, who was the most influential Marxist in the regime, to Omar Arteh Ghalib, who was openly pro-American. Somewhat unnoticed in the general fray was the Minister of Commerce, Ahmed Mohamed Mahmood 'Silanyo' (the little lizard), who managed to run away and avoid arrest. He fled to London and later enjoyed a major career in the SNM, becoming President of independent Somaliland in 2010. 'The Seven', as they were soon called, all ended up in jail, while by early 1983 the Ogadeni–Issaq fighting started to subside. The Ogadeni had asked the Dhulbahante for help against the Issaq within the supposed framework of a broad Darood alliance, but it had not worked out.[12]

Meanwhile, in June the Americans decided to cash in on their investment and arrived in Berbera to refurbish the old Soviet base and enlarge its runway so that it could accommodate B-52 nuclear bombers. The new installations were inaugurated in October 1984, providing a measure of relief for Siad Barre, who had now become a (small) pawn in the Cold War great game. But in the parallel world of Somali reality, things remained difficult: the Issaq refused to pay the *mag* the Ogadeni were demanding.[13] The Issaq argued that the usual prices were not applicable because the Ogadeni had had the support of the Somali National Army (SNA), with its artillery and armour, which had represented an unfair advantage, therefore lowering the *mag* compensation that was due. In fact, the money was mostly to compensate for humiliation because, in spite of SNA help, the Ogadeni had higher losses than the Habr Yunis Issaq and they wanted cash to soothe their hurt pride. This was another world, and even if it was geographically close to the US runway in Berbera, it belonged to a different reality.

The problem for Siad Barre was how to keep these two worlds in some kind of a relationship. It was the Hawiye clan who tried to help.[14] They offered the President a mediation committee that would address the northern problem. On 30 January 1983 they presented their recommendations to the head of state:

1. All restrictions on circulation in the north should be lifted.[15]
2. All political prisoners should be freed.
3. The old *franco valuta* financial system should be re-established.
4. Government agents who, like General Mohamed Hashi Gani, had made a career of clanic persecution should be transferred out of the areas where they were operating.
5. The President should travel to the north and stay there for a while.
6. The WSLF should be disbanded and its troops should not be used in what was turning into a civil war with the Issaq.
7. A special clanic co-operating council should be created to practically address inter-clan problems instead of just 'prohibiting' clanism in an authoritarian way.

Siad Barre rejected all these recommendations on 2 February 1983 (a week before his abortive visit to the north after the Mandera attack), using 'his' Hawiye supporters against their own clan family.[16] But then the dictator received some hope of success. In January 1983 Abdullahi Yusuf had organised an SSDF congress which turned out to be a farce. The 30 top SWP and SDLF members—the SSDF left wing—who had planned to challenge him at the congress were all arrested as they assembled. What was left of the gathering duly gave him a supportive vote but his already damaged organisation fell further apart. The following month Siad Barre offered them amnesty, and over 600 of the movement's disgruntled cadres went back to Somalia. By late 1983,

SSDF had been reduced to a powerless rump and the weak SNM remained as the only organised armed force opposing the Mogadishu dictatorship. If it wanted to inherit the mantle of the armed opposition, it had to renew itself and Sheikh Yusuf Ali Sheikh Madar was not the man to do it.

In November 1983 a new congress was assembled and it elected Colonel Abdiqadir Kosar Abdi as the new chairman. Most of the religiously oriented leadership was sidetracked at the same time. This is where the strong democratic assets of the organisation—and, behind them, of the Issaq clan family and of the 'Anglo-Somali' political culture of former colonial Somaliland—played an essential role. The SNM's political culture was radically different from that of SSDF. There were no arrests, no murders, no violence, not even expulsions. Those who were voted out left of their own accord, and others took their place. The 'military leadership' settled in and set to work. It was partly successful militarily but inefficient politically, and this led to still another change of leadership—also peaceful—in 1984. The SNM leadership was far from capable but it always successfully managed to avoid the worst curse of quarrelling guerrilla movements—violence. Colonel Abdi Kosar did a good logistical and organisational job, a questionable military job and a poor political one. He was voted out in August 1984, leaving the door open for another administration, that of the wily Ahmed Mohamed 'Silanyo', Siad Barre's former economist, who had been biding his time in London. During those years—1983 and 1984—the SNM began to take shape in spite of its drastically limited means. It started to fight, with courage but rather inefficiently, trying to survive in a sharp Cold War environment where it fitted poorly. It was supported by a Marxist power but never turned 'communist'; it dealt daily with an abominably authoritarian regime but without resorting to terrorism; and it fought a Western-supported dictatorship but without turning anti-Western. All in all, an impressive, even if often fumbling, trapeze act.

Getting it together and starting to move on

(a) Putting feet on the ground and getting weapons

The person who was leading the recruitment of the combatants was Colonel 'Lixle' ... The establishment of our bases was based on clans: Xarshin for Sa'ad Musa, Lanqeyrta for Arap, Aware for Eidagalley, Gaashaamo for Habr Yunis, Baalidheeye for Habr Ja'alo ... The first two training centres were in Baabuli and Aware ... At the time, there was no army command of any shape or form, the mobilisation was directly from the communities, there was no SNM command ... When we came to Aware, we didn't have a 'base'; there were seven of us and we just stayed in a small room in the town ... Then we convinced the Ethiopians to move to Ramaso, which is 40 km north-west of Aware. There we established a temporary base. We did not have transportation. Both our men and even the Ethiopians travelled on foot ... So this was a problem when the Ethiopians gave us 200 AK-47s. Before that we had had few guns, less than one hundred, and we carried them by hand, with a little ammunition. But these other guns were given to a Dhulbahante commander to open a base in Qararo.

There was no central depot for SNM where we could put all the guns. So we organised 100 men from Ramaso and the area to assist us and move the weapons from Aware to Ramaso. We collected trustworthy men, mainly elderly men, from the villages and we all left Aware on foot. Each man carried two guns and the ammunition pouch. But we had no ammunition at all, all the pouches were empty. The guns were new. It took us three nights to go drop the guns and come back. There was only a small incident, seven of the men ran away with the guns, but we ambushed them in a place called Quus and we got the guns back but we did not shoot the men ... At the time the recruitment was voluntary. We did not have any central message. We were helped by the environment and the situation of the country. There were young men who were tending cattle and they faced the oppression and the killings; there were also deserters of all kinds, from the SNA and from the SSDF. Then by word of mouth, our relatives also came. The Ethiopians gave us army food rations and the communities in the countryside provided us with meat ...

Our major problem was with defectors. And the problem is that they took their guns with them to sell them or give them to the SNA to be readmitted. Discipline and training were limited. Some men stole animals from the local communities, and that angered people. The challenge was that we could not verify anyone apart from his clan. We had no strong intelligence. Being all Issaq, there was no betrayal, no spying. There was high trust among clansmen. But the problem was that nobody would tell bad things about a clansman so we could not really verify the information new recruits were bringing. We did some minor interviews but this was not enough ... Training was carried out by professionals, men who had been in the army. Some had made stories for the government, saying they were forming Western Somali Liberation Front units and they needed guns and registration. They got weapons from the government but it took time ... Baabuli and Aware were the two main training bases while Ramaso became the main base for the 'technicals', which supplied vehicles to all the divisions, Eastern (Qeybta Bari), Central (Qeybta Dhexe) and Western (Qeybta Galbeed). We began to get modern weapons from Yemen (PDRY) at the time of Abdi Kosar, and also the people in the diaspora bought us Toyotas and trucks, shipped them to Djibouti; we picked them up in Jijiga, we took them to Ramaso and we turned them into more 'technicals'.

(b) The first operations

> Our first operation was from Ramaso, and it was very small. We were informed that the Ogaden soldiers of WSLF passed through 'the Cross', which is 27 km north-east of Ramaso on the Qaaxo Road.[17] This was one of Siad Barre's strategies, he mobilised the fractions that were fragmenting off the WSLF and used them to jeopardise SNM mobilisation in the border areas. We were very few and we had almost no weapons. To attack 'the Cross', we were only twelve. We slept on the road and we decided to attack in the morning. The Ogaden militia was in the village where they had slept; they had one truck and a small Land Rover. I had never fired a shot in my life but I knew maybe the day had come and I felt very courageous. We entered the town from four different directions, but we had one man who spoke good Amharic, so he climbed in a tree and started to shout in Amharic. The Ogadeni got scared as they thought this was the Ethiopian Army coming and they remained indoors, hiding. So we could walk where we wanted. We realised the truck belonged to the villagers, so we did not touch it. But we took the Land Rover and drove it out of town. There was no shooting. We had stickers we had brought with us which read: 'Victory belongs to SNM. Death to Afweyne'[18] and we glued them everywhere. We left the village as the sun was rising. The Ethiopians were surprised to see us come back with a car. It was the first car our base got. We used it later to fetch water and transport goods and people between villages ...

So this first operation was very limited, bloodless and purely propaganda. But other operations began to be improvised, without planning, entirely at the initiative of local commanders.

> Let me claim that I perhaps led the first SNM unit that shot the first bullet of the war. In 1982 Lanqeyrta was an SNM base and we raised a small local force of Arap clansmen. We knew there was an SNA tanker regularly going from Baligubadle to Gumburaha, supplying the *faqhash*[19] with fuel. So we decided to attack it and I organised the operation. We ambushed the vehicle, burned it and killed some SNA soldiers. I believe this was the first armed operation by SNM fighters ...

Then there was the Birjeex operation (April 1983), a very strange and daring operation, carried out in unusual circumstances which seem right out of a Hollywood action movie; it had a large impact, even though it was carried out by a group of less than twenty men.

During the 1982–3 period when SNM installed itself in former Somaliland, the cadres of the movement started to implant secret cells in various parts of the region, some of them working out of the various government offices, where spies and special agents used their previous social contacts to assist their underground work. Such a development created ambiguous situations of shadow action, suspicion and at times betrayal. This is what triggered the so-called Birjeex operation, which was described by one of its main actors as follows:

I have to mention the Birjeex operation. I was a coordinator for the SNM in the north at the time, and this is what happened. We sent Abdullahi Askar and Abdisalam Turki from Bura'o to Hargeisa. When they got there, they stayed in a safe house run by Mohamed Haji Yusuf Imaan, near the Aw Adan workshop. Lixle wanted them to kill Ibrahim Koodbur because he believed the false information he had received that Koodbur was working with Hashi Gani and the SNA. I was the one in charge of giving the orders to Askar and Turki.

Then let me describe the situation we got in. Koodbur came to see us, and when we were all together, it got very serious indeed when I told Askar what he had to do. Turki's reaction was to disbelieve the orders of Lixle and to defend Koodbur, saying he was a good man, not a traitor, and that we should get in touch with Lixle and get him to rescind the order. There was a lot of confusion and then we parted, and the next day Askar fell into a trap and was arrested by General Hashi Gani. Hashi Gani threw him in jail and tortured him to get information about the SNM organisation in Hargeisa. This was on 11 April 1983 and the next day was Somali National Army day and General Hashi Gani decided to celebrate that occasion in the National Theatre and exhibit Abdullahi Askar bleeding and half-naked to the audience, presenting him as the defeated SNM. But we learned about it, and Major Ibrahim Koodbur put together an SNM rescue mission and attacked the officers' mess of the Birjeex military camp where Askar was detained. There was a big gunfight, one of our team was killed and another one was injured, but the man who had been ordered to kill Koodbur was saved instead by his intended victim from the hands of Hashi Gani, and we managed to all run away and eventually to cross the border and go into Ethiopia. Thus both the Mandera prison break-out and, three months later, that Birjeex operation boosted the morale of the SNM combatants and of our supporters everywhere, and we started to believe in the possibility of victory since we had successfully attacked one of the strongest armies in Africa.

(c) Hell on wheels

By the end of 1984 Adan Shine, who was the commander of the SNM forces, wrote a memo saying that we could not grow and undertake any serious action without vehicles. So far the SNM had been using camels, donkeys and pushcarts. We had only two Land Cruisers, which were used by the commanders. So we had a meeting and we decided to consult with some of our friends who had commercial trucks going to Djibouti. When the government had stopped the *franco valuta* system, the trucks which used to transport goods between north Somalia and Djibouti ran out of business. Maybe this could work. So we talked with a man called Omar Iman who had a truck in Djibouti and we asked him to organise a meeting with his colleagues in Hargeisa ... After a week Omar came back from Hargeisa with disappointing news: the truck drivers were not interested. We were not surprised because the trucks were their only source of living, and to sacrifice them—and perhaps their lives—was a hard decision to make.

I had a cousin called Haybe Omar Jeeni who had his own truck. At times he used to fulfil some assignments for us. I told him we were at a point where the SNM struggle would be in jeopardy if we could not get some trucks because our operations could not grow. He told me he had one trip to go to Hargeisa and he will see what he can do. After a few days I saw six truck drivers in front of my office in Djibouti in the company of Haybe Omar Jeeni. Those were really brave men and they were one of our success stories as well as pillars of the SNM operations. One of the drivers, Ali Gaabi, I think he was called—I think he died later in the coastal area—told me: 'My Isuzu truck is very old but I maintain it very well with spare parts and it is in good condition; in the 1977–8 war with Ethiopia, I fought side by side with your cousin Omar Jeeni near Dire Dawa and it was a lost cause, so if you think that today I can be of any use to the SNM, here are the keys.' Within a few days we had 17 trucks and a few smaller vehicles. Among all those there was even a brand-new Mercedes-Benz truck!

Next thing, the big challenge was how to transfer 17 vehicles to Ethiopia. We got help from Mohamed Ahmed Hersi, who worked with UNHCR in Djibouti. We contacted UNHCR Geneva and informed them that these trucks were owned by drivers who are Ethiopian Somali, born in Aware and Gaashaamo in the Ethiopian Somali region. The Ethiopian Embassy in Djibouti helped us by confirming these facts to the Djibouti authorities. We got permission to go to Ethiopia but we could not get the Djibouti papers because the Djibouti government refused to give them, saying it would cause an international crisis because they would be accused of assisting a liberation movement in Ethiopia. So we drove the truck to Ali Sabieh, on Djibouti territory, trying to push through, but we were blocked at the Geestiir checkpoint, where all three borders—Ethiopia, Djibouti, Somalia—meet. We could not proceed and we had to go back to Djibouti town. So we recontacted UNHCR Geneva and gave them a letter from the Ethiopian Embassy in Djibouti and then we got the green light to send the trucks by train to Ethiopia. We did not risk sending them all at once but sent two trucks on every trip, hoping this would not be noticed by the Somalia intelligence agents spying on the Djibouti railway.

But they had found out about our plans. So a delegation came from Mogadishu, with several Issaq high-ranking civil servants in it. They met the Djibouti government and talked of releasing the Uffo detainees from jail and also freeing the SNM prisoners and pardoning them if only Djibouti promised to stop these trucks from reaching Ethiopia. Some of the Issa Somali were in our favour, and they told the delegation they wanted to help us fight the oppression of the

Mogadishu clans and they could not understand how Issaq officials could be part of that delegation. The delegation was embarrassed and they tried to meet us personally one by one, but we refused. Eventually the 17 trucks all reached Ethiopia, but at the time Ethiopia was communist and they could not understand how there could be so many privately owned trucks on these trains, and this helped the SNM image and raised the morale of our fighters because nobody had managed to stop us, socialist or capitalist. Our drivers were really brave men and few are still alive today. After the war, no one helped them and those who had senior posts in the government never bothered to ask about them, even though their trucks were very crucial for the SNM operations and they had lifted the morale of the commanders and all fighters.

These men were indeed almost fearless. I remember travelling with drivers who had already had their vehicles blown up but who kept moving along randomly mined tracks, taking their chances as they moved. I remember especially one driver who travelled everywhere with his wife, who had lost her two legs in an earlier explosion. She insisted on travelling with her husband, saying that the next time they got blown up, at least it would be together. That made him laugh and he told me: 'If the God he wants you to die, you die; if the God he wants you to live, you live.' We did not die during that trip. I don't know what happened to them later.

(d) Trying to set up a health system

I flew to Mogadishu and from there to Dire Dawa. When I joined the SNM in Dire Dawa, I learned that my family had escaped from Hargeisa. Then I travelled to Lanqeyrta, which was the main base for SNM logistics. They were planning to set up three medical centres but there were not enough surgeons ... We wanted mostly health centres with blood banks and surgical equipment for the casualties that could not wait for referral to hospitals like Dire Dawa. We visited various locations where we were hoping to set up facilities and we chose Baligubadle for its strategic position. We wanted to pay rent but we did not have enough money, so we asked the landlords to have understanding. Actually they even removed the tenants to give us houses! So I started the first surgical health facility there in Baligubadle. We had to collect refrigerators and electric generators in order to store blood. But we also had to look for desks, chairs, surgical tables and the like. But there was no place to buy these items and there was not even any place to buy wood to make all those items ... So people suggested that we build our own furniture from the wooden storage boxes that we got for the ammunition, so we started to make everything from these boxes, but they were not made of good wood. They were not strong enough and I remember terrible problems such as when the table started to break in the middle of a surgical operation ...

We tried to do the best surgery we could with this makeshift equipment, with Allah's help. We mobilised all those who had any near-medical experience and even others such as carpenters and chemists ... We built temporary shelters around the hospital houses and the community did its best to support us as the casualties started to arrive. Women were really the most helpful and they did a great job. The work was very difficult and it was hard to work with the wounded. The fighters were of two categories, trained soldiers and new recruits who had just left their camels behind and had come to volunteer. At times the situation was terrible, with people asking us where their legs had gone after we amputated them, while others were shouting and yelling at their officers whom they insulted because they considered them responsible for having put them in harm's way. I would say it was a miracle that 95 per cent of the victims survived our surgeries, it was so difficult and the environment was so bad. With time, things improved slowly as we received trained staff.

The civil war in Somalia, early 1980s

The narratives of SNM veterans, like those provided above, and my attempt here to chronicle the politics of Somalia in the 1980s occupy almost completely different worlds, sharing only a very limited overlap. The 1980s were the last days of the Cold War, a key moment when the ailing Soviet Empire, ruled by ailing gerontocrats, was being pushed into a corner. There were two African episodes in that worldwide drama: southern Africa, where the apartheid regime was struggling against its Marxist enemies in Angola; and Ethiopia, where the Derg regime, allied with Moscow, was reeling from the attacks of several guerrilla movements. In comparison with these international battlefields, the Somali civil war was a minor episode of little interest to anybody, almost a parochial conflict in what was seen as a former Cold War narrative. The fact that the Somali[20] pursued a completely national agenda in fighting the Siad Barre regime, which had been kicked out of the 'socialist camp' without being given full membership of the 'free world', was beyond the understanding (and interest) of the rest of the world. Those dealing with Somalia in the so-called international community—which had yet to achieve the all-encompassing, politically correct, anaesthetic quality it reached after 1991—were second-tier people: US generals with a narrowly military outlook or Italian bureaucrats still embodying what Angelo Del Boca has felicitously called 'the nostalgia of Empire'.[21] Somalia was definitely not front-page news.

In April 1983 the Saudi government slapped an embargo on cattle imports from Somalia, which represented 87 per cent of the country's exports.[22] In a way this was business as usual in the cut-throat relations between Somalia and the Arab world. Somalia had joined the Arab League in 1974 and had always been treated as a second-rate member. But as soon as it was sidetracked by the Soviet Union in 1977, it became the humble recipient of obsolete military equipment from various Arab armies, which considered it an inexpensive way of keeping Ethiopia in check by proxy. During the 1977–8 war, Cairo and Damascus supplied large quantities of old Russian AK-47s and 'Dashaka' light machine guns to support the Somali offensive. But this did not stop with the end of the war. Light weapons kept flowing to Mogadishu and in 1983 the Somali Army had even received from Egypt 45 old T-54 Russian tanks given to Nasser twenty years earlier by Great Britain while Abu Dhabi presented ten British Hawker Hunter fighter-bombers to the Somali Air Force. These were soon put in use not against the Ethiopian enemy but rather against the SNM guerrillas in the north-west. The US included Somalia in their list of MAP (Military Aid Program) gifts but the generals were blocked in their generosity by the International Monetary Fund (IMF), which insisted on a number of reforms of the Somali economy: devaluation of the shilling, scaling down or closing many parastatal entities, and cuts in military spending. USAID had earmarked $42 million for modernising the harbour of Kismayo but the money, just like the MAP funds, was held up to try to put pressure on Siad Barre to 'de-Sovietise' his economy. In October 1984, Washington went so far as sending a sizeable delegation to attend the 15th anniversary celebrations of the 1969 coup, dangling the pending military deliveries in front of the Somali regime as a way to pressure it to satisfy the IMF demands. Those demands that could be satisfied were—the shilling was devalued by 48 per cent and some parastatals were closed—but no reduction of military spending was even attempted, in fact quite the contrary.

By late October 1984, the SNM had managed to infiltrate up to 2,000 fighters into the large cities of the north-west—Hargeisa, Bura'o, Berbera—and small insurrectional movements had taken place in the towns. The street battles lasted until early November and the repression was brutal. Between 14 and 19 November batches of civilians accused of having helped the SNM commandos were publicly executed by firing squads, and the whole north fell under the pall of a massive military attempt to control the situation. In December 'elections' were held all over the country and Siad Barre was 're-elected' with 99 per cent of the vote. Whatever fighting still took place was limited to the north-west. The SSDF, by then a dying organisation, tried to revive military operations in the Balambale–Goldogob area which it occupied militarily in the south, but this soon ended without causing any serious problem for the Somali Army.[23]

It was at this point that a new chapter of co-operation opened for the regime when apartheid South Africa entered the scene. In fact, contacts had been taking place discreetly for some time. The first (secret) delegation from Pretoria had come to Mogadishu in February 1984 and Chief of Staff Mohamed Samantar had discreetly travelled to South Africa in May. On the side of the apartheid regime, the main actor was 'Pik' Botha, the clever Minister of Foreign Affairs who was the first Afrikaner nationalist politician to realise that segregation politics had no durable future. Botha had been the pioneer of political contacts with black African regimes and, in a way, the Pretoria–Mogadishu confluence was an alliance between political outcasts.[24] Botha might have been a 'liberal' in the South African context of the time but he was no pacifist and he knew that the way to gain Siad Barre's support was military co-operation. So in January 1985 a full-fledged mission arrived in Somalia, bringing artillery—a number of the famed South African 122 mm cannon were delivered, and soon shipped to the north—anti-guerrilla trainers and, last but not least, cash to pay the pilots and mechanics recently recruited to fly and maintain the UAE-supplied Hawker Hunters. In an unexpected addition, South Africa delivered to Somalia a civilian aircraft, a middle-range Boeing 727. The plane actually belonged to Air Comoros and had been leased to South Africa. It kept flying under the Air Comoros livery and opened services to Rome, Athens and Tel Aviv.[25] This was a way for apartheid South Africa to circumvent the economic sanctions to which it was then subject and which banned its commercial aeroplanes from most foreign destinations.

The South African connection boosted the Siad Barre regime and isolated the SNM even more. The northern Somali guerrilla force could count on no Arab sympathy, given its communist connection and, what was worse, its Ethiopian communist connection. It could not count on right-wing anti-communist connections either—even through the back door—now that the compromised 'apartheid regime' had swung behind Mogadishu. In the political atmosphere of the Cold War, political status tended to be clear-cut and brutal. Finland and Yugoslavia were about the only two examples of states which had rejected—for different reasons—the bipolar division of the world. But in February 1985 Siad Barre nevertheless tried to circumvent that division, hoping to have his cake and eat it too when he wrote to Moscow, offering to normalise his relations with the USSR and describing his relations with the US as 'limping'.[26] The main reason for the 'limp' was the fact that the Pentagon was still holding up the delivery of the $40 million of MAP that was meant for the fiscal year of 1986, even though the IMF had finally renounced its military limitation conditionality. Somalia had devalued the shilling by another 29 per cent in January 1985 and the IMF decided to let it go at that. But the Pentagon still did not want to release its MAP commitment without giving more than delaying explanations.

In that same January, in an all-round effort at marshalling more help, both economically and militarily, Siad Barre sent Vice-President Hussein Kulmiye Afrah and Defence Minister Mohamed Samantar to Rome to meet Prime Minister Bettino Craxi and Foreign Minister Giulio Andreotti, 'demanding that Italy should take up its historical responsibilities in the defence of Somalia'.[27] Italy was already the main foreign donor to Somalia but its generosity was not sufficient. On 23 January 1985 all the main donors—Italy, the US, Germany, the European Economic Community, Saudi Arabia—met in Paris for an emergency meeting: Somalia was near bankruptcy and could not meet its immediate payments. $80 million was drummed up in a hurry but this was no long-term solution. Military expenses were exploding and the main source of foreign exchange—cattle exports—was in free fall, even after Saudi Arabia eased the ban on imports. Part of the cause was the massive drought of 1983 which killed thousands of cattle, and then the transport insecurity in the north. A turning point was reached in April 1985 when the US decided to supply $25.3 million of food aid (70,000 tons) and Libya decided to resume its relations with Siad Barre. On 18 April Tripoli issued a communiqué explaining that the decision to switch policies was based on 'the necessity to face the dangers posed to the Arab nation by Imperialism'. This 'explanation' simply meant that Gaddafi's mood had changed and that he had decided, in his usual lackadaisical way, to become an enemy of his former friends and a friend of his former enemies.[28] In a panic, Abdullahi Yusuf rushed to Tripoli where he was cold-shouldered. The SNM, which had always refused Libya's money and equipment offers, did not suffer any withdrawal pains. It just went on with its provincial home-grown guerrilla force, patiently hoping for better days.

5

COLD WAR RECESS

THE MOGADISHU–SNM STAND-OFF IN AN INDIFFERENT WORLD, 1984–1988

The Mogadishu regime in slow-motion survival

By late 1984, the main problem for the Siad Barre regime was not military, but financial. The SSDF, the main and most dangerous anti-regime guerrilla force, had collapsed upon itself due to the paranoid leadership of Abdullahi Yusuf, while the SNM, which was short of everything—weapons, money, diplomatic support—had been hemmed in by the joint action of the Somali National Army and the WSLF remnants. In spite of the (half-hearted) Ethiopian support,[1] and in spite of widespread sympathy among members of the Issaq clan family, the SNM survived as a worrisome but tolerable regional nuisance. What really preoccupied Mogadishu was the economic situation, a factor aggravated by the 1984–5 drought. Total exports for 1984 had only reached $60 million while imports had peaked at $452 million, with military expenses massively contributing to the imbalance. The resumption of diplomatic relations with Gaddafi in April 1985 had not been followed by the hoped-for Libyan bonanza, and a reluctant US had provided aid as a purely humanitarian gesture: 70,000 tons of food worth $25.3 million. For Washington, Siad Barre was still seen as a former Russian ally and the promised Military Aid Program (MAP) still remained as elusive as ever.

Shocking as it may sound, the main forex resource for the regime was the presence on its territory of large numbers of refugees who had fled the Ethiopian Ogaden province in 1978. The refugees were cold-bloodedly exploited as a natural resource. In early 1985 the government officially stated that there were 826,000 refugees and in March it asked the International Red Cross for an extra $7 million, corresponding to an extra 60,000 'new' refugees who were supposed to have just arrived. But the government did not allow a head count on the ground and the Red Cross estimated that at least 320,000 of the refugees had gone back to Ethiopia. But UNHCR was not allowed to verify the government figures and its commissioners who tried to check the refugee numbers too closely were at times deported.[2] The estimated figures were 30 to 60 per cent lower than the official ones, depending on which camp-site was counted.

In August 1985, in what was considered by Siad Barre to be a major success, the US Army agreed to take part in a joint 'Bright Star' military exercise with Somalia. This brought $73.5 million of civilian aid plus another $41.5 million of military aid.[3] But as total bankruptcy loomed, Somalia's last recourse was Italy. Here, Siad Barre's most reliable supporter was the Socialist Party and its leader, Prime Minister Bettino Craxi. The link between the Italian Socialists and Siad Barre combined both *la nostalgia delle colonie*,[4] a very Italian regret for the loss of empire, and a vague, rose-coloured leftist outlook that raised the prospect for the very moderate Italian 'Socialists' of wrapping themselves in a symbolic Red Flag. One should remember that in 1970s Italy this was a useful electoral device. But more than anything, this close post-colonial relationship was a product of the so-called *lottizzazione* (repartition) policy.[5] During the 1980s foreign aid was seen by Italian political parties as a huge resource for pork barrel politics, whose benefits were parcelled out between the main parties (except the Communists, who were not allowed a place at the trough). The Christian Democrats could benefit from the budget for Ethiopia, the Socialists from Somalia while the small Republicans had to accept the slimmer pickings from what was earmarked for Mozambique. Each party promoted aid to 'its country' in the hope of getting more power, more glory and more money. As early as 1981, Paolo Pillitteri, the socialist mayor of Milan and a member of the Italian Socialist Party's Central Committee, had published a whole book of interviews with Siad Barre, which presented a rather bizarre mixture of nationalist fervour, liberal worldview and personal buddy support: 'Italy's international presence has to be solidly grounded in the framework of principles which place our country squarely in the Peace Camp[6] and qualify it as a defender of people's rights.' The conclusion was abrupt: 'In any case, we won't abandon our friends.'[7] The tool that could help 'our friends' was the Fondo Aiuti Italiani (FAI, or Italian Aid Fund), which had been created in 1979; its actual 'boss', in the murky world of Italian international aid,[8] was the economist Francesco Forte, one of Prime Minister Bettino Craxi's advisers. Fully 25 per cent of the global budget of FAI went to Somalia. It featured such opaque budgetary lines as '$2,436,000 to develop the telephone system'; payment to expatriate Italian university teachers who received $16,000 a month in Swiss bank accounts;[9] or a $250 million budget for the Garoe–Bosaso highway, which was jokingly referred to as 'the highway with the gold-plated road signs'. A lot of this aid was not exactly humanitarian: Italy provided G-222 troop transports, Piaggio P-180 light patrol aircraft, Agusta-Bell 204 and 212 helicopters, SIAI-Marchetti ST-260 ground attack planes, and Fiat M-47 armoured vehicles.[10]

In February 1986 Siad Barre was invited to Rome where he caused a scandal when he declared during his visit to parliament that he was so happy 'to be here at the seat of power where your great patriot Benito Mussolini used to stand'. The Communist MPs were shocked and wanted to table a motion asking for a no-confidence vote against Craxi's cabinet; they could only be stopped when the Socialists managed to convince them that the fall of the government would benefit the conservative Christian Democrats. Siad Barre was puzzled by the anger he had provoked but he made up for it by inviting Giorgio Almirante, the secretary-general of the neo-fascist Movimento Sociale Italiano, for a visit to Mogadishu.[11] During the meetings Francesco Forte suggested cancelling the $153 million of Somali debt to Italy and offered additional aid to the tune of $200 million plus another $340 million if an agreement over the Ogaden borders could be reached with Ethiopia. As a result of this unusual visit, the commander-in-chief of the Italian Air Force and the second-in-command of the Italian Army both flew to Mogadishu for 'technical consultations'. What the 'technical consultations' consisted of was never disclosed.

On 23 May 1986 President Siad Barre was the victim of a serious car crash. He was immediately transported to Saudi Arabia in a coma,[12] where he was joined by a 60-strong ad hoc 'Marehan Committee', which met around his hospital bed. The crisis of the dictatorship was immediate and intense. Siad Barre had been born in 1910 (even though he always publicly maintained his year of birth was 1916), which meant that he was then 76; and the whole precarious regime depended on his presence and leadership.

His wounds were serious and his death looked quite possible. So Mogadishu became prey to a slow-motion panic because the regime had no 'government' in the modern administrative sense of the word. To borrow words used to describe another neighbouring country where the structures (or lack thereof) were largely similar: 'it was not a world of institutions; it was a world of relationships ... personal interests trumped the authority of formal institutions in almost every instance'.[13] Power was in the hands of clanic and personal networks, in which tasks were distributed in a purely subjective way, with no institutional specialisation and nothing approaching a constitution or a legal system for devolving power.[14]

With Siad Barre incapacitated or possibly dying, power was up for grabs. His first wife, Khadidja, immediately moved to propel her eldest son, Meslah Mohamed Siad, into the seat of power[15] by ensuring that Abdi Nasser Haqi Mohamed, brother-in-law of the President and the officer in command of the capital's tank units, would support the young man. But her move by no means had unanimous support. The Marehan 'moderates' favoured General Omar Haji Mohamed (who had been in detention since 1982) because he was both relatively open-minded and a fellow clansman, while the 'loyalist' Minister of Defence, Ali Samantar—the constitutional Acting President—was a Sab supported by Ahmed Suleiman Abdille 'Dafle', the Dhulbahante warlord of the north who was then keeping the SNM at bay and who wanted a patsy as President.[16] Meanwhile, Aden Abdullahi 'Gabiyow', the Deputy Minister of Defence and a Kenya-born Ogadeni, courted the support of the young officers who disliked the arrogant Meslah. Immediately after the accident, the upsurge of competing factions provided a preview of the way Somalia might be heading when the strong hand of dictatorship disappeared. But this was premature. On 23 June Siad, weakened but recovering, was able to leave the hospital much earlier than most observers expected, thus putting all the thriving ambitions temporarily to rest. Then, on 24 December, he was 're-elected' for another seven-year term, with 97 per cent of the vote.

Of course, the war had not stopped in the meantime, but it had lost its capacity to represent a single autonomous path towards regime change. The SSDF was almost a bygone memory, with its unemployed fighters sitting it out in Ethiopia. The SNM hung on by the skin of its teeth, doing a bit of hostage-taking—such as kidnapping ten volunteers from Médecins Sans Frontières (Doctors Without Borders) in Tog Wajaale camp on 23 January 1987[17]—and some targeted killings, such as when they shot Colonel Ahmed Adan, the notorious NSS torturer, in Hargeisa in early January. Any such

SNM activity usually triggered demonstrations in the northern capital, and the two events just mentioned brought people out in the streets. As was also usual, the police and the army opened fire indiscriminately, killing 25 people and arresting 250.

Djibouti President Hassan Gouled was worried by these developments, which he felt could threaten his small country.[18] So French President Jacques Chirac sent his all-purpose African trouble-shooter, Fernand Wibaux, to Addis Ababa to investigate. Upon his return to Paris he advised that the situation was local and could easily be contained. This was a widely shared opinion, including in Moscow and Washington. The only foreigners who discreetly kept their attention focused on Somalia were the Italians. Their main effort was directed at trying to reconcile Addis Ababa and Mogadishu.

Just like Fernand Wibaux, most foreign observers saw the low-intensity 'disturbances' of northern Somalia as the unresolved tail end of the 1977–8 Ogaden War. That they could be the visible sign of a much deeper problem was simply not part of the international picture. Actually, both Mengistu in Ethiopia and Siad Barre in Somalia used whatever was left of 'their guerrillas' as pawns in the negotiations that were still taking place around the Ogaden problem. In March 1987 Mengistu had told the Somali that he would like to formalise the shadow talks between the two countries and invited his counterparts to Addis Ababa. Just to keep the pot boiling and to put some heat under the diplomatic talks, the Ethiopians encouraged the SNM to undertake some visible military activity. On 12 February a sizeable SNM force attacked Togdheer province around Balidhig; but Somalian security had been forewarned of the SNM attack and the force fell into an ambush, losing over 80 men and 11 tanks, which they had borrowed from the Ethiopians. The survivors crossed back over the border and went to lick their wounds in the relative security of Ethiopia.

On the opposite side, Siad Barre resuscitated some phantom groups of WSLF and launched them on a series of symbolic attacks in the Ogaden.[19] When all this was over Abdirahman Jama Barre, a cousin of Siad and his Foreign Minister, was sent to Addis to reopen the peace talks. All this was nothing new. These talks had taken place on and off for the previous two years, and since the Somali refused to provide clear and public maps of what they agreed belonged to Ethiopia and what they themselves would still claim, the meeting was another failure. For the SNM, none of this was serious and it kept on charting its own independent course.

Lone wolf: The SNM small war in the mid-1980s

During the 1980s, the main problem of the SNM was not to win but to survive in the hope of better days. It was caught in a paradoxical situation: ensconced in the north, very far from the country's power centres, devoid of any media attention, ignored by the international community, the Movement was totally self-reliant. Even its most dedicated fighters were aware of the situation: 'We had to use guerrilla fighting because the military power of the SNM was so weak compared to that of the government, our fighting was like playing hide-and-seek.'[20] And then:

> We had to keep some military activities going on. But these were only hit-and-run war tactics by young SNM men to disrupt the SNA on the border. We had to keep those going not to lose the momentum because there were so many young men who had finished their training at Baabili and they had been brought to the front areas such as Aware, Burco Duuray, Kaam Libaan. I think we had about 500 trained men. They were restless. It was an army made to fight inside the country but we hesitated to go in deeply.[21]

This slow-motion warfare took its toll in that many chose to desert after training rather than remain sitting aimlessly:

> At times the loss of recruits could be up to 50 per cent on any given batch. I remember one time we collected 70 in an Ethiopian base and only 10 or 15 came out of the training. It was a great loss for us, especially if the men left us taking their gun and ammunition with them.[22]

For lack of any better opportunity, the Movement resorted to the targeted killing of opponents.

> Given the situation, we used surveillance to track those military and police who were jailing, torturing or killing people. That's why we killed Ahmed Adan or Abdi Aziz Ali Barre. They were against SNM and they tried to steal the people's minds.[23] Also they tortured prisoners. For Ahmed Adan, the NSS boss, we studied him, found out everything about him, when he woke up, where he went, whom he met, and we decided only four should carry out the assassination. We shot him at 8 p.m. when he arrived at his office. We had sabotaged the lights, he could not see ... The people supported us because of the pain and agony in which they lived.[24]

But this support was limited, province-wide, not national, even though the war aims of the Movement remained resolutely national, aiming at regime change, which made a kind of overall tactical reassessment necessary. In this situation three things were obvious: ideology was not a significant factor;

popular anti-dictatorship was adamant and clan-based; and organisation was often the key component.

The first point, ideology, was the original element that differentiated the SNM from its older SSDF rival. SSDF had not been an ideological guerrilla force either, but it had tried to pass for one. Abdullahi Yusuf was basically a Majerteen warlord who wanted to eliminate a Darood warlord but he managed to wrap this unappetising goal into a more attractive ideological package. One should try to remember (age permitting) or imagine (if not having lived in those times) that ideology during the Cold War was a most necessary piece of equipment for membership in either the 'progressive' or the 'freedom' camp. To venture into the open ideological field without such a necessary flag (the flag was often more of a cover than a genuine item) was daring indeed, and regardless of his personal feelings Abdullahi Yusuf managed to fake it for the benefit of both Mengistu and Gaddafi, whose requirements were not the same. But for the deeply motivated SNM founders—and, later, cadres and followers—they could do without it because of the unspoken feelings of the northern mass of Issaq, who were solidly behind them. This did not constitute an identifiable 'ideology', even if, in a way, it was one—one that was not universal or transferable, but needed no text or ritual; it was immediate and essential.

This is the reason why the Ethiopian perception of SNM as a 'religious' organisation was wrong. 'Religious' would have meant 'Islamist', and this was not the case.

> In fact, there were three 'parties' within SNM: the religious one, the military one and the political one. They succeeded each other in time, with Sheikh Yusuf Ali Sheikh Madar being the first chairman, Colonel Abdiqadir Kosar Abdi replacing him in 1983, and then Ahmed Mohamed 'Silanyo' becoming chairman in 1984. They disagreed about a lot of things. But, deep down, they all agreed on the meaning of the struggle: removing the Siad Barre dictatorship and installing our own form of democracy. The SNM democratic system was similar to the traditional democracy which had always existed among clans. So there were always groups or sub-clans supporting or fighting the elected leadership. Groups like Calan Cas (Red Flag) or the nationalist anti-clan group opposed the leadership but they did not do damage to the struggle. Instead of addressing issues, it was personalities that were attacked. But the political deadlock was peacefully resolved when traditional elders intervened.[25]

This system was operationally efficient in the short term and provided a rough but successful measure of immediate democracy. During the ten years of the war, the SNM, contrary to many rebel groups in Africa (and elsewhere), never saw any violence taking place among its leadership. It sometimes came close to it, but blood was not shed and none of the five chairmen met a violent death. Abdiqadir Kosar Abdi was the only one who did not survive the conflict. His death took place in combat on 12 July 1987 in Mustahil when he fell into a military ambush as he was trying to expand the perimeter of SNM operations by travelling to the southern Ogaden where he was planning to meet some Hawiye elders.[26]

Here we should recall the remark of the native adjutant, already quoted, about his ideal political vision—'I want to be well-governed ... and to be left alone'—and the observation I made that in British Somaliland during the colonial years, the British almost achieved that prodigious policy paradox. For this is what probably lies behind the rebirth of the Somaliland colonial territory as a 'state' (albeit so far an unrecognised one) instead of sinking into the mess that the South is to this day. The South—the internationally recognised 'Somalia'—is the territory of the former Somalia Italiana, where the Italians—or rather the Fascist Governor, Cesare Maria de Vecchi—totally divorced their colonial administration from any continuity with native institutions and radically destroyed the peacemaking mechanisms that the Somali had previously used. Like most nomadic cultures, the Somali were permanently at war—about grazing rights, about water holes and about stolen cattle. Thus they had also developed, as part of *Xeer*, a complex system of (temporary) peacemaking. War was as much a part of their world as drought and camels: it therefore had to be managed. In the north, partly out of convenience and laissez-faire and partly due to legal and political philosophies, the British kept the Somali peacemaking mechanisms because it was in their interest to do so. ('Let us get the meat for Aden and let the natives govern themselves, as long as they remain peaceful.') And peaceful they had remained, from the death of the 'Mad Mullah', Mohamed Abdulle Hassan, in 1920 till independence in 1960. Not so in Somalia Italiana, where the Italians kept fighting their Somali subjects well into the 1930s and regained a fractured polity when they came back in 1947.

This past is often neglected by contemporary researchers and writers. It is paradoxical that, while pre-colonial African history has been restored to the place from which it was dislodged during the colonial period, it is now colonial history that is neglected. Both approaches are wrong, and the pertinence of colonial history in the region is obviously relevant if we look at situations like the Eritrean anti-colonial (i.e. anti-Ethiopian) struggle or the independence of South Sudan. Regionally, the very existence of the Djibouti Republic is a pure colonial construct. In many ways—politically, legally, philosophically—the SNM had a (partly) British history. Its place of birth in London was symbolic. This is probably one of the reasons why it remains today the object of strong hostility among non-Somaliland Somali: it is a half-caste political culture, part Somali and part British, which does not correspond to the nationalist epiphany envisioned by the Somali Youth League ideologues; it is 'tainted' by something foreign. Worst of all, it works. And it works because it is Somali in a way the mutilated South never had a chance to achieve. The Italians had tried for a 'European' colony, sterilised the Somali war–peace culture and failed; the British had tried for nothing but left the natives to their own devices while easing them into a marriage of convenience with the British common law system, as applied to the interactive zone of the two cultures—and it worked.

If there was some 'ideological' substratum to the SNM experience, it was this. And since its own initiators probably had only a very distant view of the question, it remained unspoken. The SNM leaders—religious, military or political—shared that same deep concept of what they wanted. It is amusing that often, in order to explain what they meant to a foreign observer, the best-educated ones would explicitly refer to I.M. Lewis's seminal work, *A Pastoral Democracy* (1961). This book is in itself a perfect example of an Anglo-Somali piece of research. Lewis, who loved the Somali culture but who was at the same time a dyed-in-the-wool Briton, wrote a very British account of the foreign culture he loved. He gave an intellectual synthesis of both and the SNM, in a spontaneous and almost unconscious way, practically carried it out.[27] It could not be called an ideology—especially by foreigners who were then Marxists or anti-Marxists—but it was a way of thinking, a manner of approaching political reality.

So in that spirit, the ideology-less ideologues of SNM approached the fourth congress (held in Jijiga, Ethiopia) and, on 9 August 1984, elected Ahmed Mohamed 'Silanyo' to the chairmanship. Actually, his very election is an example of what we have just discussed. Silanyo had been a member of Siad Barre's government before fleeing to the UK in July 1982. As it happened, the internal constitution of the SNM forbade any former member of Siad Barre's regime to hold any position in the Movement.[28] In many rebel fronts such a situation would have led either to the candidate being blocked or to him organising some kind of internal coup or power grab. But before the Jijiga congress there was none of that. Instead there was a lengthy discussion of the merits and demerits of Silanyo's application. Of course there were back-room manoeuvres and clanic negotiations, but the consensus was that the military period of Abdi Kosar had not been fruitful and that a more nuanced political approach was now necessary. So the discussion or negotiation period eventually led to a modification of the SNM's internal constitution. Was this an application of the 'pastoral democracy' system or a distant projection of Whitehall? Probably both. But this clever way of dealing with the situation, even if it was good in itself, could not produce a miracle.

What is more, the military situation remained poor. There was a need for morale-boosting and for diplomatic impact, to show 'that the SNM was not dead'. So a deliberate attack was planned in the Burco Duuray region. 'In that battle we engaged the fighters who were the first ones to have completed their seven months of training at the Aware training school … Our contingent arrived at the position facing Labi Sagaala, deployed up to Ina Guuxaa, on the Ethiopian–Somali border, in the first week of October 1984. This was a strategic mistake because this position was an obvious access route to Somalia, and Siad Barre's forces had anticipated the attack to come from that direction.' But to the strategic mistake, the freshly trained fighters added a crass lack of discipline:

> 'In addition, our troops were short of fuel, they had actually run out of fuel 45 km west of Lanqeyrta and the tankers we had assigned to provide more fuel for our contingent had stopped at Dabiile village to be entertained at a wedding. The SNA had known for the last 78 hours about our coming, and when the engagement took place at Burco Duuray, we were defeated and we suffered many casualties. Our commander, the famous Colonel Lixle, was killed on 17 October. This was our worst disaster, ever.'[29] When SNM chairman Silanyo learned the news, he said: 'Now if Lixle is dead, we all have to be like Lixle.' But it was easier said than done.

The SNM command had graduated more volunteers from the Aware school—about one thousand—and it decided to launch them, divided into three columns, on another 'invasion' of Somaliland's territory a month after the Burco Duuray disaster. The operation, known as 'the Mountain Wars', was conceived of as a test to see if the lessons of the Burco Duuray defeat had been learned. Colonel Jama Ali Elmi, who was the overall commander of the operation, told his men before they departed from Camp Libaan: 'You are going to be the probing spike; so do not assume that you are going to capture territory.'

There were three columns of about 300 men, the western one, which attacked first on 5 November 1984, was on foot led by Colonel Abdiqadir

Askar; the central one under Ibrahim 'Dhegaweyne', assisted by Abdirizaak Gamba, Abdisalam Yassin and Hassan Dayax, which attacked four days later; and finally the eastern column under Mohamed Kahin, who was the Movement's minister of defence and who moved forward on 20 November. Columns number two and three could use vehicles because they were on less mountainous terrain. All groups fared very differently: the western sector the worst as 347 combatants out of 383 were killed. The central and eastern groups benefited from the sacrifice of their comrades who had drawn all the fire of Siad Barre's troops. But organisation was still poor:

> All three forces were deployed in a disorganised manner. After the Burco Duuray disaster and the partly negative outcome of the Mountain Wars, a thorough SNM reorganisation had to be undertaken. The logistics were bad and management was poor. Some officers just disappeared and we realised the training was insufficient. There was a lot of confusion and we had doubts about how to take the struggle forward. But young men kept coming and we recruited around 1,300 new combatants after the Mountain Wars episode, questionable as it might have been.[30]

The reason for this sustained recruitment even though the Movement showed little military success was simply the hell most ordinary citizens had to live through in northern Somalia (Somaliland).

> Since Siad Barre had stopped any form of broadcasting news to the north, anyone who listened to the BBC would be arrested if found out, in order to deter people from transmitting news to others ... In the cities the curfew started at 3 p.m. Anybody caught in the street after 3 p.m. would be arrested and the women had their hair shaved, on top of the fine they had to pay. Some women were summarily raped ... Some women's long clothes were prohibited because the police feared they could be used to hide guns that could be used by SNM ... If the army killed somebody they alleged to be SNM, they brought the dead body into town, even if the corpse was decomposing and smelly, and forced us to look. If you recognised a dead relative and cried, you would be arrested.[31]

> There were no civil courts working, only military courts. So every day there were people killed without real judgment. Many were jailed in the morning and they were killed in the afternoon. We lived under so much pressure that we were ready to die just to escape it.[32]

> The government repudiated our right to live, in every way. If you were a northerner and you wanted to build a house, you had to pay taxes that would be equal to the cost of the house, if you had a car it could be taken from you at any time, you could not express your opinion freely for fear of arrest. So the government's repudiation of northerners' rights resulted in their unity and revolution.[33]

It is this situation which explains the total adherence of the northern population to the SNM. As I wrote after spending some time with the guerrillas in 1990, 'The SNM is not a guerrilla movement, it is the Issaq population up in arms.'[34] This ensured maximum support but it did not make for either permanent fairness or efficiency. Silanyo tried to plug the gaps but there were many.

> In 1989 Silanyo appointed me a member of his executive committee as finance secretary ... The administration of the SNM was not effective because the sub-clans were administering the combatants directly by providing the logistics or other support. The most effective place for efficiency was the SNM General Assembly meeting where all came and the differences were resolved by open discussion.[35] The General Assembly's functioning used to be very democratic and the election of a new chairman was always a free and fair process, contrary to other African liberation movements which were led by an authoritarian leader. The Central Committee selection was based on clan power-sharing and it was more chaotic. In 1989 the SNM leadership started to involve the traditional elders in what is known as *Guurti* (Assembly). Later the *Guurti* became formalised[36] and it became very useful to solve the conflicts, especially those between the political and military wings of the Movement ...

> When I was appointed as finance secretary, the SNM had no money in its account. But when my term ended in 1990 I had in our Ethiopian bank account 300,000 birrs ($150,000 at the official exchange rate, $43,000 at the black market rate), US$250,000 and 1.8 million Djibouti francs (about $56,000). The source of the dollars was the fishing ships seized off the Somali coast, which we fined for fishing illegally in territorial waters.[37] The Djibouti francs came from an agreement I negotiated with the Issaq merchants in Djibouti to whom I gave the right to use the port of Zeyla, in Awdal province, to ship goods to various parts of (government-controlled) Somalia after they paid a 2.5 per cent tax on the value of the goods.[38]

Silanyo managed to streamline some of the operations but he had serious problems with the integration of the Habr Yunis sub-clan of the Issaq and with the 'military party', which considered him too soft and 'too political'. Some of the army even went as far as organising a 'party' within the SNM, which they called Calan Cas (Red Flag), probably to please Mengistu.

> 'We aborted an assassination attempt on Silanyo. We uncovered a mine buried by the Calan Cas on the road he was supposed to travel ... After the failure of the assassination attempt, Dhegaweyne and Yusuf Ali Gaboobe fled in an armoured vehicle but they crashed it in Harshin and got captured. Most of the western colonels who were with Calan Cas were also jailed. The story was that it was revenge for the killing of Ali Adan Shine.'[39]

At the fifth SNM congress (28 February to 10 March 1987) Silanyo was re-elected as chairman, in spite of growing dissatisfaction in the ranks. Things were not much more hopeful on the government side, even if the feeling there was that there was still room for manoeuvre. But manoeuvring in which direction? Growing splits were opening up within the regime, which became deeper and deeper, between sullen but growing popular discontent, a morose diplomatic landscape, the bothersome SNM insurrection in the north, and a gaping economic abyss.

A peace attempt turns the small war into a bigger one

The mid-1980s had been a long journey into the dark for Somalia. Here we had a notional 'country'—in fact, a nation—whose cultural enthusiasm and political entrepreneurship had brought it from decolonisation towards an abstract unification. This was exactly the opposite of what was taking place at the same time in neighbouring Ethiopia, where the severed Eritrean former colony was fighting tooth and nail to resist reabsorption into its Abyssinian matrix. While Pakistan unity had been built on a commonality of religion, the various attempts at pan-Arabism all rested on a shared culture. Meanwhile, pan-Somalism had been perverted from a dream into a torture chamber, once the dynamics which fuelled the invasion of the Ogaden had been turned backwards by the defeat of 1978 and began to pit the Somali not against their *habash* (hereditary enemy) but against each other.

By 1987 exhaustion had set in everywhere and some kind of regime change was on its way. But which one? Siad Barre's accident and near death in May 1986 had not pointed towards any kind of principled renewal but just a free-for-all, where the barons of the regime lined up for a power grab with the best starting positions distributed—in descending order—according to family, connections and clan. Culture, language, nation—all the trigger words which had fuelled the anti-colonial unification movement forty years before—now sank into the mire of power, money and violence.

What was the challenge on the other side? The SNM was basically an anti-dictatorship movement that aimed also at clan defence and survival. This defined the essential limits of its operations. But as soon as the SNM actors—no matter how faithful or honest—veered away from these fundamentals, the core problems of Somali culture were reasserted: freedom pushed to the point of anarchy, and clanic patriotism verging on blind prejudice. The fifth congress had been a contest between Silanyo and Ibrahim

Meygaag Samatar, i.e. between Habr Ja'alo and Habr Awal. But the Balidhig disaster of February had a bad smell of clanic betrayal and the May kidnappings only confirmed the suspicions: SNM had been ambushed at Balidhig because it had been betrayed. The seven NSS agents captured in Bura'o in May denounced (under torture perhaps) around 70 Barre agents in Aware and another 50 at the rear in Dire Dawa. Silanyo gave the green light for summary executions and 60 to 70 were rumoured to have been executed.[40] So now the field battles had a 'home extension', and Colonel Adan Shine was shot in Jijiga in early June by two Ogadeni hired guns who confessed to being part of a recently formed hit squad.[41] But what was even worse than the personal executions was the growing ideological split between the majority SNM, which stuck to the overthrow of Siad Barre and regime change, and a limited but growing nucleus, spearheaded by the Calan Cas group, now openly aiming for the secession of the north.

In any case, whatever the SNM could do to undermine the regime was probably less successful than what the regime was doing to undermine itself. Most foreign aid given by donors was ineffective because it was project-centred rather than targeted by means of budgets.[42] This was because all donors over the years had agreed to foot the bill for project costs, thereby multiplying the number of those 'projects': many wells in odd locations, high-cost roads, the expansion of Bosaso harbour, refurbishing the Jowhar agro-industrial complex, a new slaughterhouse and a new tannery in Mogadishu, the Bardheere dam project. The US, the UK and Germany were highly critical of this spreading of projects, which Somalia did not have the administrative means or the trained workforce to handle, but Italy, which largely benefited from the kickbacks of otherwise unworkable projects, supported this dispersion—which had a planned cost of $1,025 million, a huge figure at the time. Meanwhile, a large segment of the population was undernourished and exports represented only 25 per cent of imports. In mid-August there were three days of rioting in Mogadishu due to the rise in the price of gasoline and the effects this had on the price of food. The IMF basically agreed with the World Bank and was incensed by the insistence of the Somali Central Bank that the floating rate for the shilling be abolished. This is what finally happened when the Central Bank was handed over to Mahmood Mohamed Nur, who replaced the incumbent governor. This nomination was the outcome of a perverse case of reverse clanic favouritism: Siad Barre had deliberately picked an Issaq to do the job, knowing full well that the poor man would agree to do anything he would be asked.[43] On 18 September he decided to suspend the forex auction and to condone the unrealistic rate of 100 shillings to the US dollar. This lasted six months before the IMF obliged the government to abandon the overvalued rate.

The succession problem also kept being handled in a similarly clumsy way. Meslah had created his own faction—popularly called the *tuttaley*, from the word *tutta*, which is used in Italian to describe the camouflaged battledress he and his associates wore in all circumstances. His father had created a special military district for him—the 77th, which comprised Mogadishu and the neighbouring territories. When the US troops withdrew from Somalia at the end of the Bright Star exercise, the equipment they left behind was given to Meslah, even though General Mohamed Hashi Gani, who bore the brunt of SNM military pressure, had been clamouring for the same weapons.[44] But Meslah behaved as if he was already President, even though he had none of the qualities required for the position. At the end of September 1987, trying his hand at 'field diplomacy', he went north following a spate of riots in Bura'o. About 90 people had been killed in skirmishes between pro-Silanyo (Habr Ja'alo) and anti-Silanyo (Habr Yunis) Issaq sub-clans, a confrontation that fitted with the Togdheer ambush of the previous February and also with the political lines ('regime change' versus 'secession') within the SNM. Meslah had come to fish in troubled waters, hoping to use the sub-clan conflict for his own benefit, but his intervention was so heavy-handed that he only managed to get the two groups to (temporarily) reconcile on the basis of an anti-government position.

In Mogadishu, the pressure was growing and an 'opposition party' had developed to try to counterbalance Meslah and his *tuttaley*. In typical Somali fashion the new group was linked to a separate strand of the President's family—the Rer Nur Dini of Dalayat Hajji, Siad's second wife—while the *tuttaley* were mostly Rer Koshin Dini, Khadidja's lineage. In June 1987, as he was coming back from one of his usual forays abroad in search of money,[45] Siad and Meslah swept into jail a number of *Desturi*[46] followers, including General Abdinassir Hajji Hashi, the commander of Mogadishu's military garrison, who was not a militant 'constitutionalist' but just somebody who resented Meslah's brutal and overbearing personality.

But the regime was in such dire straits that Siad Barre sent his Vice-President Ali Samantar to Sana'a in Yemen in October 1987 to meet with Mengistu and try to pacify him in respect of the Ogaden, in the hope that an internationally recognised peace with Ethiopia would satisfy the donors and bring cash. There were two issues, the forced drafting of Ogadeni refugees into the Somali Army and, as always, the border issue and the refusal of Siad Barre to renounce territorial claims against Ethiopia. The drafting issue was dealt with but the Somali government kept postponing the release of maps in which the Ogaden borders would have been clearly defined.[47] Nevertheless, these signs of diplomatic improvements were enough to get Siad Barre invited to the Franco-African summit at Antibes on 10 December 1987. Here the French hinted at promises of international support to help the dictator with his delicate position vis-à-vis the World Bank and IMF. Upon returning to Somalia, Siad carried out a broad cabinet reshuffle in which General Samantar was neutralised through the creation of no less than three 'Second Vice-President' positions,[48] while the Ministry of Defence was assigned to Cdr Aden Abdullahi Nur, a close associate of Meslah. At the same time, Siad's half-brother, the hapless Abdirahman Jama Barre, was transferred from Foreign Affairs to Finance, a position he had coveted for years and which he was fully incompetent to occupy. This would leave the actual control of the Finance Ministry in Siad's own hands.

At the same time, having reorganised his own camp in the simplified way he saw as a transition towards a controlled succession, Siad decided to impress what he considered to be 'the enemy'. To do so he brought back before the courts the accused members of the so-called Group of Seven, who had been detained without trial since June 1982 and who represented the only credible group of unarmed opponents. Among them were the former Vice-President Ismail Ali Abokor, the former Minister of Foreign Affairs Omar Arteh Ghalib, three former MPs, the human rights lawyer Yusuf Osman Samantar 'Berda'ad', and the former Minister of Health Omar Haji Mohamed. These men were all very well known—Omar Arteh had even been a candidate for the UN Secretary-Generalship—and all could claim to form part of some democratic alternative to the dictatorship. Bringing them back to court under charges of treason caused a world-wide sensation. The trial lasted five weeks and was handled clumsily, in a way that exhibited gross rigging of the procedure. The accused (all Issaq) were condemned to death but, after the resulting international outcry, were 'pardoned' and remained in either detention or house arrest. This absurd treatment of the matter resulted in the government looking both barbaric and further weakened. But these considerations of internal politics, important as they might have looked at the time, would soon be pushed into the background by radical military developments in the region.

The Eritrean war of national liberation had started in 1961 and gone through the ups and downs of military victories and defeats. But twenty years after it began, three factors radically affected the nature of the struggle:

- The central government of Ethiopia had to accept the idea that the country was not a nation-state as both Emperor Haile Selassie and the military–communist dictatorship which had replaced him assumed. By 1987, given the number of ethnic insurrections—by the Somali, the Tigrayans, the Oromo, the Afar and several Nilotic African groups—it had become impossible to keep asserting that this Amhara-based empire was actually an 'Ethiopian' nation-state in which diversity was blended in harmony.
- The Eritrean struggle, far from being an oddity or 'foreign-inspired', was now perceived as part of a 'nationality problem' which the 'proletarian' revolution had failed to address. The foreign support—both 'Arab' and 'Communist'[49] received by the Eritrean insurgents—had been an addition to the problem but not its cause.
- By the late 1980s, the Eritreans were not fighting alone any more. Prior to the early 1980s the other rebel groups had all been fighting Addis Ababa separately. But the Tigrayan insurrectional front (TPLF) had progressively developed a tactical and political alliance with the Eritrean People's Liberation Front (EPLF), and it was this alliance which eventually brought down the military–communist junta in Addis Ababa in 1991.[50]

In late 1987 and early 1988 the allied Eritrean–Tigrayan forces were on the upswing and had reinforced their positions in northern Ethiopia. And then suddenly, on 19 March 1988, the Ethiopian front cracked in Af Abet. This victory, which at the time went largely unnoticed worldwide, was in fact an important milestone in African warfare and, more broadly, in the geopolitics of the late 20th century. Throughout the 1980s the Soviets, who were experiencing simultaneously the financial effects of 'Star Wars', the impact of the war in Afghanistan and the shocks to their economic base, were already engaged in a desperate withdrawal in which they tried to rescue what could be saved and jettison the rest. In what concerned the Ethiopian part of their alliance network, they had withdrawn most of their advisers, stopped paying their satellite forces (Cuban, South Yemeni) which used to bolster the Derg, and concentrated the mechanised equipment (tanks, artillery) of their main battle force in a strategic position where their army could make the best use of it. But the location—Af Abet—was a mistake because it was within reach of the EPLF. And on 19 March 1988, Af Abet fell into the hands of an EPLF offensive, with its strategic treasure trove completely intact: over 200 pieces of artillery, 320 tanks with their spares, and 80 mobile fuel tanks. The war would last another three years but it had already been lost that afternoon in Af Abet.[51]

While this catastrophe was taking place, Mengistu, who was ignorant of it, was in Djibouti to discuss the Somali question with President Hassan Gouled and his nephew Ismail Omar Guelleh. He flew back to Addis on 22 March. But the collapse in the north continued. On 26 March the EPLF took Tessenei and Ali Gidir and the TPLF occupied Axum that same day. Then on 28 March the Eritreans took Agordat while the Tigrayans entered Adwa. On the 31st the TPLF completed its takeover of Tigray by occupying Adigrat. There were still 60,000 Ethiopian troops in the Ogaden, and by then the communist regime needed them in a hurry to plug the gap in the front and close the road leading down to Addis Ababa, which was now under threat. Mengistu immediately dispatched his Minister of Foreign Affairs, Berhanu Bayeh, to Mogadishu on 1 April to sound out Siad Barre about the possibility of signing an immediate peace agreement between Ethiopia and Somalia. The Soviet Deputy Minister of Foreign Affairs, Anatoly Adamishyn, simultaneously rushed to Mogadishu and representatives of the two heads of state[52] met in Djibouti on 3 April and signed a peace agreement.

Basically the agreement kept to the essentials: Somalia recognised the Ogaden as an integral part of Ethiopian territory, and both countries agreed on cancelling any help provided to the rebel movements of their rival: Mogadishu cut off support to the WSLF (or what was left of it), to the Oromo Liberation Front (OLF) and to the SALF, which was not in much better shape than the WSLF. But Siad Barre refused to repatriate the Ogaden refugees then on Somali territory. They were worth their weight, if not in gold, at least in food aid, and it was out of the question to see them heading home, peace or no peace. Addis Ababa reciprocated by stopping any aid to the nearly dead SSDF and promised to do the same for the very much alive SNM. As a first measure the Ethiopian police closed down the offices of the two Somali rebel movements in Addis Ababa as well as the studios of Radio Halgan,[53] which was a joint SSDF–SNM venture. Some Ethiopian liaison officers were dispatched to the SNM camps on the border and Mengistu received Silanyo in private. On 6 April Muhamad Sheikh Ibrahim, the Ogaden National Liberation Front (ONLF) leader in charge of information, then in Kuwait, rejected the Ethiopian–Somali peace treaty because 'it accepted the Ethiopian occupation of the Ogaden'. In Addis, Mengistu had called an emergency meeting of the politburo of the Ethiopian Workers' Party (EWP) and decreed 'an absolute and total mobilisation'. Troops were already evacuating the Ogaden by road and by plane, Asmara airport had been closed to civilian air traffic, and boats were ferrying more soldiers between Assab and Massawa. For the SNM, a decisive point had been reached.

> In April 1988 Ethiopia and Siad Barre signed an agreement in Djibouti, and this created the biggest defining moment in SNM history ... Mengistu basically ordered the SNM and Silanyo to follow the terms of the accord to the letter ... Even though this was a dark moment for the SNM, it also had a good result in uniting the ranks for the first time ... The Djibouti agreement was the biggest unifier at a time of large internal discord. Colonel Ahmed Mire, Colonel Hassan Yunis and myself, we escaped with a few others from Dire Dawa in the middle of the night in order to avoid having to obey the orders of the Ethiopian government. We arrived at dawn at Camp Abokor, which was the main centre and command post of the SNM on the border. There was a common popular decision to prepare for an overall offensive. All the SNM members had mobilised themselves without much prompting. Silanyo was in big trouble at the time because Mengistu had ordered him to move the SNM forces from the border areas and demobilise them. He knew that this would not go down well with the SNM, particularly with the armed youths who had been joining us recently and who wanted to fight. So Silanyo came to the front accompanied by Ethiopian military commanders. They brought fuel with them and orders to move our forces back to three bases inside Ethiopia: Aware, Harshin and Gaashaamo.

> Silanyo arrived and went to stay in the Ethiopian Army camp. He summoned the SNM commanders to give them orders, but nobody could be found because the day before his arrival we had moved the command post right up to the front lines, to avoid him. The SNM military command had already prepared a plan for the offensive. So instead of sending the colonels whom Silanyo had requested, we sent him fuel tankers asking for fuel, supposedly to move the troops back. But when the fuel arrived, we used it to move our forces inside the border with Somalia instead of back to Ethiopia as we had been ordered. So Silanyo decided to replace Colonel Ahmed Mire from the command due to his insubordination in defying orders to bring the troops back. Silanyo was advised to replace Ahmed Mire with Colonel Jama Ali Elmi, which he did. However, Colonel Jama Ali had decided to follow the same line as Colonel Ahmed Mire. So once Silanyo realised that there would be no change in the popular decision to invade, he asked at least for a postponement of the offensive for a few days in order to allow him to leave Ethiopia, as he feared that Mengistu would put him in jail.[54] ... So the decision to liberate the north was made in reaction to the Djibouti agreement and it was not, as it was said later, for secession. This was not even part of the original SNM plan.[55]

The date set for the attack was 27 May and three separate forces were regrouped. The two main ones—3,000 and 1,500 men—were supposed to attack from the west and the other from the south. The main one was led by

Colonel Ibrahim 'Dhegaweyne' (who had been released from jail where he had languished since trying to kill Silanyo) and the southern one was led by Colonel Hussein Dheere. The third force (of 1,200 men) was supposed to attack Bura'o and was led by Colonel Ahmed Mire. Given problems of fuel delivery, the Hargeisa attack was postponed by one day and took place on Friday, 27 May 1988. 'The three attacks were supposed to take place all at the same time, but of course the timing was not achieved. It was only the Bura'o attack which took place at the planned time.'

The SNM forces that took part in the attack were low on both fuel and ammunition, and the key to success, as Colonel Jama Ali told them when they launched the attack,

> was to get our resupplying from Siad Barre's forces. The Hargeisa attack was delayed for a variety of reasons. But the key attack was on Adadley weapons depot. The men who took Adadley then shared their supplies with the two other forces in Bura'o and Hargeisa. They captured about 30 armed vehicles, which were then split in two with the two other attacking groups. After we took Bura'o, our forces were overwhelmed with recruits, more than 30,000 men who came by spontaneous recruitment. Every able-bodied man took his gun or got one from a looted military store or captured one from an enemy soldier. Later this incoming crowd was popularly known as 'the Friday recruits' because 27 May was a Friday and they all took arms and came on that day. The trained SNM fighters were overwhelmed by the new recruits, and that later caused several problems ... On the afternoon of 28 May we entered Hargeisa after another heavy battle at Werarta, to the south of Adadley. But on the evening of 30 May we got bombed for the first time by the South African mercenary pilots. We shot down one plane but we took serious losses.[56]

This was a radically new situation. The Djibouti 'peace' had led to a new war, which would be much more violent than all that had preceded it since 1981. In 1960 the population of British Somaliland had been independent for five days before it renounced its new-found freedom in the blur of an idealistic dream that would later turn into a nightmare. This new war was going to allow Somaliland to regain its independence, but only on a truncated basis. May 1988 was the first stage on a long road whose end has not yet been reached.

6

AND SUDDENLY ALL HELL BROKE LOOSE, 1988

The decision to launch the battle of the cities

April 1988 had been a time of waiting. Ethiopia and Somalia, the major proxies of the two Cold War camps facing off in the Horn of Africa, had signed a long-awaited 'peace agreement'. Of course, this had nothing to do with a strategic change of perspective or, even less, with a sudden flowering in human hearts of humanitarian sentiments. The 4 April 1988 Djibouti Peace Agreement had been a pressing necessity for adversaries who, in many ways, had reached the workable end of their previous policies. After the battle of Af Abet the Ethiopian Army witnessed a massive expansion of the military means available to its enemies. It now knew the extent of the potential catastrophe: the EPLF had grabbed, in perfect condition, nearly 80 per cent of the deliveries of heavy Russian weapons made to Ethiopia over the previous twelve months. This included numerous pieces of artillery of various calibres, from heavy D-30 122 mm howitzers to rugged B-9 82 mm mortars; BM-21 multiple rocket launchers fitted on trucks; and over 250 tanks ranging from old T-54s to state-of-the-art T-72s.

In the strategic thinking of the allied EPLF and TPLF, it was the latter organisation which should inherit the mass of equipment. This was because its territory was positioned further south than that controlled by the Eritreans and, with some effort, it could put them within reach of the capital Addis Ababa. The anti-Derg rebels were now thinking in terms of ending the war through a total military victory, a previously vague idea which had now become thinkable. The Derg's protector, the USSR, was by then bleeding as a result of too many battlefields or strategic involvements, from the war in Afghanistan to the massive support it gave to its Middle Eastern allies (Iraq, Syria, Libya), from its African allies (Angola, Ethiopia, Guinea-Bissau) to those countries that were not at war but were living in a 'post-war' economic condition (Cuba, Vietnam, South Yemen) and had to be kept alive by constant care. The USSR did not have an economy that could satisfy its own citizens, and extending its sparse resources to so many beneficiaries world-wide was becoming more and more untenable. The accession to power of Mikhail Gorbachev in March 1985 had begun the slow retreat of the Soviet Union's global hegemonic dream. Within that context, Ethiopia was increasingly a disposable unit and Mengistu realised it. The Russians (and their allies) had gone as far as they ever would in protecting the Ethiopian communist regime from its rebel enemies.[1]

On the other side, the problem was different. Former Soviet ally Siad Barre had abandoned the communist 'Peace Camp' when he attacked communist Ethiopia but he had not managed to have his bona fide accepted in the US-protected 'Free World'. He was still suspect owing to his former association with Moscow, and Washington did not trust him. He benefited from a minimum guarantee from the US ('we won't let the bear tear you apart but do not expect more than that from us') where titbits of (largely obsolete) military equipment were delivered, while privately engaged US allies such as Italy (and to a lesser extent Germany)[2] gave a much lower level of aid than what could have been expected from a Cold War superpower. Such aid could not be compared to the large weapons deliveries from the Soviet Union to Ethiopia. But for both countries—and much more so for Somalia—the main problem was economic. War is expensive, both countries were poor and their limited resources were drained no longer by a mutual conflict but by a series of internal conflicts, partly funded by the main adversary. During the 1986–8 period the weight of these little wars grew heavier and heavier, and the states—even Mogadishu, which benefited from its IMF status—could increasingly less afford to continue. This was particularly so for Ethiopia, where the EPLF–TPLF alliance had reached a level of military performance that their two Somali equivalents—SNM and SSDF—had never achieved, and was now in a position to seriously threaten the central government.

So the Af Abet defeat and the massive capture of heavy equipment by the rebels finally tipped the scales. Half abandoned by the Russians, Mengistu had no other option than the 'total, absolute mobilisation' of his national forces that he had called for upon his return from Djibouti. The small SNM had no choice either: if it accepted the withdrawal from the border and the dismantling of its military structure, which the Ethiopians had promised Siad Barre, it would have disappeared, like the SSDF before. But the SNM had one trump card in this increasingly dangerous game: the broad commitment of its frontline fighters for a war to the end. There were problems, of course, with some of the cadres of the movement, the assassination attempt against Silanyo being a clear case of institutional blowback;[3] but these problems did not seep down to the level of the rank-and-file fighters. The process, demanded by the Ethiopians, of withdrawing first and negotiating later was not acceptable, not only for the soldiers themselves, but for a majority of their officers. These simple men had first-hand experience of the Siad Barre–Somali Army–SRSP tyranny. Official measures could be announced but nobody believed in them and this discredited in advance any negotiating position.

> When IGADD[4] was established in 1988, one of the prolific writers of the SNM called Said Ali Giir had written an article in which he predicted that the real objective of IGADD was conflict resolution rather than drought (what can be done about that?) or development. In fact, this was prescient because soon after we heard rumours and we saw articles in newspapers that said that the Siad Barre government had agreed to bring northern government employees all to the north and to put them into local government positions. All prisoners were to be released and those who had fled the country were to be forgiven. The military in the north would be replaced by northern officers. We heard that 300 to 400 northern civil servants, businessmen and armed forces officers were going to be brought to the north.[5] But these were all rumours and lies. Siad Barre and Mengistu had agreed to end the hostilities, terminate all opposition, and try to make it nice by announcing measures that would have assuaged the northern bitterness. We did not believe it for long. So the army developed a new strategy, from the bottom up. Three regiments—named Mecca, Medina and Central Front—would be prepared and aimed at attacking Adadley, Mandera and Berbera and then move on to capture Bura'o and Hargeisa. But the plan was changed at the last minute by the High Command.[6]

In fact, this change of plan, which favoured the symbolic capture of the northern capital over a logistical blockade, was one of the basic reasons which added a year or eighteen months to the war. In spite of periodic light attacks, Berbera remained solidly in government hands till the end of the conflict and was used as a beachhead for receiving troops and supplies from the south or from abroad, unloading them and redistributing them to the whole region. Berbera, a key strategic point, was neglected for the symbolic benefit of temporarily holding (and later of besieging) Hargeisa.

On 27 May the Medina Front forces had carried out the plan and attacked Bura'o. But unfortunately the western Mecca forces were still behind in their preparation. As the Hargeisa attack had also been delayed, 300 men decided to attack Adadley to relieve the pressure on the SNM forces then attacking Bura'o.[7] Adadley hosted some of the biggest SNA defences in northern Somalia and it also held a large amount of equipment. On 28 May the Seyid Omer Brigade had reached a place called Debis, which is the mid-point on both the Hargeisa–Bura'o road and the Hargeisa–Berbera road. The aim of taking control of that road crossing was to prevent SNA troop movements between the three cities. On the 29th the Sayid Ali and Barkhad Brigades from Central Division attacked Adadley and secured the ground ... But the Somali Army sent reinforcements from its First Division to Werarta to prepare attacking Adadley and retaking it ... But we decided to take the battle to them in advance. We walked all night, arrived at dawn and attacked them suddenly. Many were killed and the others ran away. We captured a lot of their material ... but then we received reports from Mandera saying the garrison there was preparing to kill all the prisoners so that we could not free them ... Then we sent men and when we reached Abdaal we ambushed these reinforcement convoys sent from southern Somalia. The field guns and the jeeps we had just captured at Werarta were used there and we attacked Mandera to free the prisoners. We had gained a huge number of vehicles and heavy weapons, and we were in a position now to help the other forces in Bura'o and Hargeisa ... It was at that stage that we discussed again the plan to capture Berbera or else send reinforcements to Hargeisa. And we decided to go for Hargeisa.[8]

Experiencing the violence of urban warfare

As soon as the operation was launched, it became fragmented battlefield by battlefield as it involved almost exclusively urban fighting, i.e. it was geographically quite focused and limited.

On 27 May 1988, after we refused to comply with the Ethiopians' plans, Colonel Ahmed Mire and his forces entered Bura'o early on Friday morning, starting the first of the battles to seize the major cities of the north. After our unit commander was killed, I briefly became the commander. But the Brigade decided to send us an experienced officer, they sent us Mohamed Ali, and I became his second-in-command. Mohamed Ali was an experienced fighter and also a very religious person. He never missed a prayer even in the midst of fighting and it made me confident to be at his side. We got a warning from our command that government forces were leaving Hargeisa to come to Bura'o as reinforcement for their men. We had to stop them, so we left in the evening with five vehicles and enough combatants and organised an ambush on the Hargeisa–Bura'o highway. We spent the night there and the fighting with the reinforcement column started at dawn. It was bloody and we lost quite a number of our men because of the new M-16 rifles the Siad Barre forces were now using.[9] M-16 were better than other guns and their wounds were often fatal. We won and the enemy retreated and went back to Hargeisa, leaving all their wounded behind. Many of the wounded claimed to be Hawiye. As usual we gave orders to leave them unharmed and the wounded soldiers were surprised because what they had heard from their officers was that we would torture and kill them. When they recovered from their wounds, we used to send them back to their villages and ask them not to join the government forces again. At times it happened that these soldiers, when they realised the SNM would not harm them, they even showed us places where guns were hidden and they would give them to us.

After the battle we continued our march and we reached the Omar Kujoog halfway crossing between Berbera and Hargeisa. At that point we saw a convoy of armed vehicles with government soldiers travelling from the direction of Berbera. Later we found out they were on their way to Mandera prison to execute the Issaq political prisoners. We started shooting and we destroyed two of the vehicles. The other two managed to escape but they were quickly attacked by government planes which had received the information that SNM units were approaching Hargeisa. So they mistook their own force for us and their planes destroyed their own armed vehicles.

After this bit of luck, we continued our march until we reached the hill over Adadley, the strong government military base and depot. In Adadley, the Hussein Dheere fighters and those of the Sayid Ali and Barkhad units had attacked the government garrison from several sides. We could not see what to do, so we watched the battle for a while. But by midnight Salaan Abdi Shide had a lucky shot when he put an RPG-7 shell right in the middle of a warehouse where millions of rounds of ammunitions were piled up side by side with armoured vehicles and other military supplies. Everything exploded and then it went on burning all night long till dawn. The next morning our commander, Mohamed Ali, asked me to lead a patrol of four and go into the village of Adadley to see how things had developed. When we reached Adadley we were surprised to see our combatants sitting down with the villagers and enjoying breakfast. But they told us another strong government force was heading towards us from the south, with heavy artillery. So we went for the garrison, which was demoralised, and we surrounded them. They just ran away and we did not even try to stop them. As we entered the compound we found the dead body of the commander of the Adadley base, who had committed suicide by shooting himself through the head when he realised that his big military base had fallen into the hands of SNM.

Then Mohamed Ali decided we had to march on Mandera prison. He feared that the prisoners would all be killed. So we marched through the hills on foot all night and at dawn we started the attack on Mandera prison. But we could not penetrate through the armoured metal doors, and since the walls were solid concrete and in spite of using all kinds of ammunition, we could not knock a hole through them. But Mohamed Ali, who was a former inmate, knew a place where there was a soft spot and we blew it with the Jeep gun [105 mm recoilless]. When we entered, the commander of the prison, who refused to surrender, was shot on the spot. Many prisoners were chained to the walls and there were at least one hundred of them, chained or not, in each prison cell. Some of the prisoners recognised us. The ex-mayor of Hargeisa, Barre Langadhe, was one of them. Mohamed Ali recognised some of the businessmen, such as Abdirahman Hassan Rakoub, who were imprisoned there. We released 664 prisoners, including 34 Ethiopians and people from south Somalia ... We helped the Ethiopians by giving them a letter and a vehicle to transport them to Jijiga. We had lost ten combatants, including officers, and we started treating our wounded. We gave our prisoners the choice to go anywhere they wished, and those who wanted to join us were immediately given guns.

After the Mandera operation we returned to Adadley and we discussed our next plan. We had the option to join either the group fighting in Bura'o or the one fighting in Hargeisa, but Mohamed Ali suggested that we should rather attack Berbera because all the supplies and reinforcements for the government were coming through Berbera. But the rest of us rejected the idea[10] and proposed that we join the forces in Hargeisa or Bura'o ... Mohamed Ali preferred then to join our men in Bura'o because the reinforcements for the government would come from the east. I agreed because he was my commander and he was experienced, and we changed our direction to Bura'o. We avoided the government garrisons of Oodweyne, Warabe and other strong points and we reached Bura'o to support our forces that had been weakened through losses. Our reinforcements were useful but the government also got more reinforcements from Oodweyne and we tried to push them back, and it was during that confrontation that our commander Mohamed Ali was killed in the battle. Then the government planes flown by Rhodesian mercenaries[11] arrived and they started to bomb the city.[12]

Due to the delay in the fuel supply, the SNM units attacked Hargeisa slightly later than they had attacked Bura'o.

Hargeisa was attacked on 31 May 1988 and I was among those who went in. We infiltrated everywhere, we captured the headquarters of the 26th Division,[13] we collected the ammunition from the Birjeex depot and we saw the SNA as they were running away and dropping their uniforms on the ground. Then we moved to the radio station where we wanted to announce that we had captured the city. But even though we had captured the headquarters of the 26th Division, Birjeex and the surrounding area, when we surrounded Radio Hargeisa we were faced with a huge resistance of the SNA who were inside the radio station perimeter. They bombarded us with heavy artillery and tanks, and so the force that was assigned to take the airport fell back and decided to go fight in Adadley.[14]

Those of us who had invaded Hargeisa were estimated at 500 men, equipped with 84 vehicles. But we had left the vehicles parked outside and some were taken by those going to Adadley ... So by the time we entered the city with our small force, we had only 14 vehicles left. The senior officials that were leading the invasion of Hargeisa were Mohamed Ahmed aka Dayib Gurrrey, Musa Bihi,[15] Abdirahman Aw Ali Farah, Adam Cade, Mahmood Haybe Goodhadh, myself, Mohamed Kosar and others. The fighting lasted 73 days and nights, with constant ups and downs. We had different brigades assigned to various parts of the city area. There was a lot of fighting around Dabada Caddaada, the section around the slaughterhouses, and there we had a lot of support from the Arap sub-clan. The Sa'ad Musa were fighting in the north and west and around Radio Hargeisa. But there was so much fighting that after some time almost all of our senior officers had been killed or injured and most of the injuries could not be treated right on the spot. Practically all the survivors had some injury or other. It came to the point that when the SNA got reinforcements and started to seriously push on us, we had to give up and we retreated to safe areas like Baligubadle, Gumar and other places that were free of an SNA presence. We survived and the SNA ended up trapped inside the cities, they could not get out because we had ambushes on all the roads.

We managed to improve our medical services to take care of our many wounded. Little by little we remobilised for the struggle once again, we fixed our 84 vehicles and carried our wounded combatants to the field hospitals. We mostly put our new facilities in Geed Debleh, we had lots of wounded. But we had a huge problem with the civilian refugees that were streaming out of the city. They filled the roads, they also had a lot of wounded, and we could not refuse helping them, but this made a great confusion for our combatants. We had wounded people everywhere. Since the planes were strafing us all the time, we had to try hiding the wounded. So we put them up on trees, hanging there, suspended between the branches. With the shade the planes did not see them. Otherwise they would kill anybody, they would even finish off the wounded ...

But we kept attacking and harassing the SNA reinforcements that were coming from Berbera. The SNA began to panic and, when they were fleeing, they regrouped themselves on a clan basis. Those who were of the Hawiye clans went over to Birjeex while those who belonged to the various Darood clans went over together to another side. Ahmed Omar Jess was called to lead them, but this was before he properly became chairman of the SPM.[16] We allowed them to pass through safely, from Hargeisa down to Baligubadle and from there on, towards their final destination in the south. Those who supported General Aydid ran away from our cities and gathered in the south in the name of USC;[17] they had their armoured vehicles and tanks, and we called them and told them to leave before we would murder them. Then Abdullahi Darawal led his combatants to the west and deserted from SNA.[18] ...

One thing that facilitated our fighting, even though we were most of the time numerically inferior, was the fact that most of us were from the very army we were fighting, the Somali National Army (SNA). We knew each other well, we knew their tactics and their positions, and as their morale was falling apart, it became easier and easier to fight them. They had no more morale, even committing all those crimes against civilians got them money but no heart and caused them in the end to be defeated.[19]

Actually in the general confusion of May–June 1988, the only people who paradoxically were quite clear about what side they were on were the refugees from the Ethiopian Ogaden.

General Siad Barre and his regime used the Somali refugees from Ethiopia in many ways. They used them as security personnel to guard installations and they used them as SNA levies when the need would arise; the international agencies supporting the refugee camps were the main source of income, jobs and supplies, and the refugees monopolised 100 per cent of the available resources. The number of refugees living in the camps was inflated by the Somali Refugee Agency, and the rations and supplies supplied by UNHCR directly went to the Somali National Army. Therefore the refugees were not only a source of security for the government but they also fed the government's army.

Another way of using the refugees was intelligence. All these refugees had relatives living in places like Jijiga, Dhagax Buur, Aware, and they could easily gather information on what SNM was doing in these bases on Ethiopian territory. The Ethiopians knew this and therefore they forced all refugees, from our side as well, to settle in Harta Sheik where there was no access to water. This was to push people away from Jijiga where access to water was easy. This forced UNHCR to supply the camps by means of water tankers. Before the battle of the cities, all refugees were from the Ogadeni, i.e. from the Darood clan family and therefore allies of Siad Barre. Siad Barre had circulated information among the refugees in the camps near Hargeisa that he would replace the Issaq population from Hargeisa with refugees from Ethiopia after oppressing the people so much that they would leave. This is one reason why many people feared joining SNM: they felt that in their absence the government would take their houses and lands and give them to the refugees. Some of these refugees were assisted by the authorities to start small businesses in Hargeisa so that they would become permanent settlers. When the battle of the cities started, the refugees joined the SNA as they thought all the non-Issaq would be chased away or killed if the SNM won.[20]

In fact, some of the immediate consequences of the SNM attack against the cities could almost be viewed in that light. It started, logically, with the army.

Even before the offensive, many Issaq officers in the military, including the air force, were transferred to the south: well-known officers like Shaqale,

Abdullahi Darawal and others too. But after the offensive, the lower-level ranks of the military—and also very many civil servants—were simply put in prison or directly killed.[21]

The SNM offensive immediately extended the policy of targeted ethnic repression which had been rampant for months, if not years:

Hundreds of men were arrested. They arrested anyone they feared could contribute money, experience or military knowledge to the opposition: in short, anyone they thought could provide some kind of leadership. They began by detaining all the people they had arrested in the past, i.e. a significant proportion of Issaq men in northern cities. There was no escape. We thought of going to Mogadishu but we heard on the BBC that Issaq men were also being arrested there. There seemed to be nowhere to go.[22]

The conditions of detention were completely contrary to usual practice because, when the mass arrests of Issaq started, there was not enough space in the jails for all these human beings. So, in order to make room for the new prisoners, all non-Issaq were released, including people who had been sentenced to death for civil crimes, people jailed for life, drug dealers, and so on. Many of those who were young enough were given arms and became the guards of the newly detained Issaq. The others joined the SNA and participated in the ongoing war.

Another effect of the SNM offensive was the immediate looting of all properties by the army, the Gulwadaayal[23] and the recently released criminals from the jails.

I saw them go into a big shop in front of our house that belonged to Suleiman Amin, a wealthy trader, and empty the shelves of food, tins, clothes, everything they could lay their hands on. At least Suleiman Amin remained alive but many others were first looted and then shot.[24]

But soon the looting began to look like a lesser evil. The soldiers or allied militiamen started to break into houses, looking for SNM fighters who might be hiding there. If the occupants were slow in opening the door, the soldiers would start shooting and then would break into the house.

When the soldiers came to our house, there was a big group of us gathered there, family, friends and neighbours. They banged on the door. One of the men, Osman Jalle, panicked and hid inside a cupboard. They broke the door. They searched under the beds and finally the cupboards too. They found Osman and shot him. The soldiers were arguing among themselves to decide whether or not we should all be shot. But they decided to take us to the Hangash[25] Centre and there they decided not to kill us. So we requested an escort to walk us home and protect us from the other soldiers. The soldier who accompanied us back home was grumbling and telling us it was foolish for so many civilians to have stayed behind because we could not defend ourselves and in the end we would all be shot.[26]

The looting, arrests and executions were now taking place all over the northern cities, whether or not SNM had attacked. According to a man[27] who had been arrested on 29 May in Borama, where no fighting was taking place, and was taken to the regional military headquarters:

There were hundreds of soldiers and civilians detained there, mostly men, but there were a few women as well, who had been accused of cooking for the SNM or giving them water. There were also a number of mentally ill people who had been rounded up. I was there for eight days. Everyday there were executions of Issaq,[28] both civilians and military. A number of CID officers (police) were also shot. The smallest number of people killed during any day would be 30 but usually it was much higher, In one day alone, 80 Issaq soldiers were shot, 40 from Gabiley and 30 from Dararweyne, a base near Naasa Hablood[29] ... and ten from Boqol Jireh, the headquarters of the anti-aircraft artillery. When there were so many to kill, they were put in a truck and taken to the banks of the dry riverbed because there was not enough room for the pile of corpses. The bodies were left outside.

In many other towns—Erigavo, Sheikh, Arabsiyo—the same type of massacres took place even though there were no SNM forces engaged in combat there.

In terms of deliberate cold-blooded violence and civilian casualties, the worst happened in Berbera, the north's second city, which the SNM had deliberately left aside to concentrate on Bura'o and Hargeisa. Most victims in Berbera had their throats slit and those who tried to escape were shot. Most of the killings took place at night at a site about 10 km out of the town, near the airport.[30] People were killed in batches of 30 to 40.

The overwhelming majority of the victims were seasonal labourers from Hargeisa or Bura'o or the nearby villages, hired for loading livestock for export and unloading goods at the port. We never identified most of them because they were temporary workers and they had no locally surviving relatives.[31]

The mechanics of destruction

As early as the third day following the attack on Hargeisa, and as soon as the SNA had regained control of the airport and could airlift supplies, Mogadishu started flying heavy artillery and shells into the north.[32] This new equipment, Russian, Italian and South African, was to have a frightful impact on the ongoing battles. Batteries of big-calibre artillery were towed up the Naasa Hablood hills overlooking Hargeisa, aimed at the city area and fired. The shelling was systematic and relentless. It was impossible to consider this use of artillery fire on a thickly populated urban space as anything short of a war crime. Given the situation, the SNA had to flush the SNM out of Hargeisa, for such are the needs of war. But heavy artillery used for street fighting is an absurdity. Armoured vehicles, machine guns, mortars, howitzers and, of course, combatants on foot, yes. But a 122 mm gun aimed at three men hiding on a street corner three miles away is not only brutally cruel, but also rather ineffectual. It is more likely to knock down a whole residential building and kill a score or two of civilians while missing the trained fighters lying flat on the ground. But as a genocidal tool, massive use of artillery fire on a populated city is reasonably efficient.

Even though the 'big g-word'—so easily bandied around since the Rwandan genocide of 1994—has not been used to describe what happened in northern Somalia in 1988, it is difficult to avoid.[33] In January 1989, Community Aid Abroad (CAA), an Australian NGO, produced the first report ever on the northern Somalia situation, commenting: 'The government response to the attack has been particularly brutal and without any regard to civilian casualties—in fact there is ample evidence that civilian casualties have been deliberately inflicted so as to destroy the support base of the SNM, which is mainly comprised of people from the Issaq clan. Following the SNM attacks on the major towns of Hargeisa and Bura'o, government forces bombed the towns, causing over 400,000 people to flee the atrocities across the border into Ethiopia where they are now located in refugee camps, living in appalling conditions ... A scorched earth policy has been applied to the villages in the vicinity. There the displaced people are hiding in the bush without any adequate access to food or medicines ... Genocide is the only word for it.'[34]

But was it such a surprise? In the so-called letter of death dated 23 January 1987,[35] General Mohamed Said Hersi 'Morgan', the regional commander of the northern region (26th Division), had written:

> We took punitive measures against the positions jointly occupied by the 'Qurmis'[36] and the Ethiopians, resulting in losses for them and the obliteration of villages such as Dibiile, Rabaso, Raamaaale and Garanuggle ... But unless the guerrilla opposition and its supporters are subjected to a campaign of complete obliteration, there will come a time when they will raise their heads again.

The 1989 SNM attack provided the government not only with an opportunity to attack the guerrillas, but to finally launch the 'campaign of obliteration' recommended by Morgan. The artillery was an obvious instrument but so were aircraft. The Somali Air Force still had the remnants of the planes it had used during the war with Ethiopia in 1977–8: a few Mig-17s, three Mig-21s and the survivors of its one complete fighter bomber squadron of Shenyang F-6, the Chinese version of the Mig-19, assembled post-1978 when Siad Barre was trying to find alternatives to the lost Russian connection. None of these aircraft were very useful, partly because lack of spare parts had grounded most of them and also because they lacked both pilots and mechanics. This is why the key air element in the brutal city war of 1988 had nothing to do with the flying archaeology inherited from Somalia's communist period. A few of the Migs or Shenyangs still flying took part in the Hargeisa butchery but they had only limited airworthiness and the pilots had low morale.[37] The key squadron was made up of the eight Hawker Hunters which had been given by the United Arab Emirates after the 1978 defeat to help Somalia rebuild an air force.[38] But the deadly edge of the air attack was provided by South Africa whose Foreign Minister, 'Pik' Botha, had approved the recruitment (and paid the salaries) of a team of six (white) pilots and mechanics from South Africa and Rhodesia. There were later some discreet additions, such as a British woman who did observation and liaison work with a light Cessna four-seater and a couple of (black) Botswana pilots. There were enough parts to keep the whole flying circus airborne and operational for a few months.[39]

And it was fiercely efficient. 'When it was the Migs, we were not afraid, they would fly too high and miss when they bombed. But with the Hunters, it was quite different. They were deadly. The best was Mr John.'[40] 'Mr John' had a hellish tactic. After taking off, he would spiral upwards to gain a high altitude. Then he would turn off his engine and dive, pointing towards a place reasonably distant from Hargeisa proper. He would then level off and fly horizontally, silently, at a very low altitude. In this way he would come as a surprise and pick off his targets at his own pace, one by one. He would machine-gun columns of refugees heading on foot towards Ethiopia, knock off the odd vehicle, kill wounded fighters hammocked in the trees, and even slaughter cattle so as to increase the food shortages of his targets. When his momentum began to slow down, he would restart his engine and regain altitude. It was war of a very special kind. Strangely enough, the refugees I talked with had a certain grudging admiration for Mr John: 'He flew very low and we tried to shoot him down. We hit him many times. But he never gave up. He kept coming back and killing us. He had courage.' A very Somali kind of praise.

The international community was largely blind to the drama then unfolding—the United States blind to the point of culpability. On 28 June 1988, in the middle of the fiercest fighting then taking place in northern Somalia, with massive killings of civilians and 400,000 refugees trekking over the border to Ethiopia, the Pentagon delivered 1,200 M-16 rifles with two million cartridges. In addition, the shipment included 300,000 .30 cartridges and half a million .50 for heavy machine guns.[41] The MAP delivery had been approved in November 1986, during a somewhat quieter time. But then, two years later, somebody in Washington who probably never read press dispatches decided to fulfil the requirements of the agreement without any concern for what was actually going on at the time—and without any idea of how that gift would be used. Since Siad Barre had (reasonable) doubts about the reliability of his troops,[42] he immediately laid hands on the American shipment and passed the booty to five of the fourteen Ogadeni refugee camps: Gallikar, Bihin, Adi Adeys, Dam Sabad and Arabsiyo. The President knew he would have no problem with them: they would kill as many enemies as they could, without bothering unduly whether they were 'civilians' or 'combatants'; in either case, they were all Qurmis.

But just as the Pentagon was absent-mindedly pouring oil on the fire, the Refugee Bureau of the Department of State was busy digging up another half-forgotten problem, the repatriation of the Ogadeni refugees. There had been a 'peace treaty' signed on 4 April, which included resettlement of the Ogadenis in Ogaden, although right now this seemed to be the last concern of either the refugees themselves or of their host, President Siad Barre. Actually, far from wanting to head home, the 'refugees' were fighting fiercely and the President was hanging on to them, pretending there were 840,000 of them, a figure the UNHCR did not consider realistic. In May 1988, UNHCR had stopped food deliveries, then resumed them at the end of June, only to stop them again in February 1989 with a phasing-out scheduled for June of that year. By that point the Somali government's relationship with the UNHCR had become so stormy that on 2 August 1989 the agency's High Commissioner was expelled from Somalia.

In the meantime, this had not stopped the State Department's Refugee Bureau from recruiting a very experienced researcher, Robert Gersony, to go out to Africa and investigate. Since the man was a realist, he wrote about what he saw and not about what he should have seen. After spending about ten weeks in the field in rather rough circumstances, he emerged with an explosive report that shook the complacency of the United States and, indirectly, of the rest of the international community.[43] So just as the weapons deliveries were exacerbating the crisis, the counter-logic of the US bureaucratic and information systems began to expose the massive violence in northern Somalia. The Gersony report was a first step and it was followed by the report of the US General Accounting Office. But both were administrative documents with a very limited distribution and circulation. Nevertheless, they both contributed to the wider impact of the Africa Watch report, which was published in their wake.[44] This was the beginning of the mediatisation of the Somali problem, a regional crisis which has continued periodically to grab the news for the past forty years and which still refuses to go away.

In the short term, the focus of the emergency moved from the violence itself to its consequences. And the main consequence in the short run was the one present in Gersony's title: 'flight'. Huge human streams issued from the gutted cities and converged towards the Ethiopian border.

> The Issaq refugees began evacuating the cities of Hargeisa and Bura'o by the end of the first week of the fighting (early June) and it appears that the evacuation was completed by the end of the month ... They gathered by the thousands on the outskirts of the cities, assembling their families and relatives. A number of the refugees indicated that while gathering their families, they were strafed by Somali military aircraft.[45]

Actually the air attacks were a lot heavier than the coy mention in the GAO report conveys.

> When the people fled the towns, they went after them in planes as they could not chase them all by foot. The planes used were British-made Hawker Hunters, Chinese-made Mig-19s and Russian Mig-17s and 21s. There were also slower Italian-made planes for observation. The smaller Italian planes identified the long caravan-like rows of people and located them. Then the warplanes came and would drop their bombs. The Hunters made nine to twelve rounds every day and the Migs would come five or six times. They would fly very low because they knew the civilians did not have any anti-aircraft guns. Some days the planes were at it non-stop 6 a.m. to 6 p.m., hitting some areas again and again. They also killed the livestock so we would have nothing to eat.[46]

> When the aerial bombardment started, we decided to escape. We had no idea where we were going but we had to escape the bombing and the shelling. We went towards Geed Debleh, about 10 km from Hargeisa. We arrived there after a seven-hour trek. One had the impression the entire city was there. But then the shelling started as well, although the SNM was nowhere to be seen. Real pandemonium broke out. People were even more desperate than they had been in Hargeisa. It made them feel they could never escape. Many people were killed,

some by the bombs dropped from the airplanes, others shot by the machine guns they were firing, even more by the shelling and some by being trampled underfoot by the panicky crowds. Family members lost each other and some parents were separated from their children. For me I lost my mother-in-law and I only learned much later that she eventually got to Djibouti.[47]

Two weeks after the fighting broke out in Hargeisa, the conditions became unbearable and we fled to the north of the city and trekked to Annayo. We lived there under the shade of the trees on the river embankment ... There were several air raids a day in this little place. The shortage of food was such a serious problem that people were forced to sneak back into Hargeisa to find something to eat. Each time we went back, we would see additional dead bodies and more homes destroyed. In late July we decided to cross into Ethiopia. We tried to cross to the west of Hargeisa, at Abudleh. There was a contingent of the Somali Army stationed there, and if they got you, that was it, you were dead. Five times we tried crossing but we were forced back when the soldiers fired at us. The army was in all these places to prevent us from crossing into Ethiopia, and this in spite of the fact we were unarmed civilians who had nothing except our barest possessions. They killed many and then robbed the bodies. I witnessed the killing of many women and even children, I even witnessed the shooting of an old man who was nearly blind.[48]

The lack of resources available for the fleeing people rapidly became a nightmare.

Soon after we arrived at Annayo, we ran out of food and out of money. In any case, there was nothing to buy. The only food available was either what the SNM could give us or what was brought by car by people who were daring enough to steal back into Hargeisa at night. So we decided to go to Ethiopia before we died of starvation. But we did not have transportation and there was a fierce struggle over the vehicles. When a truck agreed to take people, they would spend the entire day guarding it. Families with adult men were in a stronger position, they could fight for them. But we only had two young boys. So much of their transport had been destroyed by the warplanes that the SNM was reluctant to let all the vehicles they had left cross into Ethiopia. Even though we were so hungry, our fear of the bombings was such we were even prepared to try to walk. Finally, the SNM provided 40 trucks when they realised how bad it was. There was havoc as people scrambled for space. They put goats or bags on top of you, but it did not matter as long as you had a place. People were hanging out the sides of the vehicles. All the trucks were in a bad state and the terrain was rough. In order not to attract attention, the headlights were turned off and it was dangerous on that mountainous road.

The shortage of water was terrible and we had to fetch water very far and in secret to avoid the soldiers. We stayed six days. Food was scarce and children and babies were very weak by then. We divided food into tiny portions so as to give them the illusion of being fed regularly. But their hunger was obvious and it was painful to watch your children getting weaker and weaker from hunger. The bombings continued but hunger made us less and less concerned for our safety. The only thing that mattered was reaching the border. As trucks broke down, more and more people took to walking. They kept a hand on the mouth of children so they would not cry. Many didn't make it and some groups were killed by soldiers as they tried to cross. The SNM escorted the bigger groups, but they could not escort everyone because of the size of the fleeing population. Finally, we got to Ethiopia, one by one in some cases because of the broken-down trucks.[49]

One of the strongest testimonies available about that time of horror is that of a man who saw it from a very special perspective, that of burying—or rather removing—the dead.

One day in the evening I returned to my house and on my way I met a tall military captain from the Issa Musa Habr Yunis,[50] who gave me a lift. But then we met a well-known officer, Colonel Mohamed Alin, who told me to come with him without explaining anything. We arrived at their military camp, and the colonel told me to take one of the bulldozers and bury the dead at the Malka Durduru site. There were a few dead bodies and I buried them. Then the colonel took me to the soldiers who were there and he said they had to guard me; if I disappeared they would all be shot. I was so precious to them because I was the only person who could handle a bulldozer ... Then I parked the machine properly but they would not let me go. I argued with them, so they accompanied me to my home and they did not leave. They stayed to guard me and in the evening I could hear their footsteps, they did not trust me and they remained awake all night.

The next day when I came back to Malka Durduru, I saw dead bodies stretching for almost 150 or 200 metres. Most of the people massacred at first were soldiers and officers of the Issaq clan. So I started to bury these dead bodies near the dry riverbed. I lifted the dead bodies slowly and lowered them into the hole slowly, trying to avoid dumping them like trash. I usually left the scene exhausted. But I had to finish my task on that day otherwise, if I left the bodies behind, they would have been a feast for the hyenas and the roaming dogs. They would shoot the people in the late afternoon, till sunset. I could hear the machine guns when they were shooting and I worked that way for many days, burying men in uniforms and also civilians. The officers had their pens in their pockets, their watches and their boots, and strangely enough those who shot them did not loot their property. It was an impossible mission and I felt pain beyond normal endurance. My only consolation was that by burying the dead I was doing a good deed. In Islam burying the dead is a good deed and a responsibility for any grown man. In any case I could not escape because they would have killed me immediately as they were watching over me day and night.

One day, near the Somali Armed Forces headquarters in Hargeisa, I was burying some dead bodies shot in the evening. While I was moving the dead to the mass grave, an officer from the Ogaden clan called me and told me to bury a dead body which was lying away from the rest of the other bodies. I told him to bring the body to the area where the mass of the dead bodies were lying so that I can bury them together. He became furious and started abusing me and calling me names like "Qurmis" and "son of a filthy father", asking me how do I dare bury this soldier who was from his own clan and loyal to the government, with this SNM filth. I replied and told him that for me there was no difference between the dead bodies. Hearing my answer, he pulled out his pistol and shot at me. I was lucky, the bullet only grazed me and went through my shirt, but there was no blood. Colonel Mohamed Alin, who was close by, threatened the other officer that he will shoot him if he tries to kill me.

Another day while I was burying more dead, a truck stopped near me with eight bodies. I looked closely because these bodies looked different from all those I had buried since I started working on the mass graves. They were the bodies of teenagers in secondary school uniforms. There were no bullet wounds on their bodies nor any other type of wounds. I asked the truck driver whether those had been strangled with ropes. The truck driver was crying and could not answer my question for some time. He finally replied and told me that their blood had been drained completely till the last drop and showed me the medical plaster on their arms where the blood had been drained from. It had been taken out for transfusing the army soldiers. The faces of those dead children looked different from those of adults who had been shot to death. They looked as if they were in a deep sleep because they had not died violently.

Another day while I was burying the dead, I saw one man lying among the dead, crying and asking me for help. He was still alive and was asking me to untie him. Without hesitation I took my knife and got down from the bulldozer and moved towards the man who was calling for help without realising the risk I was taking. Immediately the soldiers ran towards me and stopped me, with their guns pointing at me. They lifted me up in the air and threw me under the bulldozer. Then they all turned towards the man who was crying for help and they started shooting at him from different sides, they were crazy with anger and they shot so many bullets that they set a large patch of dry grass on fire. I got back to my seat, feeling depressed and demoralised, and went to the garage to park the bulldozer, and I left the place in a terrible mood.

I kept moving the dead that way for 28 days straight and then the number of the massacred people decreased because many people had escaped from Hargeisa and moved to the outskirts and the rural areas. The number of dead soldiers and officers decreased and I started to bury more civilians. I used to dig the mass graves starting in the morning, after the morning prayers, and I started to get bodies from different areas of the city to the three major graves. There was one near Malka Durduru, another one near Abu Sita milk factory and the third one was in Sinai. The dead were transported by trucks from different areas and they were dumped in the mass graves I had started to prepare in the morning. Some of the dead fell in the graves while others would fall outside, and it was my duty to make sure they were all buried properly. I remember one area called Doqonmawaaye near the head office of the telecommunications and the old bridge of Hargeisa where heaps of dead bodies had accumulated and the soldiers used them as a shield against the fire of the SNM fighters. Among the dead I saw a child who was hanging to the body of his mother, and I believe the child must have died when the mother was breastfeeding him.

In the end I was burying less and less people because all the civilians had fled the city and the fighting was between the SNM and the armed forces. I used to collect the military dead from the Hargeisa Group Hospital. After the war, I was interviewed by many foreign agencies and human rights activists, and I usually told them that what I am telling them is the truth and I asked them what they were going to do about it. They did not know what to answer and they spoke in general terms.[51]

'In general terms' the battle of the cities had mostly petered off during July 1988. There were still sporadic skirmishes in Hargeisa and around Berbera. The Somali government was then calling on the Arab countries for help, with the discreet underlying message that this was a 'fight for Islam'. Egypt, the UAE, Libya and Kuwait all responded with dribbles of military aid and a bit of cash. In spite of (limited) Ethiopian support for the SNM offensive, the pretence of respecting the 4 April Djibouti Agreement continued. On 26 July 1988 the Ethiopian Minister of Defence, Mesfin Gebre Meskel, went to Mogadishu and proceeded to exchange 3,507 Ethiopian prisoners for 229 Somali ones.[52] On 17 July the SNA recaptured Bura'o, but this did not stop the relentless air attacks on the refugee columns by the Hawker Hunters. Nevertheless, if the 'war of the cities' had been a clear tactical defeat for the SNM (with the civilians paying the highest price), it began later to turn slowly into a strategic victory.

This happened in two ways. Firstly, the exhausted SNA was in the process of breaking down into its clanic component units, with parts of regiments not fully deserting but rather breaking ranks and rejoining their clan brothers in order to reconstitute clanically coherent units, where the soldiers felt safer because they were shoulder-to-shoulder with people they considered relatives.[53] These new, increasingly autonomous units held out in the northern towns they had reconquered but were surrounded by a hostile countryside. Secondly, those military clanic elements that felt ill at ease with the new quasi-genocidal developments originating from Mogadishu began to divorce them-selves from the 'national' army. This was the case in Somalia proper for the Majerteen, for the Hawiye and even, in the end, for large segments of the Ogadeni. In the 'Somaliland North', the Issa and Gaddabursi in Awdal (west) and the Dhulbahante in Togdheer (east) began to chart their own course, distinct both from those of the government and the SNM.

This clanic disintegration was a complex phenomenon. There were, of course, feelings of moral disgust towards the crimes perpetrated by the ill-named 'security forces'. But more than anything else, there was a growing fear that the regime was now on a course of accelerating collapse, progressively losing control of more and more areas of legitimate authority. The economy was a wreck,[54] the army was dissolving, and the very clan structure on which Somali state politics had been precariously perched was beginning to wobble. The implosion of pan-Somalism, which had been triggered by the 1978 defeat, started to impact on its initial component factors. After 1988, 'Somaliland' was back, even though many of its actors were neither aware of this nor willing to adopt this course. But the May–July 1988 northern horrors had dealt a death blow to what we called earlier 'the Dream'. How could the Somali 'dream of unity' survive a situation in which genocidal violence had rolled over the land like a torrent of blood? The SNM leadership was still largely united. But by then the ordinary northern population had entered into a quiet divorce and the next few years were only going to deepen the divide. As for the rest of the country, the clanic scramble, which started in the wake of the northern 'war of the cities', soon began to turn into a free-for-all. As the national government started to slide into a slow-motion collapse, the various clans began to look for clanic safety nets, each territory turning itself into a protective zone. The unravelling of Somalia had begun.

7

THE LOCAL WAR IN THE NORTH GOES GLOBAL, 1989–1991

Since the Somali defeat of 1978, the international community had become accustomed to seeing the conflict in former Somaliland turn mildly chronic and morph into a feature of the Horn of Africa landscape: 'Those Somali! ... Hard to govern! ... What a problem!' In the commonly accepted international view of the 'problem', the greatest danger the Somali represented for the international order was their quixotic desire to break down the existing borders and march forward to the unity of a 'Greater Somalia'. Thus the northern war was seen as a mild annoyance, fought 'for tribal reasons'. Besides, the outside view of the conflict was almost completely seen within a Cold War framework. This meant that the SNM was perceived as both 'tribal' and 'communist-aligned'. As a consequence, the failed invasion in 1982 of Balambale–Goldogob appeared like the last hurrah of the 'communist allies'—even though SNM had taken no part in the offensive—perhaps even as *the* last hurrah of such adventures anywhere. The reason for this was that the Cold War was progressively winding down all over the world, peaceful coexistence was slowly spreading and, apart from exotic outposts of the Revolution, such as Nepal or Colombia, Marxism-Leninism was progressively becoming outdated. Ethiopia, now no longer having any relevance, was being progressively evacuated by the Russians.

But considering SNM and the war in the north as an extension of what was happening in neighbouring Ethiopia was plainly wrong. And so was the 'folkloric' view that attributed the Issaq rebellion to some genetic incapacity of the Somali character to develop an intimate form of law and order. It was both much less and much more than that. What the explosion of May 1988 had brought brutally into view was the relativity of the concept of culture. Yes, there was a 'Somali culture'; and it shared an enormous number of common traits across a vast expanse of territory spread over four countries. But it was not a solid homogeneous bloc. Did that cause a problem? Yes, indeed, it did. The Somali world is not the juxtaposition of deeply different cultural units agreeing to harmonise, like Switzerland. Nor is it a de facto multicultural commonwealth of people agreeing to disagree, as in many African tribal countries or even in India, because it is in their well-calculated interest to do so.

On the contrary, it is a largely homogeneous cultural entity extraordinarily selective about the means used to make the pieces of the puzzle fit together. You don't rule over the Somali, even in the mild way a European democracy can rule over its own people between elections. Instead you run along a constantly modified track which needs the agreement not only of the engine driver but of most of the passengers, who all have their own views about where the train should be going. Does this mean constant anarchy? Definitely not if you can patiently give, take, repair, threaten, seduce, adjust, modify if needed, and rush to enforce if there is consensus. Governing the Somali is an art and a constant headache. They themselves know it so well that *Xeer*, the clanic law, is the ultimate standard of practical legal decisions, not the Islamic Shari'ah, even though everybody is Muslim. The general attitude is that Shari'ah is the embodiment of Islamic perfection, so perfect in fact that dragging it down into the murky affairs of this world is not quite proper. *Xeer* can do that, *Xeer* is tough and age-old, and can be used without becoming dirty. If you can reconcile *Xeer* and the spirit of governance, then you have reached a starting point.

This explains two things. Firstly, the south never had a chance in trying to run (govern) the north. The south had been thoroughly administered according to the old Italian colonial system. It was initially rough and it became even rougher after 1922 when the Fascists tried to remodel the colony in terms of their simplified political philosophy. That meant force and especially the frontal destruction of the Migiurtina, the north-eastern Majerteen territory which had been the most resolute clanic or geographical area in standing up to the forceful Italian onslaught. In a milder spirit but following a basically similar approach, the post-war AFIS administration had carried on with an attitude of rigidity tempered by corruption. In this still Italianate atmosphere the UN-sponsored organisation tried to rigorously apply Romanic law to the rubber-like universe of clan relationships—and it failed. It also tried to advance post-colonial Italian interests and it failed to do that as well.[1] Corruption, both Somali and foreign, plugged the gap between abstract legal ideals and practical *combinazione.*

Secondly, pan-Somalism was a dream of perfection, a family reconciliation, an ethnic epiphany. It did not belong to this world, particularly when its practical implementation was subcontracted to the African incarnation of a Mafia *capo di tutti i capi.* 1978 had been a reality check for the pan-Somali worldview. But the worst was not the military defeat, but the dream's ideological collapse. It happened when the liberated Ogadeni 'brothers' suddenly turned into invaders, with the Darood leaders becoming thugs and the Issaq *Xeer* dignity being dragged into the mud after it had been praised as a component of the pan-Somali struggle. Thus the May 1988 invasion (backed by the Ethiopian Christian enemy) was the battering ram that finally brought down the whole imagined pan-Somali dream. The Darood—and those non-Darood that believed in 'national unity'—raped, killed relentlessly and destroyed the material life of their 'brothers'. Culture had not succeeded in trumping politics—and, even less, economics. In the wake of the brutal attacks and civilian massacres of May–July 1988, another social and political order needed to be rebuilt over the ruins of the collapsed dream. In the north the direction could not be forward anymore, given the abyss into which pan-Somalism had sunk. The only pattern left was that of the stern and ungainly shape of old Somaliland, the territorial arrangement that had been produced by a foreign hand—something that very few 'Somalilanders', even within the SNM, had ever contemplated before.

'Nothing is the same anymore'

In the short term, as the SNM offensive fell apart, a series of complex and uncoordinated battles developed on secondary fronts. In late August SNM forces occupied the harbours of Hiis, Meid and Bulhar, while residual (but intense) fighting lingered around Borama. The SNA started to crack apart, not so much under SNM pressure, but rather because of internal fissiparousness aggravated by the recent fighting. Omar Jess and Morgan were at daggers drawn in the north, Jess having managed to obtain the support of Gabiyow who, as Defence Minister, still retained a claim to a broad army establishment. But this claim was increasingly theoretical since the minister was not even in charge of the 26th Division troops, who were the core operational force in 'Somaliland'. In spite of being of cabinet rank, he had been put under the operational orders of General Ahmed Warsaw, who was a Marehan (i.e. the President's clan), while Gabiyow himself was Ogadeni. This clanic reordering of the army's command structure began to spread like a crack in a windshield as 1988 came to a close. In Mogadishu, Khadidja, the President's first wife, had put together a kind of 'Darood inner caucus' whose members were supposed to cut across the SNA ranking order and superimpose another—clanic—order over the formal military hierarchy. Suleiman 'Dafle' was a key member who had been drawn in to circumvent General Samantar— who remained in theory the Chief of Staff—and to keep the Dhulbahante on the regime's side.[2] Another role of the 'caucus' was to sideline Gabiyow and to cut down to size all of the Ogadeni sub-clanic groups. The minister took a quick trip down from Berbera to complain to the President, telling him that if the north was still in the government's hands, it was due to those Ogadeni who would instinctively side against the Issaq.

But the situation was also collapsing in Awdal where the Issa and the Gaddabursi were now fighting to steer their sub-region into different directions. Both were anti-SNM, as befitted two minority clans standing in the way of a larger clan family; but being anti-SNM was not, in itself, a coherent political choice. Discreetly egged on by Ismail Omar Guelleh, President Hassan Gouled's nephew and head of the Djibouti secret service, the Issa had created the United Somali Front (USF, in fact a clanic movement), which engaged in preparations for an eventual secession of this westernmost part of Somaliland. But this line of action came into direct conflict with that of their Gaddabursi neighbours, who were the local proxies of the Mogadishu regime. Nobody wanted the SNM, but the two clans had different views of the future and pursued their options militarily.

On 19 September, President Hassan Gouled flew to Mogadishu in the company of his nephew Ismail Omar Guelleh (secret service) and Moumin Farah Badon (foreign affairs), to meet with Siad Barre. The three Djiboutians asked that the Somalian head of state intervene and separate the fighting clans, something he hardly could do and did not seem to want to attempt. The final communiqué spoke about 'further cooperation in ensuring peace and stability in the Horn of Africa'—definitely a highly optimistic goal given the circumstances.

'Peace and stability' were eluding the regime, whose economic collapse was pushing it to extremes. In mid-September 1988 the Kenyan paramilitary force GSU[3] had to battle it out with Somali government-sponsored elephant poachers. Killing elephants for their tusks had become a steady income stream for Mogadishu since hunting was officially outlawed in 1978. The elephant population in the Tsavo border area fell from 35,000 in 1973 to 5,363 in 1987,[4] most of the killing being the work of Somalis. In February 1989, the US Fish and Wildlife Service put an embargo on Somali ivory since it estimated that, over the previous three years, Mogadishu had exported or stocked more than 25,000 tusks, while the total Somali elephant population only amounted to about 4,500 heads.[5] But the government was barely surviving, with total imports worth $510 million against exports worth $88.1 million. Inflation had reached 42 per cent.[6] The IMF had suspended all aid and private donation programmes had also been stopped, with the exception of Italy ($16 million) and Saudi Arabia ($5 million). Germany, Japan, the US and the International Bank for Reconstruction and Development had all put a halt to their programmes and during 1987 total foreign aid plummeted to $67 million. In December, Siad Barre flew to Tripoli where Gaddafi, the usual lender of last resort for desperate authoritarian regimes, agreed to make some more arms deliveries.

In January 1989, the first international effects of the massive fighting and massacres of May 1988 began to be felt. At this point, it is perhaps necessary to remind the contemporary reader that in those pre-Internet days communications and news took a lot more time, not in being researched or issued—print media journalists did a magnificent job—but rather in being distributed and therefore 'digested', i.e. becoming capable of impacting on public opinion and therefore policy decisions. The present immediacy of every newsworthy fragment of reality was still in the future and large events, particularly if they came from the margins of the 'developed' world, took a few months to ferment and achieve significant effects. Thus the small, unremarked war in Somalia of the early 1980s only began to shake and shock the public in late 1988 and early 1989. The connection between the 'exotic' local situation and its broader Cold War context started to emerge slowly, even though local perceptions changed rather quickly. The main transformation was the growing clanic and regional segmentation of the SNA, which remained 'national' in name only.

At the international level the constant toing and froing of both the regime's leaders and their foreign backers became frantic. In January 1989, Second Vice-President Hussein Kulmiye Afrah was in Paris and Brussels; in February, Italian President Francesco Cossiga came to Mogadishu, while General Abu Bakr Yunis, Libyan Chief of Staff, visited four days later; and Siad Barre himself flew to Abu Dhabi shortly after. And this was only the foam on the surface of the soup, while the pot kept boiling underneath, mostly at the clanic level. Gabiyow had been dismissed in January, while the Ogadeni refugees were massively re-armed. When the SNM attacked the refugee camps, the UNHCR decided to regroup the core of the refugees still inside Somalia in camps around Borama where the pro-Siad Barre Gaddabursi militia provided a back-up protective force. In London, the diaspora organisation Ogaden Action Group launched demonstrations in March to protest against the forced recruitment of refugees to the 'national' army.

Then, on 15 March the Ogadeni refugees who had been incorporated into the Somali Army and who were garrisoned in Kismayo, mutinied, killed the town's military governor, looted the armoury and took to the bush. During April, the Ogadeni insurrection spread to Buale, Lugh and Bardheere, resulting in the creation of a new anti-government movement, the Somali Patriotic Movement (SPM). On 20 May, the Ogadeni Colonel Omar Jess, who was defending Hargeisa against the SNM, deserted, switched sides and joined the newborn SPM. For the SNM, things were going almost too fast.

> In the early years, there were combatants trained in camps in eastern Ethiopia, and after the completion of their training they were assigned to different fronts, regardless of which sub-clan they belonged to ... But after the big 1988 fighting in Hargeisa and Bura'o, the fronts (*Aags*) broke into sub-clans and SNM became less centralised; each group was fighting in the front which corresponded to his sub-clan. They became less dependent on the SNM central command and started to undertake independent operations. The reason was that all the people from the major cities of the north were either in refugee camps in Ethiopia or displaced in rural areas. And it was at that time that very large numbers of young people started to join SNM. They could only do so at their local sub-clan level because, after the signing of the 1988 peace agreement between Mengistu and Siad Barre, the Ethiopian government had stopped its support for the fighting movement. So, with this decline of the central command, it was the clan elders of each region who mobilised their own sub-clan in providing food, arms and logistics to the young people who had just joined the war. Before the 1988 explosion, the funds donated by SNM supporters living abroad were centralised and kept in an account in Addis Ababa. But after the city fighting, each elder communicated with the members of his sub-clan abroad and the funds were directly sent to each front (*Aag*) and they all became more and more decentralised.[7]

Paradoxically, victory and defeat were less important than process, and both processes went into the same direction: away from formal organisation and back to the clan, sub-clan and even sub-sub-clan. The SNA 'army' was disintegrating into its component parts while at the same time the SNM was ballooning into a 'mass organisation'. But the reality was that the SNA was less and less of a 'national' army while the SNM was less and less of a (proto-) 'national' revolutionary movement. The clanic organisation had antedated both, and it outlived both.

> Another effect of the 1988 fighting was the foundation of the *Guurti* [Assembly].[8] There had been an embryo *Guurti* before, but the first formal *Guurti* was held in Adarosh in that same year 1988. The struggle had become more loose and a new mobilisation had to be developed along these lines ... Fifty-two elders met in Adarosh and Ibrahim Sheikh Yusuf Sheikh Madar was chosen as chairman of the new assembly ... Then the *Guurti* became part and parcel of SNM when it was added to its structure. We were mandated for fundraising and for the mobilisation of the communities. We had good relations with the officers of the SNM even though we were not mandated to take part in the politics and management of the movement; we had no role in the decision-making process. But when there were assemblies or meetings, we were invited as an observer group ... The livestock was the backbone of the economy and the *Guurti* played a leading role in collecting and distributing livestock resources ... Our best opportunity was that we met in a period when the struggle was at its peak and the war was all over the cities of the country ... Therefore those who were asked to pay funds for the struggle, and many others who were paying without having been asked, were so numerous we could not count them all ... Later we extended the Council from 52 to 82, so that the clans from the east and the west of Somaliland could be part and parcel of the Council and of the country as a whole.[9]

'Part and parcel of the country as a whole': these words were uttered in earnest but they were spoken 27 years after the fact and they probably better represented the sentiment of the speaker at the time of the interview than at the time of the events described. This was because within SNM, before the March 1987 fifth congress, the main emphasis was not on any 'Somaliland national unity' but rather on an effort to unite as many different clan representatives as possible. The well-known Hawiye lawyer Ali Mohamed Ossoble 'Wardigley' had been chosen as vice-president, while seven other members of the Hawiye clan family had been elected as members of the Central Committee. There were also one Dir (Gaddabursi), two Darood (one Majerteen and one Dhulbahante) and one Rahanweyn. In the mid-1980s the emphasis was on fighting the Siad Barre regime, and any help in that common cause seemed positive. A branch of SNM called SNM South or SNM Southern Front was organised and it fought in Hiiran and Mudug provinces. But Wardigley complained that Silanyo was keener on northern military operations and that this preference smacked of rampant secession-ism. The Hawiye front progressively dried up and the 1988 fighting only strengthened the feeling of the southerners that there were in fact two SNMs, the real one, which was an armed expression of the Issaq clan family, and another, which only amounted to a propaganda booster. To escape being held hostage in an organisation he felt was heading in the wrong direction in January 1989 Wardigley created in Rome the United Somali Congress (USC), in theory a multi-clanic organisation even if it was in fact largely dominated by the Hawiye.

As we saw above, when the Ogadeni mutinied they had joined neither the SNM South nor the newborn USC but had created their own SPM. Parallel with the breaking up of the old Somali state, the delineaments of its successor structures were beginning to emerge. The impression was so strong that even in the Mogadishu regime, within the vertical dictatorship structure inherited from its Marxist-Leninist origins, the impression was now growing that decen-tralisation of power had to be embraced rather than resisted. The name had, of course, to be different since that systemic outline had to be sold to donors, who might shy away from endorsing a *Guurti*-like structure. On 17 July 1989 the Central Committee of the SRSP rejected the proposal that multi-partyism should be introduced as a constitutive part of the regime.[10] And then on 30 August 1989 that same Central Committee unanimously voted for a return to pre-October 1969 'democracy'.

But what had happened during those fateful six weeks? The clanic clashes between the Marehan core of the army and the Ogadeni insurgents had mul-tiplied around Dhobley. Hundreds of young people were arrested after the Friday prayers when they protested against the detention of twelve popular sheikhs, and many had been shot in what later became known as the al-Jazeera massacre.[11] The government admitted to 24 deaths and 59 people wounded but there were at least 400 victims.[12] At the same time the ghost of SSDF came back to life in Hiiran, under the label of SNM Southern Front, when it attacked Belet Weyn. And to top it all, the Rahanweyn announced the crea-tion of their own new rebel movement, the Somali Democratic Movement (SDM), which started to attack the 'national' army in the Upper Juba valley. During the month of August, Meslah Mohamed Siad, the President's son, travelled to Moscow, Tripoli and Havana, desperately trying to muster some support, without finding help anywhere.[13] And then in September, the first USC units swung into action on several fronts at the same time (Hiiran, Galguduud and Mudug). That last-mentioned uprising was momentous. Just as the Issaq clan family is the 'core population' of the north, so the Hawiye are the core population of the centre-south. Their decision to go into armed opposition was critical and the war suddenly took on a radically new aspect. It was not the disaffected margin of the 'Grand Somalia' project challenging the centre, but the centre itself challenging the project. It meant regime change and perhaps even more.

Trouble from the margins moves to the centre

On 29 September 1989, a group of prominent US Congressmen with a continuing interest in African affairs[14] wrote to Secretary of State James Baker, questioning the financial aid which would allow Mogadishu to repay its IMF arrears, a measure that would keep Somalia's access to IMF financing open.[15] Baker listened to the admonishment, particularly in view of the reports of human rights violations coming out of Somalia at the time, and in February 1990 the decision to supply financial aid was eventually cancelled.

Why was this financial episode so essential for the overall evolution of the conflict? The reason has to do with what has already been said about the absence during the long history of the Somali of anything approaching a 'Somali state'. Somali culture is fissiparous, not because its component parts want to avoid each other but because they deeply refuse any submission to another clan, and consequently no acceptable mechanism has ever been devised to fit the various parts of the Somali puzzle into an identifiable unitary structure. The only things that can—in a way and for a while—unify Somali clans are a common outside enemy or economic interest. Now that European colonialism had gone, in the absence of any other bond, money was the last thing that remained as a toe-hold for some kind of 'unity'. Is this peculiar to Somali culture? Yes, in a way. It has to do with the fierce social egalitarianism of the Somali. A Somali will bend to force if it is a matter of survival. He will also bend to economic interest if necessary, though he will never accept this as a normal and lasting proposition. Having lost the war with Ethiopia and squandered the political capital pertaining to Greater Somalia in the north, Siad Barre had no force left to rule over a polity of hyper-democrats. Beyond his own clan and a handful of *gaashaanbuur*[16] allies, there was nobody anymore. This was a very costly proposition to hang on to and in addition he had lost both the support of foreign patron states and any way to make money independently beyond smuggling a few poached elephant tusks. This left the struggle for international financial support essential, not only for his own regime to survive but also for any form of 'national' statist power to exist. Without money or an external enemy, and with a broken dream as as a sole asset, the fate not only of the 'Afweyne' regime but of the whole state structure now looked grim.

But as usual, when unexpected major changes were in the making, the international community kept its business-as-usual attitude. On 20 July the European Union (then EEC) announced the opening of a $66 million fund to build a Gelib–Bardheere road. It was described as a step forward in the development of the country's infrastructure. In the short term, though, what really preoccupied the Somali regime was its collapsing army. The last element of support came from Libya; in October the SNA received 32 T-55 tanks, 20 BM-21 truck-mounted multiple rocket launchers, and an unknown number of D-30 122 mm artillery pieces.[17] This equipment was sorely needed as the military situation was collapsing in slow motion. During November 1989 multiple clashes developed all over: Belet Weyn was attacked by loose groups of Ogadeni and Hawiye deserters, in Hiiran province the Hawiye sub-clans of Hawadle and Habr Gidir attacked each other over water and pasture, and the SNA did nothing to stop them. In Togdheer province Dhulbahante and Issaq clashed along more or less SNM lines of conflict, and the same happened in Awdal between the newly created Somali Democratic Alliance (SDA, which was Gaddabursi) and western SNM regiments. The situation was so confused that not even the SNA general staff was able to keep precise track of what was happening. On 11 November the SNM and the newborn SPM, which were equally lost, issued a joint communiqué asking for the unification of the opposition.

Now that the Ogadeni refugees had become almost officially part of the war, the UNHCR was equally worried. After screening the refugees—it was the first time their exact numbers had been allowed to be counted[18]—the UN agency offered them three possible options: going back home to Ethiopia with some cash and a one-year supply of staple food; becoming Somali citizens (less cash and only seven months of food); or remaining as refugees, an option that was strongly discouraged. The estimated cost for UNHCR was $50 million and, given the military situation, all programmes in the northern provinces of the former Somaliland had been suspended in August 1989. The main problem for the UNHCR concerned those Ogadeni incorporated into the SNA, who were both refugees and combatants. Under pressure from the SNM, they tried to join the newly created Islamic Front for the Liberation of Oromiya (IFLO) and walk back into Ethiopia, where the war had taken enormous territory from the Derg regime and was approaching Addis Ababa. There was a similar problem for the Afar Liberation Front (ALF), which, without having reached the same degree of integration with the Somali Army, nevertheless benefited from its help in fighting the Derg. ALF leader Sultan Ali Mirah had first gone to Mogadishu and then rushed to Borama, where his men had seen a drastic change when the Hawiye Colonel Mohamed Hussein 'Garrileh' rebelled against Siad Barre and took over the town. ALF fighters were caught there and Mogadishu's word was not much use any longer in the town. ALF fighters, who were ideologically very distant from the IFLO boys,[19] chose the same form of exit and walked back towards Jijiga, bowing out of a conflict which was not theirs anymore but had become purely Somali.

On 19 December the USC and the SNM issued a joint communiqué, demanding that Siad Barre step down. The two organisations implicitly spoke as if they were some kind of future constituent assembly for a national unity government, but the USC was basically a Hawiye front (and the Hawiye clan family was far from being united) while the SNM had only seven non-Issaq in a Central Committee of 47 members. A national critical mass was far from having been achieved. Then on 2 January 1990, a meeting of the Issa clan family took place in Djibouti. The tone was belligerent and clearly anti-Gaddabursi, even if both clan families feared that Mogadishu's defeat would usher in a regional Issaq dominance. The main question during that conference was the degree of Djibouti state support which the Issa group could claim and how the two armed militias—the Issa USF and the Gaddabursi SDA—would deal with each other. The debate took place as if the Somali government had already disappeared and as if Somalia 'state territory' was up for grabs by other non-Somalia Somali.[20]

On 9 January Siad Barre dissolved his cabinet and, after a few days of floundering about, he re-formed it with the same Mohamed Ali Samantar as Prime Minister, after having approached twelve different respectable political figures[21] and been refused each time. A new cabinet was finally put together, mostly made up of young unknowns. Only seven of the old ministers accepted positions in the new government, whose military actions, in the absence of new funding and equipment, had become more and more sporadic. In late March the SNA had retaken Zeyla, Lughaya and Loyada in order to discourage the ambitious attempts of USF and SDA militias to claim pieces of the dying country. The SNA was helped in its operation by the 'Horyal' (Vanguard) Gaddabursi militia, which was so unsure of its status that in 1991, when the Derg was overthrown, it turned itself into an 'Ethiopian' political party. On 3 April the SNM retook the three towns to make a point: that the Mogadishu state was on the way out but minor clan militias were not going to be allowed to position themselves and detach micro-clanic areas from the collapsing structure. The SNM was Issaq and the SNM represented the demographic majority.

In a desperate bid to regain some popularity Siad Barre abrogated the law on *qat* in May 1990, a measure that came much too late and had no great social or economic impact. The *qat*-trading networks, like everything else, had adapted to the war and were now operating completely outside the state circuit. On 11 May, Susanna Agnelli, the Italian Deputy Minister for Foreign Affairs, offered to mediate between the government and the rebels. It was very late for such an offer to be made but it was not inconsequential because, as the state and army progressively fell apart, there was a parallel effort at structuring the opposition. In addition, the idea developed that there might be one last chance at a 'grand negotiation' between the rebels and the government. In fact this was perhaps a bit of wishful thinking because the very person of Siad Barre was a major obstacle. A 'grand negotiation', if such a thing were possible, could only have been about the terms of Siad's effacement and the groundwork for a transitional government. Siad's own obduracy prevented this possibility from turning into a reality.

What of the reorganisation of the opposition? It started in February 1990 at Baligubadle, a small town on the Ethiopian–Somali border where the fifth SNM congress had been convened. There was change in the air, even in the choice of delegates. The gathering revealed the typical weariness of ageing political establishments. Silanyo had been chairman for six years and there was a desire for renewal, which, this being Somalia, was expressed in clanic terms. Silanyo was from the Habr Ja'alo and another clan family, probably the Habr Yunis, were ambitious for the position. But there were also more fundamental issues. Deserters were multiplying and a problem had developed around the handling of them. The 'first-generation' SNM fighters felt a certain amount of hostility towards the newcomers, accusing them of being lukewarm rebels and opportunistic latecomers, and more discreetly resenting them for not being Issaq.[22] But true as these accusations might have been, many of these latecomers were also well-trained soldiers, some with useful specialised technical skills. Silanyo tended to favour these newcomers and promoted some of them (as officers) above the heads of many less well-trained Issaq veterans.

A third issue with great potential for future trouble was the attitude towards independence. Independence was the lingering problem the SNM had never wanted to discuss, largely because it was not important within the higher circles of the organisation. But after the massive 1988 battles the SNM had morphed into 'a political organisation fighting a people's war'.[23] The views of the 'higher circles' became less relevant and these 'higher circles' had to take popular feelings more into account. During long conversations at Baligubadle with the SNM leadership in February 1990, repeatedly came back to the question of independence and I repeatedly got the same answer: we do not want secession. The motivations for this refusal were threefold. Firstly, we can't leave Mogadishu because we are the biggest landowners in that city. They would confiscate the houses and lands if we seceded (an almost unanimous answer). Secondly, Somaliland by itself lacks sufficient natural resources to survive. In addition we would have problems being recognised internationally (a frequent but not a majority position). And thirdly, 'I believe in the pan-Somali ideal' (the answer of very few, including Silanyo himself).

At the same time, practically every ordinary person I could manage to speak to (it was difficult because of language problems and my official translators disliked the question) gave me the opposite answer: 'We don't want these southerners ruling over us, they are killers and thieves. They use this pan-Somali propaganda but what they do is the opposite.' A sub-theme often mentioned was: 'They are communists. They want to take our cattle from us.' And then the usual comment: 'You are talking with the big people. They'll tell you they don't want separation and they will lie to you; but us, the small people, we don't want anything more to do with these southern criminals, we want freedom, our own life. Don't believe what you are told.' Some translators were sympathetic to this line of argument and translated without problem. Those who were linked to the SNM establishment tried to skirt around the issue. But they often finished by translating fully, under pressure from people (especially women) who, without speaking English, knew enough to know what was going on. After translating honestly, the pro-establishment interpreter would usually comment: 'They don't know any better, they are simple people, uneducated. But this is not SNM policy.'

The Baligubadle conference did not lead to any major changes apart from doubling the numbers of the Central Committee members (in order to include representatives of those who had recently joined). On 5 June a new military organogram was issued, with Arap Dualeh as Chief of Staff and the unconventional Ibrahim 'Dega Weyne' as his number two and, of course, the replacement of Ahmed Mohamed 'Silanyo' by Abdirahman Ali Ahmed 'Tuur' as secretary-general of SNM. But in terms of national choice Tuur was as much a Unitarian as Silanyo was, if not more so, so this did not lead to any change in overall SNM strategy.

But something had changed at the Baligubadle conference; not SNM policy, but something more subtle, less visible or subject to structural analysis than a political programme: unspoken independence had become a subject of discussion. Silanyo favoured unity as did Abdirahman 'Tuur', but they did not operate in the same environment as in the early 1980s. There was, of course, the clanic switch, with the Habr Ja'alo having to take more of a back seat and the Habr Yunis sitting in front. But pro- or anti-secession did not follow clanic lines; it was a personal option. Supporters of continued unity—who were just as anti-Siad Barre as their counterparts—now had to argue to defend their position.

The main political event of that period came not from the armed rebellions but from a group of peaceful dissidents who issued on 15 May what quickly became known as 'il Manifesto'[24] since it had been issued in Rome. The group of 114 signatories were extremely distinguished, comprising the lawyer Ismail Jumaale Ossoble; former President Aden Abdulle Osman; former Director of Police, General Mohamed Abshir Musa; the well-known businessman Jirde Hussein Dualeh; and the pre-1969 parliamentary Speaker, Sheikh Muktar Mohamed Hussein. In fact the roster of names attached to the manifesto resembled a Somalian Who's Who. The only one missing was Ali Mohamed Ossoble 'Wardigley', who had died of natural causes in Rome at the end of April, after working tirelessly in drafting and issuing the document. Siad reacted with typical churlishness, first asking to meet all the signatories who lived in Mogadishu and then arresting them after reproaching them for 'intruding in the gradual process put in place by the government for making room for political pluralism'.

Meanwhile, since the US was busy launching the first Gulf War against Iraq, the Pentagon, which did not have any special policy for the Horn (except discreetly supporting anti-Ethiopian initiatives), set in motion the process that would renew its lease on the Berbera military base.[25] The main problem for the democratic opposition was Italy, where Foreign Minister Giovanni De Michelis had declared that 'there is nothing much wrong with Somalia, and if we cut aid there because of these human rights problems, we would have to cut it off in 42 of the 47 countries of black Africa where we have aid programmes and where human rights are not respected either'.[26] De Michelis said that he was ready to act 'together with the Egyptians where President Mubarak has offered us a common approach'. Then, the following week, the general commanding the 21st Division was killed by new USC levies while fighting in Hiiran province. A month before, the former Somali Ambassador to India, General Mohamed Farah Aydid, had taken control of the military branch of the USC, based in Ethiopia, and received large donations from Mengistu. The Ethiopian regime feared a secession of Eritrea and wanted to preserve its access to the sea through Berbera. Aydid was quite open to the idea of Somalia becoming a second Djibouti for Ethiopian commerce. All options were on the table. By then borders were beginning to collapse menacingly all over the Horn of Africa.

Could war be ended through peace negotiations?

As the disintegration of the Somali state kept progressing, there was a continued denial that its very existence was now in doubt. We must remember the times. The Soviet Union still seemed indestructible and Yugoslavia was still at peace. In Africa neither Eritrea nor South Sudan had gained independence, and Gaddafi ruled a rich and aggressively united Libya. Twenty-five years ago, states joined and collaborated; they did not 'exit' a previously unified structure. But on 28 July 1990, there were 500,000 mourners at the burial of Ismail Jumaale Ossoble, after his death of a heart attack in Rome. Ossoble—like Wardigley—had been the living symbol of a reasonable 'diplomatic' solution to the expanding catastrophe that Somalia had become and the USC had been so far a 'reasonable' guerrilla force, open to negotiations. But now both Wardigley and Ossoble were dead, Mohamed Farah Aydid had taken solid control of the USC, and on 6 August the SNM and the SPM signed an agreement for common operations with the USC. In that communiqué, which explicitly rejected the Italo-Egyptian negotiation initiative, Aydid insisted that he wanted to overthrow Siad Barre by force and leave him no chance to negotiate a compromise way out.

Siad Barre, who did not always seem to realise how far things had gone, was still dealing in symbols. While there were pro-Iraq demonstrations in the streets of Mogadishu,[27] the dictator asked Saddam Hussein to withdraw his troops from Kuwait. The Somali population had, of course, only limited interest in what was happening in the Gulf, but pro- or anti-Saddam moves were destined for local consumption. Siad still calculated his moves within the framework of the Cold War, without realising that it was increasingly obsolete. The region was in the process of moving rapidly from global to local. Siad was also trying to operate at that level when, on 3 September, he replaced Samantar with Mohamed Hawadle Madar, an Issaq, as Prime Minister, without realising that, at this point, the man's clanic origin was not in itself sufficient to be a symbol of political détente and opening. He also promised the organisation a constitutional referendum for 31 December 1990 and invited Africa Watch and Amnesty International to visit the country. But officially, just for security's sake, the dictator left Villa Somalia, his official government residency, on 15 September and moved to Aviazione, the headquarters of the air force, near the airport. In early October the planned December referendum was discreetly 'postponed'. Whether because of oversight or denial, the Western powers still carried on in a strange parody of business-as-usual. The US Army was working hard on the Berbera military base, refurbishing it for use in the coming Gulf War,[28] and Italian Foreign Affairs Minister De Michelis was still going ahead with his planned Italo-Egyptian conference arrangements.

On 2 October the USC, the SNM and the SPM announced that they would keep working on the unification of the opposition and that they would never negotiate separately.[29] But even the opposition was losing ground to direct actions from the unorganised population. On 22 October there were violent demonstrations in Mogadishu against the increase in fuel prices from 500 to 900 shillings a litre. Gas stations were looted, and trucks attacked. The police shot indiscriminately into the crowds and the victims were not credibly counted. Mohamed Ibrahim Egal, the man who had been the first Prime Minister of the briefly independent British Somaliland, later an architect of north–south unification and, finally, the last Prime Minister of unified Somalia prior to the 1969 coup, chose that moment to step in and offer his views of the situation. In November 1990 he published an 'Open Letter to the Nation and Its Friends', which gave what was probably the clearest and most realistic view of where things had got to:

> Somalia is now facing most difficult problems which would tax the very fibre of this nation's genius, its wisdom and even its will to remain a nation ... The pillars of organised society are beginning to crumble ... We have months, perhaps only weeks, before we reach a point of no return ... There has never been a more urgent need for compromise ... The alternative is anarchy and descent into warring tribal fragments ... The men who have brought down Siad and his regime are the armed insurgents, not the politicians ... There is no possibility that anyone could now grab power cheaply in the streets of Mogadishu ... The men who have made millions under Siad ... should lie low and be grateful if they are forgiven and left alone ... The SSDF, the SNM, the SPM and the USC have waged a long war and suffered numerous atrocities during their armed struggle ... They

simply would not allow eleventh-hour arrivals to snatch the trophy of their bitter struggle! The hard fact Siad has to accept is that there are only two options open to him: he can be either a Habré[30] or an Arshad.[31] He should choose the example of the latter and go before it is too late.

Egal finished his three-page letter by asking for the establishment of a provisional government under the existing Prime Minister, for complete negotiations with the insurgent forces, and for a minimum of two years for a transitional government. In spite of these reasonable and informed proposals, the international community continued in its denial of the situation. The International Development Agency launched a plan for the rehabilitation of the national communications infrastructure (roads, ports, telecommunications) and started by setting aside a first tranche of $18.5 million for implementation, even though undertaking large-scale construction work in this situation was completely unreasonable. Meanwhile, Rome asked the EEC to give support to Siad Barre's theoretical plan for constitutional reform, something to which at least Paris and London objected. But the Italians did not give up: in what was a near-surrealistic move, Mario Raffaelli, a leading member of the Foreign Affairs Committee of the Italian parliament, met on 20 November with UN Secretary-General Boutros-Ghali and got his support to organise a 'round table for national reconciliation' to be held in Cairo on 12 December.

In Mogadishu, General Mohamed Said Hersi 'Morgan', nicknamed the 'Butcher of Hargeisa', had become Minister of Defence. The northern SNA, completely surrounded by SNM, was by now cut off from its national bases and only in contact with Mogadishu by radio, boat or plane. The USC was pushing its offensive all the way to Afgooye, 70 km from the capital, and Meslah had gone over the top, shooting dead a Marehan general who had refused to accompany him to Jowhar, where the SNA and USC were engaged in battle. While pro- and anti-conference rebels were discussing in Rome how to respond to the Italian–UN call, the United States recommended that their citizens in Somalia depart. A week later (20 December) the leaders of the Manifesto group who were still in Mogadishu were all (re-)arrested as they were about to fly to London in a bid to convince the SNM leadership to attend the last-chance Cairo conference. By then there was shooting on and around the airport and an Egyptian cargo plane, which had landed to deliver weapons, was blown to pieces by mortar fire. Abdel Rahman Duale, one of the few SNM leaders of Issa origin, had gone to Djibouti to meet Ismail Omar Guelleh and begin to coordinate more closely the collaboration of the United Somali Front (USF) with the Djiboutians.[32]

On 28 December 1990, USC troops reached Mogadishu and fighting developed in the streets. The USC vanguard was mostly made up of Hawiye of the Abgaal sub-clan and was led by Colonel Mohamed Abdi, a long-time Siad Barre loyalist who had recently changed sides, General Ahmed Mohamed Sheikh 'Nero' and his friend Colonel Hussein Dheere, who had created an independent Abgaal militia outside the USC. Mohamed Farah Aydid, who by then realised that power was going to be won through Mogadishu street fighting, gathered all the troops he could muster (7,000 men) both in Mudug and in Ethiopia, and made a dash for the capital where the final act would be played out.

The degree of clanic dissociation was extreme. At the end of December, Siad Barre realised that even if every single Marehan fought for him, it would not be enough. So he gave weapons to the Galgalo sub-clan of the Hawiye–Habr Gidir,[33] provoking a massive popular retaliation not only against the Marehan but practically against all Darood and the Hawiye as well. This triggered the entry into the conflict of the Hawiye Abgaal under Ali Mahdi, leading to an apocalypse of violence.[34] On 15 January SPM elements led by Omar Jess occupied the Balidogle Air Base and then Afgooye. The South Yemen PDRY in Aden recognised the SNM and the USC as the new Somali government. In the following days USF elements negotiated separately with the SNA in the north to recover their weapons (they had been disarmed) so that they could cross the border into Djibouti and be ready to return in fighting formation at a moment's notice, should the government's army totally collapse in Somaliland.[35]

On 21 January, Siad Barre fired Hawadle Madar and replaced him with Omar Arteh Ghalib. Omar Arteh, whom he had arrested years before and later condemned to death before freeing him conditionally, accepted anyway. A traditional diplomat, who had many good contacts with the Rome faction of the USC and with the Manifesto group, he was hoping that, as the internationally best-known Issaq,[36] he could count on implicit SNM support. His view of the situation was, in the typical perception of a Western-oriented diplomat and statesman, what could be called statist. He, like all international diplomats, was a product of the Westphalian worldview which had given birth to the United Nations in 1945. In spite of his dislike for Siad Barre and his dictatorship, any action he undertook would aim at some form of survival of the Somali state since he could not reasonably accept the dismantling that was taking place before his eyes.[37]

But in the short term, in spite of a call for a ceasefire, his nomination had no direct effect. The SNM occupied Sheikh and Bura'o and launched attacks on Berbera, as the 'Ethiopian refugees' in the south moved in huge numbers back to the Ogaden.[38] Many of the government's ministers and high-ranking civil servants were fleeing to Kenya. The Siad Barre regime was by then a government in name only, definitely without a monopoly of force and with only a shadow of legitimacy. But the street fighting was intensifying, and for the ageing dictator it was becoming a question of physical survival. On 25 January President Siad Barre boarded a tank and fled southwards towards Garbahaarey, deep in the heart of Marehan territory, the core of his clanic homeland. There he would try to reassemble a partial pan-Darood alliance, something which could evoke some kind of a Somali political logic but not a Somalia national legitimacy.

8

NORTH AND SOUTH BREAK UP AND FIGHT AMONG THEMSELVES

An attempt at a quick snapshot of 1991

The flight of the dictator was of course a key marker in the fifteen-year-old conflict. But it was not the end of the war. On the contrary, the conflict festered. Paradoxically, this was because of the turning point represented by the 'peace agreement' signed in Djibouti in April 1988. The plan was to try making peace by insisting on an end to Somalia's military pressure in the Ogaden borders through its support for SALF, the WSLF and even, marginally, for the TPLF, in exchange for a reciprocal Ethiopian disengagement from its support for SNM and SSDF. At the time, the SSDF had shrunk to a ghost of its former self but the SNM was hanging on steadfastly and represented a serious military threat. And while SSDF had little to lose—it was already lost in its own contradictions—carrying out the provisions of the agreement would have been political and military suicide for the SNM. This was what invalidated the deal. As we saw earlier, the SNM doctored the truth to retain local support for a policy diametrically opposed to the tactical withdrawal Mengistu had chosen. On the other side, SALF or WSLF, having very little autonomy and independent resources, remained largely appendices of Siad Barre's regime.

But the SNM was the key problem, the square peg that would not fit in the round hole. It had the means to carry on fighting and the collective will to do so. But it was far from Mogadishu and there was no realistic way it could get there. In spite of his rapid weakening—the press had nicknamed him 'the

133

Mayor of Benadir'[1]—Siad remained the centrepiece of the international legitimacy game. This is why the USC and the SPM[2] played the key roles in the fall of the regime. Why them when the real military battering ram was the northern SNM? Well, exactly for that reason: the SNM was northern and Mogadishu was in the south. Both rebel organisations had had initial support from SNM, particularly in the case of the USC.[3] Both were based on clan families that had either been pro-Barre or loosely allied to the Darood clan cluster, which underpinned the Siad political system. But these two organisations were 'young', and they had been quickly put together after the massive 1988 battle in the north began to show that the days of the regime could be counted. Siad had reacted clumsily to the Issaq threat. Instead of broadening the clanic appeal of his regime, he battened down the hatches, surrounding himself increasingly with men of his own Marehan clan and marginalising Hawiye and Ogadeni allies. But given the peculiar nature of Somali society, which makes any fighting force a clanic tributary of the civilian environment in which it operates, the main rebel force—the SNM—could not go all the way to Mogadishu through hostile territories to deliver the *coup de grace*. And those who could—the USC, the SPM—were new to the rebellion, poorly organised and divided along sub-clanic lines.

The year 1988 and its massive slaughterhouse effect had broken open the clanic fault lines that lay under all the various armies involved in the civil war. Now it was every clan for itself. The SNA stopped being 'the government's army', splintering into clanic and sub-clanic regiments. The SNM, through its initial success and subsequent failure, became highly visible, resulting in the massive recruitment of untrained Issaq clansmen who naturally followed their traditional elders or their local sub-clanic 'strongmen' rather than the disciplined officer corps which had led the movement until the 'battle for the cities'. For different reasons but with similar consequences, just like the 'national' army, the SNM morphed from a tight, professional war machine into a much larger but much more unstable instrument. In the more polite words of Horn specialist Patrick Gilkes, 'it went from a small professional revolutionary movement to a larger group fighting a people's war'. The overall result was that all competing forces ended with the same problems: weakening of hierarchical structures, increasingly clanic recruitment, a switch from global to local objectives, and a ballooning size. The only force that saw its numbers decline was the Somali National Army (SNA), as many of its men deserted to join the various rebel guerrilla groups and as it became itself one of the loose contenders for power, under the name of the Somali National Front (SNF).

So by early 1991 Somalia had literally broken asunder, with the former government itself having turned into a militia and with each local clan or sub-clan attempting to position itself in the free-for-all to defend its own group interests. It was a war of shifting alliances, where today's enemy became tomorrow's ally. But violent as this Hobbesian war of all against all had become, it was never meaningless in the narrow sense. Past history still weighed on the present, and logical threads—admittedly quite intertwined— were still being followed by the actors. This was, of course, a perfect recipe for absolute misunderstanding on the part of the international community because foreign states operating on the Westphalian pattern were almost completely blind to the Somali logic. This was not a case of 'good' or 'bad' (even if these adjectives had indeed fields of applicability) but a question of cognitive perception, of different paradigms. And it was made even more complicated by the fact that SNM and the 'Somalilanders' were odd Somalis marching to a different beat, lying in-between the one common to all Somalis and the foreign one. SNM partook of both and belonged to neither.

The south: Falling from the main battle into secondary ones

Siad Barre's flight was immediately followed on the next day by a clash among his victors, Mohamed Farah Aydid on one side and Mohamed Nur 'Galal' on the other. Both were Hawiye (but from different sub-clans). Aydid led the USC radical group and Galal supported the more moderate USC Rome/ Manifesto group.[4] Four days later, Ali Mahdi was named (or named himself) 'head of state', something in which not even the USC had a part because it was by then deeply divided into the two main clanic branches, the Ali Mahdi branch and the Mohamed Farah Aydid branch. Ali Mahdi is an Abgaal Waiisle while Mohamed Farah Aydid was a Habr Gidir Sa'ad. Both clans are part of the Hawiye clan family but they were deeply divided and the only thing the two branches of USC could implicitly agree on was fighting the Darood—and eventually even the Issaq.[5] This had led the Omar Jess-led fraction of the SPM to occupy Afgooye at the beginning of February. The Ogadeni—Jess's clan—were being killed systematically in the capital. Jess expressed dismay at having to keep fighting, especially against anti-dictatorship forces, but his ally in SPM, Adan Abdullahi Nur 'Gabiyow', told him: 'Forget about any talk of negotiations. There can be no settlement, we will talk through the gun.'[6] Jess cut off Mogadishu's water supply and stopped the selling of milk and vegetables, thus effectively starving Mogadishu.[7] So on

10 February a USC–Ali Mahdi force counter-attacked and pushed him out of Afgooye. He retreated south and went to Kismayo where he met with Mohamed Said Hersi 'Morgan' and joined forces with the man who had been his colleague, commanding officer and later enemy. They both received help from Siad Barre, still holed up in Gedo.

Two weeks later Aydid, who saw himself not as part of the new government he wanted to create but as its leader, attacked Galkayo where remnants of the SSDF had been trying to set up some kind of regional authority. Because of geographical proximity, attacking Galkayo was a red rag for the Majerteen; but the Majerteen are close relatives of the Harti, who populate the coast between Benadir and the Lower Jubba. Incensed by this USC–Aydid attack in the north-east, the local Harti population turned against the USC occupiers of the south and retook the string of southern harbours (Marca, Brava, Gelib) which the USC had just taken. The Harti–Majerteen alliance then became de facto a former government ally. They kept moving and reached Afgooye, where the USC, which saw the danger, 'reunited' (even if this did not last long) and beat them back (at the battle of Afgooye on 20 March 1991). The USC being thus preoccupied, the SSDF counter-attacked and occupied Shalambot and El Bur.

What was the SNM reaction to all this confusion? First of all, it tried to assert itself in the north, but still without any explicitly secessionist agenda. Berbera had been occupied on 30 January and Hargeisa, Bura'o and Borama in early February. But even though secession was still on the cards, reinforcing oneself vis-à-vis the south was present in the minds of most men of the various Issaq clans. There were constant contacts with the former Dhulbahante enemies and a preliminary meeting was held between SNM and Dhulbahante elders in Bura'o in February, stressing their common 'Somaliland' heritage vis-à-vis the southerners. Those who were still actively trying to support a unitary cause in the Ali Mahdi–Omar Arteh 'government'[8] had a difficult job in this game of competing loyalties. In order to try to attract the northerners, Omar Arteh (himself an Issaq Habr Awal Sa'ad Musa) had tried to get the Hawiye hardliners with whom he was now allied to accept some northern representatives. He managed to include Garaad Abdigani Garaad Jama and give him the position of Minister of Foreign Affairs. Garaad Abdigani was a Dhulbahante, i.e. a member of the Darood clan family, and Arteh hoped this would make him more acceptable—a dubious calculation given the ethnic cleansing of Daroods by Hawiye in the capital.

Garad was a clever man and he quickly realised that his position was symbolic, not real. So on 3 February he discreetly left and became the

Dhulbahante representative at the big *shir* of the northern clans in Berbera. That *shir* was in fact the venue where representatives of the various Somaliland clans began discussing publicly the issue of the possible independence of the former British colony. It was, of course, a move of northern self-assertion but it was certainly at least as much a reaction to the madness of clanic war in the south. This was a policy of 'small footsteps' but a reasonable one, in view of the mess in the south, if a similar anarchy was to be avoided in the north. The lurking danger could swoop down at any time.

On 9 February SNM units skirmished with the USF on the Djibouti border and the SNM leader Suleiman Mohamed Aden 'Gal' felt it necessary to warn both Djibouti and Rome about non-intervention in the post-Siad Barre conflict.[9] On 27 February the SNM called a meeting of Issaq, Gaddabursi, Warsangeli and Dhulbahante elders, which issued a communiqué criticising 'the unilateral creation of a non-representative interim government' and demanding that a big *shir* be held at the national level on 27 April. The SNM declaration also asked for a re-examination of the 1960 Act of Union. In the same communiqué the SNM refused in advance to take part in the so-called Conference of National Reconciliation which was due to be held on 14 March.[10]

Meanwhile, in the south, the clanic war situation was becoming more and more confused. After the Harti–Majerteen offensive against the capital and its failure in Afgooye at the hands of the USC, for the next two months the two armies were toing and froing along the southern coast, with minimal strategic results and maximum numbers of civilian casualties.[11] Then, superimposing itself on this catastrophic situation, the two branches of USC started to fight each other in the streets of the capital, for purely clanic reasons. The Hawiye had emerged as city bosses following the ethnic cleansing war in Mogadishu, and now their two main branches, Abgaal and Habr Gidir, were fighting it out for control of what was left of the capital.

Omar Arteh, the man who was still officially the Prime Minister, was then permanently stationed in Djibouti for fear of being kidnapped and held hostage by one faction or the other. He kept visiting all the capitals of the Arab world in the vain hope of securing a viable mediation. In this confusion Siad Barre managed to put together a broad Darood coalition and to counterattack in the direction of the capital. In early April he came close to reoccupying Mogadishu, reaching all the way to Afgooye before being defeated by the USC, which again briefly abandoned its internecine quarrels to fight its reemergent former enemies (3–13 April 1991).

Seen from the north, the whole thing looked like madness. This was the moment the Italians chose to send a military delegation to Berbera in a bid to marshal the SNM into the broad 'unitarist' conference they kept trying to promote; but the Italian delegation was politely refused entry. The day before, in fact, Mario De Sica, former Italian Ambassador to Mogadishu, had been strafed at the Kismayo airport by a USC Mig (he escaped unharmed) while conferring with the Darood forces of the former dictatorship. This Darood alliance—representing in fact the surviving forces of the fallen dictatorship—could sense they had the support of the international community because, in the Westphalian perspective typical of the West, they seemed to represent the only resistance to the dual forces of catastrophe in Somalia, viz clanic anarchy on the one hand and secession on the other. These forces behaved as if, in a way, they still had some form of legitimacy and, by force of habit, the regional authorities seemed to follow them. The Darood forces, operating under the organisational label of Somali National Front (SNF), were based in Gedo, buying their fuel and their ammunition in Kenya. Kenyan President Daniel arap Moi declared: 'It is impossible to say who runs that country (Somalia) since anybody you talk to says that he is in power.'[12] Fighting continued in Nugaal and in the Lower Jubba, with USC fighting both the Darood alliance and the regrouped remnants of SSDF.

On 3 May 1991 Mario De Sica and Sami Heiba[13] flew to Hargeisa, asking Abdirahman 'Tuur' to participate in a recycled version of the now-mythical Cairo National Reconciliation Conference. Both men knew that a large Somaliland *shir* was about to take place, and they both rightfully feared that this meeting would have on its agenda the unspoken but predictable question: independence. Tuur did not want it and his close associates did not want it either; but what was the alternative? The south was still a hornet's nest where the fighting clans had nothing to offer, except more violence and an aim of renewed domination. The northern 'unitarians' were directly at odds with their own public opinion, with their own political base and with the rank and file of their military forces. The question was bound to be tabled and remained controversial.

> The issue of secession was not part of the SNM ideology and it was not written in its constitution. But it was a hidden agenda for some SNM leaders and for some Issaq sub-clans. The central goal of the SNM was to overthrow the dictatorship of General Siad Barre and to liberate the country from oppression. The leader of the SNM during the last phase of the liberation struggle in the north was Abdirahman Ahmed Ali 'Tuur', who was strongly against the secession of the north from the rest of Somalia. He rather supported a loose confederation

like the Emirates in the Gulf. The ex-chairman of the SNM, Silanyo, on his part, supported a union where the Issaq and the Hawiye would form an alliance.[14] But the announcement of the presidency of Ali Mahdi in Mogadishu in 1991 without consulting the SNM gave a boost to those in the north who supported the secession of Somaliland. This is one of the factors that influenced strongly the Bura'o conference in May 1991.[15]

The north: Trying to manage a fragile peace

Thus the Bura'o conference with its proclamation of independence was neither a foregone conclusion nor a careful plot of—(here insert your choice of villains, from Israel to Ethiopia and from enemies of Islam to the CIA), as Somali nationalists or international supporters of the Westphalian state system would have it. It was a complex convergence of historical, political and cultural circumstances to which we will have to return. But first we have to describe how the 'day after' (i.e. after the flight of Siad Barre) looked from the north's perspective. The most painful question was vengeance.[16]

> There were two trials of SNA and NSS personnel, but one of them is not known to the public. There was the official one which sat in Berbera later and another one which took place in Abdaal village in the last days of the war. During the four days we spent in Abdaal before we attacked Berbera, we had captured many prisoners belonging to the regime. The court that was formed was basically illegal and ordered the execution of many people. My estimate is that 50 to 60 people were considered guilty and given death sentences, which were carried out by the SNM. The judges were only two men, one of them a school teacher, and their judgment was based on this question: what would these accused men have done if they had captured us? ... But I believe it was a wrong sentence.
>
> The real court in Berbera later had a legally appointed judge who was an SNM commander, called Abdul Hakim Sumuni. There was a proper prosecuting process and there were many witnesses who attested to the innocence or guilt of the prisoners. Each conviction was based on hearing at least ten witnesses on each case. Those who were recognised as innocent were treated well and escorted to a safe place. We took some of these to very far places, like the Ogaden or Gedo for the Marehan. All the Warsangeli prisoners were also taken to their clan territory and escorted there by Issaq clan elders. I know that some people were killed illegally outside of court. But we were in a war situation. This is why we had to escort those who were not guilty, to protect them.[17]

So there were executions, but not many, and almost none for members of the non-Issaq Somaliland clans. But there was a special problem for the Ogadeni, who are not 'native Somalilanders' but who reside part-time in Somaliland's Hawd region and who were massively involved in the war after 1978.[18]

> The Ogadenis fought against us very hard in the areas they occupied. But a few of them had joined SNM so we told those: 'Anyone who surrenders to you and hands over his gun to us, let them get out without suffering any harm. But if they don't surrender, let's crush them with artillery.' They fought as long as they could, but when they saw the government declining, they got away, went back to Ethiopia ... After we captured a lot of them as they fled, we had this conflict among us about whether or not to release them. This was in Jijiga.[19] But when we let them go, remnants of the SNA army even robbed these poor fleeing people. Our only targets were those with guns. We never killed those with no guns and we ordered our young fighters not to kill those without weapons, but in some cases they did not tell their officers and they killed them anyway. But if we captured them, we gave them some clothes and medicine and released them. Also we never tortured them, even if we suspected they were spies. But the SSDF, they tortured anyone they captured.[20]

Right after vengeance—less compelling but more important in the medium term—came the question of security and organisation.

> The SNM had no programme when it took over the country. There was also disorganisation and chaos among the SNM members themselves, who were weak and unprepared for the situation they were faced with. On the other hand, the aid brought by foreign NGOs was well meant but it added to the chaos because it caused competition and looting. This is how the port of Berbera became a bone of contention because it was overflowing with goods when nobody had anything.[21]

This was the moment when the Mogadishu 'government' chose to send a delegation to the SNM in a bid to use diplomatic means to keep the country together.

> The delegation of five members arrived at Berbera airport, which was controlled by the SNM combatants. The delegation was immediately arrested and kept in a room at the airport, where they were called traitors who conspired against Somaliland in favour of Mogadishu. After an intervention from the SNM commanders, they were released and booked in the only decent hotel left, the Hotel Shide. In the beginning Chairman Tuur refused to meet the delegation because he knew them all very well and he knew their agenda did not agree with what the SNM believed. Tuur asked his executive committee to meet with the delegation but the delegation refused to talk to the committee. So he went to meet them anyway. The delegation informed him that everybody in Mogadishu was looking towards Hargeisa for leadership and that the SNM could announce Hargeisa as the new capital of Somalia, for nobody in Mogadishu would object.

They concluded that the SNM had a blank cheque and that it could demand all they had missed in the thirty years of unity with Somalia. Abdirahman 'Tuur' did not disappoint them but promised that the issue would be presented to all the clans living in Somaliland during the coming conference, though he was not very much convinced by all that information. Therefore Tuur and his administration decided that they needed to hold a consultative meeting to discuss the future of the north and the relationship with southern Somalia.

In March a consultative meeting for all the clans of Somaliland was organised in Berbera in the absence of the chairman, who was still in Addis Ababa. But the meeting was stopped by a number of SNM insurgents, not because they wanted to prevent the conference from taking place but simply because they wanted to loot. They stole all the vehicles belonging to the delegates of the Dhulbahante and the Warsangeli. In the end, the meeting finally took place and issued two key conclusions: first, the fact that the non-Issaq accepted for the time being the authority of the SNM in the country; second, that a period of peace and reconciliation was planned, with the establishment of two committees, one for the western region and another one for the east. Sanaag region, in the far east of the country, was the last region to be liberated from the forces of Siad Barre. The situation there was conflict-prone because during the years of unity the Issaq who lived in the east had been deprived of their lands and now they wanted revenge. So Ahmed Mire, the SNM commander in Sanaag, had a big problem. The Dhulbahante and the Warsangeli had sent their elders to this Berbera conference to present their case to the participants in the meeting, and when they came, they had been robbed.[22]

The proposal of the delegation from Mogadishu was both symptomatic and impossible. The delegates did not even want to challenge the SNM position but, on the contrary, made fantastic propositions that they knew were unrealistic. There was both a recognition of the situation and a complete lack of realism in trying to deal with it. The contrast with the situation of the March conference in Berbera was striking: then there was no pretence—everything was a mess and everybody knew it. And so it began on a real basis, with looting, rebellion and theft in the foreground. The only way clanic catastrophes could be avoided in the north was if they were acknowledged from the start as a high-risk possibility.

This possibility almost became reality with the battle of Dilla, in the west, which is populated by non-Issaq clans.

Dilla is on the highway to Borama and the SNM forces reached there first. The Siad Barre forces, which had fled Hargeisa, had reached Dilla but of course the people of Dilla were not defending them but rather they were defending themselves and their properties. Dilla was a cattle market and densely populated. At the same time the people were well armed and prepared to resist any external force. The battle of Dilla was bloody but in the end most of the population escaped to the Aw Barre refugee camp, just over the Ethiopian border. As a result the town was looted and the people of Dilla accused their bitter enemies and neighbours, the Issaq sub-clan of the Jibril Abokor, of having carried out the looting.

During the SNM struggle against General Siad Barre, the clans living in Awdal had fought against SNM on the government's side. Therefore, when the SNM forces reached Awdal in early 1991, local people were concerned that the Issa and the Gaddabursi would come to fight the Jibril Abokor clan of the Issaq since they were neighbours and the Jibril Abokor wanted revenge. In fact, it was not so bad because the SNM unit that first reached Awdal was the Koodbur regiment.[23] Abdirahman Aw Ali, the SNM commander, was later accused of being responsible for the looting even though he was not even there. He came later when he heard that the Koodbur force had met with difficulties. And in addition, he is not even Issaq, he is a Gaddabursi of the Rer Jibril Yunis sub-clan. But he is from Borama, so the people of Dilla say he protected his kins-men but not them.

The difficult situation in Borama was exacerbated by hunger and lack of food. When Abdirahman Aw Ali reached Borama (after the battle of Dilla), the peo-ple saw the SNM forces as the best solution to the unbearable situation in town. Abdirahman Aw Ali, in collaboration with the elders, ordered the merchants to reopen their stores and sell their commodities at a reasonable price. Before, they had closed in the hope of raising the prices of the dry rations.

Everybody was armed and ready to fight. There were militants of the SDA,[24] of the Oromo,[25] of several Gaddabursi sub-clans. But Abdirahman Aw Ali called the heads of the clan militias to a meeting in Goroyo Cawl to negotiate a peace deal with the SNM. Finally all the participants agreed that the SNM should pull out of Awdal and the SNM agreed since their man, Abdirahman Aw Ali, con-trolled the situation in Borama. The number of people who died during the confrontation in Borama (actually Dilla) was 300. So this allows the Gaddabursi to respond to the Issaq when they talk about genocide by the Siad Barre govern-ment and also claim that they have been massacred by the Issaq and that they also have their mass graves. But the numbers have nothing in common.[26]

This was the situation in the west. The other non-Issaq area of Somaliland was at the other end of the territory, in the eastern region of Sanaag.

When I reached Erigavo in March 1991 the town was in the hands of two Issaq clans, the Habr Yunis and the Habr Ja'alo. The two local Darood clans, the Dhulbahante and the Warsangeli, had retreated to their territory for security reasons since it was their side which had lost the war. The clans were separated by a thin band of people called Sharubo Libaax (the lion's whiskers) There was also a group called *Gaadishi*, armed men who moved in the bush and attacked their enemies by surprise. They came from all clans and had no political aims. Their purpose was only looting. Some SNM regiments also took part in the looting because they said now it was their turn. But the Issaq elders did not want this to continue. They maintained that since Siad Barre and his supporters had committed crimes against us and we had consequently taken up arms, therefore this was the reason why we should not be committing the same crimes against them after we defeated them in the war …

The communication system was mostly through HF radios, which were available in most villages. The women were also the ambassadors who connected community leaders on all sides. It was the community leaders who continued the communications to keep the peace and monitor the ceasefire situation. At times the women carried written messages. Later on frontier committees were established on both sides of the demarcation line; this was to monitor the ceasefire and maintain peace when violations were taking place. The other reason is that the rangelands having been neutral for a long time, the grass grew and this attracted livestock, something which made all sides want to get closer to the red line and ready to cross it. The need for these permanent monitoring committees was essential. The committees from both sides used to meet in some villages and this was very scary (I know, I was part of the process) because all sides had negative and hostile perceptions of each other. However, starting with these committees, the sides gradually gained confidence and slowly the trust increased. Everyone was armed and there was no active police service. We were the police. The two sides agreed to keep the peace and to inform each other if there were unsanctioned activities posing a threat to the security of the other side. This included the movements of the *Gaadishi* (bandits). We might also tell the other side that a few days ago, some young men had disappeared from our side and we did not know now where they were and what their objectives were. Therefore please stay alert and watch out for them because they might intend to harm you.

A basic reason also for these committees was that on both sides there were politicians who were not happy with the ceasefire and were not in favour of improving relations with the other side. Some units of the SNM were even sabotaging each other in order to compete for economic and political power. But the elders rose to the challenge, given the visible weakness of the SNM. The elders organised peace meetings in Berbera and other locations. They supported the agreements with the non-Issaq clans and convinced their own clans to forget and to reject plans for revenge.[27]

This careful handling of the situation must be seen against the background of a near-total destruction of every material structure and the mass confusion of the civilians.

After I heard that the refugees had begun to move back, I went to a village called Waribraan and the local people helped me with whatever they had to survive and help my three children ... Later, when the Somaliland government was being put together, I travelled back to my home town of Bura'o. Everything was devastated, houses were destroyed and those that still stood had been looted and their walls were pockmarked by bullets. There were still dead bodies lying around and decaying. For those who didn't flee and had stayed in the town, you could see the pain and effects of the war showing in their faces. For that reason, it took some time to adapt to the town.[28]

The return to life of normal society was made more difficult by the fact that social structures, even if they had not been as damaged as the physical infrastructure, were far from having been untouched by the nearly ten years of violence.

The SNM had no effective plans or resources to avoid the rush of refugees, those coming from the south and from the bush back to the liberated towns, which were basically rubble. The people were emotional about the liberation and everybody was looking forward to the promises liberation evoked. Hence, the discrepancy between the expectations and the reality faced by these dispossessed and deprived people was shocking to them. This situation created chaos, resentment and competition among the people for the meagre resources that were available at that time. This was the basic reason for the civil strife that developed later. There was an intense competition for any resource or even the hope of some. It was to get at these resources that people competed for control over the seaports, the airports and the limited flow of international aid that was coming into the country. The more the competition, the more hardened the positions of the various clans, sub-clans and even individuals became. In the absence of adequate resources and of an effective administrative system, the people were basically reduced to being scavengers. The other social change that was created by the consequences of the conflict was the fact that men lost their position and role in the families and that women became the breadwinners of the households. This had a profound effect on the conduct of men. Men became disoriented and lost, something which became a basic ingredient of violence.[29]

In this post-apocalyptic landscape, it was not (yet) possible to deal with the situation as a whole. In any case, the SNM had no 'grand plan' for a real peace process and the clanic nature of Somali society made such an approach—later favoured by the international community—unrealistic. What could be done was one conflict at a time, one peace deal at a time. And it was a delicate process, with material arrangements and a step-by-step follow-up being crucial.

I remember the peace meeting between the Warsangeli and the eastern branch of the Habr Yunis at Jidali in 1992 when I was the secretary for the meeting. The Habr Yunis were the hosts and I was therefore responsible for three things: food, lodging and security. Some of the regional leaders (including our own local SNM commanders) were not happy with the peace process. These fellows stayed in Erigavo and did not even come to Jidali. After the meeting concluded with the peace agreement, our team[30] was worried about trying to keep our side of the agreement since the SNM commanders were not happy with our participation and might want to spoil the deal.[31] Firstly we were relieved when we saw that the other side had reached their territory safely after departing because we were worried that they could be attacked by anyone, especially people from our side, while we were responsible for their security. So our group which had signed the peace agreement decided to work hard to implement the terms of the arrangement. Our action plan included promoting public awareness of what had been signed, debating with our own people opposed to it, and a continuous monitoring of the situation in order to be able to warn the Warsangeli in time. This proved to be successful because the people genuinely wanted peace in spite of the spoiler individuals.

But the most difficult meeting was the one in Dararweyne between the Habr Yunis East and the Dhulbahante. I was also a secretary for that meeting. First, convening the meeting was in itself a big challenge. There was a basic lack of trust between the parties. There again the Habr Yunis were the hosts, but then the Dhulbahante were not sure they were really ready for talking peace. A basic reason for the difficulties was that there were two Issaq sub-clans among the Habr Ja'alo in Sanaag which had started to fight each other, and this led the Habr Ja'alo to make an alliance with the defeated Darood clans—both Warsangeli and Dhulbahante—to fight each other and to keep the Habr Yunis from making another peace deal. The three clans—Habr Ja'alo, Warsangeli and Dhulbahante—held a number of meetings in Garadag and Shimbirale and agreed to attack Erigavo or the Habr Yunis together. But we were lucky because although they wanted to attack us, they could not trust each other deeply. The Dhulbahante had this commitment and had difficulties in making a decision about participating in the Dararweyne peace meeting that we were trying to organise. There were hard-line members in each of the clans and there were constant quarrels between those who wanted to continue the confrontation and those who supported the conclusion of hostilities.

It took a long time for the Dhulbahante peace faction to win the day and get their fellow clansmen to come. Eventually they arrived at the venue. It took us one month and seven days to conclude the peace agreement. We had to endure the conditions in this barren land where there was a shortage of water, and whatever water there was of poor quality. It was a very isolated and difficult place to stay in but we had to tolerate these conditions because peace was the more important issue at the time. The overall strategy during the holding of the peace meetings was to initially let the two sides and the aggrieved individuals talk as strongly as possible and relate all their grievances. Thus the attitude of the speakers who took turns showed hostility and appeared heated. At times there were occasions when Mr So-and-so blew up and left the meeting. In the early days, it was all very negative and aggressive. But this was to let people get the opportunity to say whatever they wanted and therefore to find relief. There were also informal sessions that would take place all night. This gave the participants time to get to know each other and to learn each other's backgrounds. Thus there was a chance to improve trust and build individual relationships which could help healing the war injuries.

After some time we got to the more technical phase and subcommittees were set up to deal with specific issues. If the subcommittees reached a deadlock, we used the sultans to unblock these issues at a different level, solve the issue and take the process forward. Some issues were particularly sensitive, especially the question of landownership. Sanaag had a tradition of private rangelands owned by families, and these rangelands had changed hands during the war. The Habr Yunis, being with the SNM dominant force, had captured lots of rangelands which were claimed by the Dhulbahante. Therefore it was a big challenge for the Habr Yunis elders to convince their own clan members that they had to evacuate these rangelands they occupied, even though they had won the war and the Dhulbahante had lost it.

The other approach that facilitated the success of the meeting was the common agreement that no reparation or blood money would be paid for all those people who had died on both sides during the civil war ... This peace meeting helped allow the movement of trade and of people beyond their clan territory. It re-civilised the people and reduced the militarisation of the communities. The clans agreed to hold a Sanaag-wide peace process in Erigavo in 1993. Although there were some international NGOs present that supported the conference (Action Aid, Oxfam UK and others), this was basically a locally owned and managed process. The slow pace of negotiations is part of the Somali traditional culture, which allows all individuals (in fact mostly males) to participate and have their say. The other reason is that there was a need to account for the events which were not always commonly agreed upon. And revisiting the past was necessary so that all finally agreed on what had happened. The Erigavo grand conference was held in 1993 and lasted for four months. Some of the agreed terms were:

- A peace charter that brought all remaining hostilities to an end and recognised the right of all individuals to move freely across the boundaries of all clans;
- The return of all the large assets (houses, vehicles, some animals) which could be identified;
- Forgiving the losses of the war, including those killed in the conflict;
- Creation of a committee to oversee the implementation of these agreed terms; and
- Heavy sanctions against the peace violators.[32]

The Grand Sanaag Conference was the penultimate peace conference in the north.[33]

Paradoxically, the problem for peace in the north did not come so much from former adversaries. Both in Awdal (west) and in Sanaag (east) there were non-Issaq, non-SNM clans with their fighters and, as we just saw, clear-sighted men managed to organise meetings and conferences where those who had fought each other managed to agree on processes to bring about, first, a cease-fire and, later, reconciliation. But the core problem came from the broader Issaq masses, from people who were either members of SNM or its sympathisers. The key words were misery and anarchy.

The civilians and the veterans were running alongside each other. Looting, robbing and killing because of ordinary arguments were very common as there were no resources and everybody had guns. The veterans commonly robbed *qat*. The doctors had no salaries and no direction. We started self-organised 'food-for-work' for doctors at a house behind the presidential house in Hargeisa. The doctors used to sleep in that house and to go to hospital every morning. The hospital had several wards, including two wards that were for people of the fallen regime. Everything was looted, including the shipments of food arriving from Berbera that were destined for those at the hospital and for the wounded. When I received a message at seven in the morning that the veterans' and the patients' food had been hijacked, I had to send a group of armed injured veterans to Awbarkhadle with a vehicle, so that they would bring the shipment back to the hospital. The food had been taken by other veterans. But since they knew each other, they talked and they managed to bring back the looted supplies.

The logistical problems were massive. There was a lack of trucks but also a lack of fuel. We used to ask some of the injured veterans to go out and stand in front of the hospital to collect fuel from their fellow veterans driving military vehicles. Since they all knew each other, they would manage to collect a couple of litres from each vehicle to make up twenty litres and run vehicles during the next night.'[34][35] The word 'insecurity' hardly captures the situation. 'Things were out of hand. Everyone was armed and there was no respect for any government or law. I once saw a young boy of nine or ten carrying a gun the same size as himself and ordering us to give him money at the checkpoint he was managing. I felt devastated by that incident. Another time, I was at a store downtown. A man came running to our store and asked for his gun which somebody had left with us. We asked him what was happening. He said: 'Give me my gun! give me my gun! these trucks were stolen.' I asked him not to take the gun and fight. Some women told him they would buy his trucks back. I insisted and other women joined me and we convinced the man not to fight. Finally he agreed, and he even promised us to stop the fight among the others. In fact, the trucks were brought back on the second day and that man is still alive today ...

Some incidents were outrageous. The young men who had come back with their arms without respect for any law or anyone were the biggest threat the country faced. It was a volcano ready to erupt at any minute, and that was even before the civil war started. I remember one day while I was standing in front of the house, gunshots and heavy artillery started firing all over the town. The sound was deafening. Everybody started to run for their lives and I thought I was done for. We went into hiding for the next six hours and at around 10 p.m. people came from the downtown area and told us what had happened. They said it was because of the wedding of one of the fighters, and even the heavy artillery was a sign of celebration for his wedding. I could not believe it. I told my mother, who could not believe it either. Someone was celebrating. That was the level of insanity we had reached in this country.

It was the time of the colonels, they were at the centre of every issue. You could hear people saying, 'This colonel did this, that colonel did that, the colonel is coming, this colonel got killed, colonel, colonel, colonel.' This shows the level of governance and rule of law we had descended to. One colonel from my clan, Jama Ali Elmi, had refused to take part in the civil war [of 1995]. But instead of being saluted, he was looked down upon and condemned for not supporting his clan. This was the situation of the country ...

I also remember another incident. I submitted a proposal to Oxfam Novib, which they accepted. They sent us a woman to travel with us to the site. She came to Bura'o and Yirowe and saw the devastation and the suffering. When we came back to Sheikh to have breakfast, she refused to eat. We came back to Hargeisa and stayed at Mansoor Hotel, which had only twelve rooms at the time. She was crying throughout the journey and we were ashamed. She told us. 'I am crying because of the suffering you have caused yourselves.' The civil war was a lesson for us. Towards the end of the last civil war, I remember the big conference in Ceel Xume by the Habr Yunis. The women who were cooking for the meeting told the young men who were guarding the conference not to let any of the delegates to come out if they fought inside the assembly. They told them to send them back and keep them inside till they reached an agreement. The dust finally settled towards the end of 1996 and the final peace agreement was signed.[36]

Not only were the basics of life deeply affected by the recent fighting, but the ordnance left behind kept causing casualties. The British company Rimfire was contracted by the UN to remove what mines they could; it operated after 1991. During a couple of years of work it removed about 50,000 mines but reckoned that many more remained.

There were mines everywhere particularly around the Hargeisa airport and the various police stations. The first groups that worked for Rimfire were very superficially trained but they managed to remove most of the mines in Hargeisa itself. There was no census of how many died because of those mines, but in every town or village you went there were people missing arms or legs.[37]

9

INDEPENDENCE, HUMANITARIAN INVASION AND SAILING INTO THE UNKNOWN

The road to the Somaliland (re-)declaration of independence

(a) Taking stock of the post-war situation

As we saw in the preceding chapter, the collapse of the Siad Barre dictatorship was not followed by any form of embryonic new administration. On the contrary, the various insurrectional movements which managed to dismantle the last remnants of a 'government' were themselves simplified fighting systems without either ideology or administrative capacity. They were designed to destroy the dictatorship, and though they did the job, they did nothing else. None had thought about how to follow up on their own success.

Even though the situation was not much better in the north, what made the difference with the south was the presence of the SNM. Not the SNM as a political and military organisation, although in this aspect it remained a factor. Unlike the USC, the SPM and other southern organisations in which the military completely overshadowed the civilians, the SNM had always been a civilian-led organisation and had embryonic civilian-run structures. Its long history of congresses accompanied by a broadly accepted authority had created a civil culture and atmosphere. But was this a cause or a consequence? The SNM was a complex entity but, even if some of the fighters imposed themselves on civilians, most of the fighters remained civilians deep down because the SNM was an organic product of oppression. Bottom-up 'insurrectional democracy' had been part of its political DNA ever since its modest beginnings, both in the UK and among the various diaspora communities in exile.

Another advantage of the SNM compared with the more recent anti-Siad Barre insurgent groups was longevity. The SNM had been a long-distance fighter, accumulating experience for most of the 1980s at a time when the pan-Somali dream was practically dead among the Issaq since they had to pay the price of the 'refugee invasion' from the Ogaden in 1978. Caught in the iron vice of the Cold War, the SNM was in a poor tactical position. The SNM was no Vietcong, even its Calan Cas faction was not really 'communist', and it was not in the front ranks of the Cold War. It was a minor player. The help it received from the Communist bloc was meagre and incidental and completely subcontracted by Moscow to Ethiopia. By force of circumstance, it had to be self-reliant and it learned how to do so, over many years. It knew that victory, a real victory, would be a long-drawn-out affair and could not be a quick 'fruit of the moment' move. But the result was an extreme fragility, partly due to the instability of its recent allies, the newborn guerrilla movements of the south.

It is useful at this point to return to the prescient 'Open Letter to the Nation' written in November 1990 by Mohamed Ibrahim Egal, which was quoted earlier. 'There has never been a more urgent need for compromise ... The alternative is anarchy and descent into warring tribal fragments ... The men who have brought down Siad and his regime are the armed insurgents, not the politicians ... There is no possibility that anyone could now grab power cheaply in the streets of Mogadishu ...' The man who had written this was in a strange position: a political leader of the north (from the Issaq clan family), he had willingly adhered to the pan-Somali ideal, saw it head into dictatorship, paid for his mistake by years in jail, and was at the time an opponent without any organisational membership since he had not joined the SNM even though he had every reason to do so. But he had a clear vision of the situation and particularly of what could not be done. He was not self-deceiving, having personally shared most of the errors and illusions of the Somali political world. He wrote his letter just at the time when the irruption of the newborn guerrilla groups had totally changed the situation. They did not have the SNM experience and, even though they were also Somali, they were the carriers of a political culture substantively different from that of the northerners. They were the by-product of a reaction against (while still being influenced by) the Italian Fascist colonisation and, later, by the well-meaning obfuscation of AFIS. Given the physical catastrophe that accompanied and followed the war, they saw their weapons as 'normal' shortcuts to power, without even thinking what power could mean in East Africa in the early 1990s. Egal knew this, partly because he had made another mistake by not joining the SNM. This is why he did not talk about it in his Open Letter. He was much more concerned—and rightly so—about the men who thought they could make a quick dash for power, and about those who thought they could stand in their way.

This was the general situation in the south where the active guerrilla forces, those who de facto occupied the ground, were barely a year old. But in the north 'the new officers who arrived after the 1988 offensive had to make a choice about how to liberate the territory. Among them were men such as Colonel Ibrahim Ahmed Ismail, Colonel Musa Bihi Abdi, Ibrahim 'Dega Weyne' or General Ali Hussein. Hassan Kayd, who had been the leader of the 1961 coup in Somaliland, was the commander of the Sanaag eastern front. With the exception of Dega Weyne, the rest of the officers were newcomers ... But the challenge to any SNM administration right after liberation was the proliferation of brigades (*aags*), which were based on different sub-clans and lacked any organisational structure. Each *aag* was independent from any other sub-clan and there was no joint command linking them together, even though the commanders were picked by the chairman. Though this was not a real issue during the fighting, it became a serious hindrance after the victory. The idea of having a united armed unit[1] was opposed by Calan Cas and other military officers who had influence, because they had been with SNM since the early 1980s. By uniting the SNM army they would have lost the authority they enjoyed over the *aags* through their sub-clans.[2] This was a dangerous trend because, for them, using their clans and sub-clans as levers to power was a tempting road to take.

As we saw in the previous chapter, when Abdirahman 'Tuur' had to deal with the one and only delegation the northern administration ever received from Mogadishu, his dilatory answer enabled him to buy time in dealing with the south. He decided to hold a meeting to consult about how to deal with the USC 'government'.[3] A first meeting was held in Berbera in March 1991 but it was inconclusive. So another was organised the following month in Hargeisa.

At the conference the most controversial resolution was to form a government in which the Issaq would have 77 per cent of the delegates and the non-Issaq only 25 per cent. Chairman Tuur protested and said that he was 70 years old and he wanted to spend the remaining years of his life peacefully in Hargeisa and not to be known at his age as the person who had divided the Somali. Suleiman 'Gal' was the only one who backed the chairman but the other ministers supported the controversial resolution. Many of us understood that it would be difficult to secede from Somalia and we were also aware of our organisational constitution that did not contain any mention of trying to achieve an independent entity. But then we had to ask ourselves, What was it we were fighting for? How could we get our rights back after thirty years of seeing them violated by Mogadishu? Abdirahman 'Tuur' talked to the participants of the conference and told them that he disagreed with their solution of making Somaliland secede from Somalia and that his own preference would have been to have a loose federation like the United Arab Emirates within which both Somalia and Somaliland could live as autonomous entities. But the participants did not change their minds and the initial resolution was finally accepted.[4]

In fact the situation was very contradictory because the formulation 'the resolution was finally accepted' stood for something more complex. The Calan Cas faction was basically anti-Tuur, i.e. anti-unity. But it was also secretly in favour of keeping the various army brigades autonomous so that the sub-clanic militias could keep control of them. Tuur wanted a unification of the real (as opposed to the official) army command. Opposing Tuur—who was against secession—would mean supporting the idea of a unified army in the medium term.

But Colonel Halac and his colleagues from Calan Cas were already organising themselves to hijack the conference by declaring an independent Somaliland. Most of them did not support the secession, but as chairman Tuur was for unity, they opposed Tuur's stance, saying that he was aiming at a federal union with Somalia. They mobilised SNM combatants, and before any decision could be made by the participants, they threatened Tuur and his allies with their guns, asking them to approve the independence of Somaliland, and the conference finally agreed to become an independent entity known as the Republic of Somaliland. The delegations which had come from the non-Issaq clans supported the resolution but they rejected the division of power to 25 per cent only for the non-Issaq clans ... So finally the next Bura'o conference approved the suggestion but did not specify whether it would be applied during the first two years during which government was under an SNM mandate or only after the SNM transfer of power to civilians in 1993.

In our next move after the Bura'o conference, we decided during a cabinet meeting to send a delegation from Somaliland to Somalia and start a dialogue. Five from the cabinet and five from parliament were selected for the mission to Mogadishu. All the members of the delegation were chosen from among those who still supported the union with Somalia. We wanted to give them the opportunity to explore what could come from a dialogue with their counterparts in the south. But they did not even meet with the new government in Mogadishu. They were just sent back with some used computer and office equipment and two billion newly printed notes in Somali shillings, which was supposed to be Somaliland's share from five billion of newly printed Somali money. Obviously this showed that Mogadishu still considered Somaliland to be part of Somalia.

But this visit caused confusion and suspicion among the public. Rumours started to spread that the Tuur administration had thrown Somaliland to the wolves. The rift between the military factions increased, and added tensions developed among the sub-clans. The first plenary meeting of the parliament (previously the Central Committee of the SNM) ended in chaos and disintegration, and the government stopped functioning. Almost immediately major fighting started in Hargeisa and some clashes developed in Berbera and Bura'o. In Berbera the International Federation of the Red Cross (IFRC), which was running the only hospital in town, decided to evacuate when the shooting started. The Issa Musa and the Musa Abdallah started fighting over the spoils, mostly the vehicles left behind by the IFRC. In Bura'o the Habr Ja'alo and the Habr Yunis sub-clans started to loot their own common armoury and began to fight each other with the proceeds of the looting.[5]

Barely independent, the former British colony seemed to have fallen victim to the same post-dictatorship disease that had already spread among its southern relatives. A post-civil war civil war seemed to be starting.

(b) Trying to implement the Bura'o proclamation

Basically, the new conflict was caused by the 'scavenger' situation we mentioned in the previous chapter. This does not mean that there was no clanic factor involved in the outbreak of the 1992 civil war. In all the interviews gathered here, the respondents are forthright about the fact that 'the SNM units were organised along clan lines'. But there was a difference with the south in the hierarchy of causalities. First of all, the term 'clan' is too imprecise. The 'clans' mentioned here are in fact clans and sub-clans of the same clan family, the Issaq. The tense stand-offs between Issaq and Dir (in Awdal) or Issaq and Darood (Sanaag) resulted in one battle (Dilla) and some light clashes around Erigavo. But both of these situations matured fairly rapidly into peace, and that second-stage peace proved durable. There were none of the massive war crimes that took place in the south during the clan cleansing of 1991 by the Hawiye or the repeated massacres inflicted by almost everybody on the Rahanweyn in 1991–2.[6]

In the north, the 'clanic' fighting was real but its cause was not a breach in deep clan relations but a much more superficial 'slash and grab' attitude.

The three bouts of civil war in the north—1992, 1993 and 1995–6—were largely cases of thuggishness rooted in misery. And their toxicity was largely mitigated by the fact that all combatants were real or purported members of SNM. The clan reality plus an opaque organisational superstructure, which was at the heart of the problem in the south, did not apply in the north. The basic cause of the fighting in the north—and here it is not certain that the term 'civil war' is apposite—was a combination of extreme material deprivation and too many weapons in too many hands.

> Everyone was armed and lawlessness was the order of the day. Many people who had never taken part in the actual war against the Siad Barre dictatorship now grabbed weapons and claimed to be real fighters so as to join sides and steal.'[7] But once this fighting-for-looting had started, it was easier to maintain if dressed up in clan loyalties and political grandstanding. The very proclamation of independence on 18 May 1991 could have been the basis for a 'true' civil war, complete with ideological preferences and political globalisation. Some of the actors actually seemed to want to rationalise the conflict along these lines. 'With the difference of ideas during the campaign for the leadership,[8] several senior politicians were known to have links with Somalia, and we were divided into two groups, one that fought in the hope of independence and the other group which did not fight for that and which I called the Somali Firsters. It was now up to the constituents to choose between these two groups and to act accordingly.[9]

But real as that cleavage might be, it was not along these lines that the fighting broke out. It had started as pure and simple theft for survival and then was amplified by clanic solidarity. In other words, the clans were not the cause of the fighting, but the reason why it spread and why it lasted. This is why both the spread and the duration were extremely variable. The first 'civil war' lasted a few months, the second a few weeks and the third almost two years.

> At Baligubadle, the last candidate standing against Abdirahman 'Tuur' had been Mohamed Hashi Elmi, and most of the delegates of the Calan Cas group, who hated Tuur, voted for Hashi Elmi. Tuur only won by 145 to 140. But there were no complaints or protest and the final result was accepted by all.[10] ... This is how Abdirahman 'Tuur', who was against independence, became the first President of Somaliland and Hassan Eissa Jama, who was a Habr Garhadjis and pro-independence, became his Vice-President.

> But even though there was no criticism at the end of the Bura'o congress, the administration got stuck and everything was jammed. Small things got completely out of control. In Bura'o the civil war erupted when the Cimraan sub-clan of the Habr Ja'alo left the other Habr Ja'alo to join the government army, which at the time was made up mostly of Habr Yunis soldiers. Then the other Habr Ja'alo told the Habr Yunis to give back the vehicles the Cimraan had taken

with them. This is how the conflict began. In Berbera, the fighting centred around the control of the harbour. The local Habr Awal clans did not consider the 'government' as an administration but only as a group of Habr Yunis who wanted to take the customs revenue from the harbour. To mobilise militiamen, you needed to appeal to their sense of tribe (i.e. clan). Tribes were keeping their weapons and the government was trying to demobilise the militiamen but no one at the time agreed to give up their guns. The war kept dragging on till it was finally half resolved through negotiations and peace-building conferences that were held in Sheikh and later in Borama towards the end of the Tuur administration. Traditional leaders convened these conferences and all Somalilanders were involved indirectly through the funding which came from businessmen, politicians or local communities. We had no foreign money.[11]

These 'peace conferences' organised by clanic elders took place in the north and they worked, to some extent and locally. But, eventually, as we will see, they ended up by putting an end to the overall violence, something which did not take place in the south, where even today acts of violence still take place on a recurring basis.[12]

(c) North–south: Two ways of dealing with the post-conflict conflicts

Let us be clear: the situation was not a question of 'southerners bad and northerners good', but rather one of how, when and why. We will come back to an examination of the northern versus southern parameters but for now let it suffice to say:

- The situation of violence and anarchy was roughly comparable in both north and south at the time of Siad Barre's flight from the capital.
- Clashes large enough to qualify for the term 'civil war' developed in both cases.
- In the south there was a pretence of normality leading to the proclamation of a new 'national' government. It was challenged both internally and externally.
- In the north the situation was radically addressed by a declaration of (re-) independence for the former British colony which had joined the former Italian colony in June 1960.
- In the south the 'civil war' went on unabated up to and during an international foreign military and humanitarian intervention in December 1992.
- In the north a series of local and Somaliland-wide peace conferences took place. Their success was limited and new instances of large-scale armed

clashes kept occurring. But no international conference took place on the subject.

- After a large 'nation-wide' conference had been held in Addis Ababa (in January 1993), the UN signed a 'peace agreement' with an array of 15 different organisations, excluding the SNM. Many of those had little or no control on the ground. The agreement had no real impact.

- In the north a nation-wide *shir* led to a gradual re-establishment of government in Somaliland (January–May 1993). The last civil war did not stop immediately but it decreased in intensity. It would eventually stutter to a halt three and a half years later and was followed by territory-wide peace, starting at the beginning of 1997.

- Various attempts at local *shirs* in the south led to more inter-clanic conflicts. The UN clumsily tried to supervise them all, failed, ended up being a party to the civil war itself and finally evacuated the country in 1995 after a near-total failure.

- This evacuation opened a long cycle of complex insecurity which, in spite of renewed foreign-supported military aid (AMISOM), has not yet subsided at the time of writing

It would be beyond the scope of this book to provide a complete history of what happened both in former Somalia Italiana and in former British Somaliland during the twenty-five years that followed the collapse of the Siad Barre regime. But the main question that has to be asked—and which the preceding paragraphs outline—is this: how is it that two segments of a contiguous geographical entity that shared the same language, the same everyday customs, the same overall culture and the same religion were able in one case to put an end to their civil conflicts—difficult as this may have been—and in the other case remained dependent on foreign support, both materially and diplomatically, while the party that had ended the war benefited from neither? Direct foreign support started by failing, and when it was later resumed, it ended up by creating a lasting dependency. So before trying to assess in a concluding chapter the internal reason for that state of affairs,[13] we should first give a short summary of the facts and events that set the stage in 1991–7 on which the internal factors played themselves out.

(d) The south: An unprepared foreign intervention feeds the chaos[14]

While the north was involved in its various peace conferences, the south, initially abandoned to its fate at the end of January 1991, became the focus of international attention. United Nations involvement in the Somalia crisis had started in January 1992 with the adoption of UN Security Council Resolution 733, which called for an arms embargo, UN humanitarian aid and a ceasefire. However, there was little implementation of this resolution in practice. The subsequent Resolution 751 (24 April 1992) created the United Nations Somalia Mission (UNOSOM), which was to send 50 military observers to monitor a ceasefire accepted by the warring parties on 3 March 1992. The first observers (Pakistani soldiers) were deployed to very limited effect. Permanently threatened by all warring parties, and somewhat lost and isolated in a hostile environment, they remained holed up at the international airport, doing very little. In an effort to break this deadlock, and as a result of the alarming deterioration of the humanitarian situation after an offensive by General Mohamed Said Hersi, the UN Security Council passed Resolution 775 (28 August 1992), which provided for an increase in the number of observers and the creation of four 'zones of intervention'. The resolution called for a humanitarian airlift but remained rather vague as to what the contents of the 'intervention' should be. The UN was hesitating on the edge of full-scale involvement.

What finally prompted President George HW Bush to announce a major American military intervention had to do with the provision of humanitarian aid in the worsening crisis. This came about after a major lobbying effort by a coalition of humanitarian agencies. While this author was travelling during the autumn of 1992 across the United States, it was fascinating to see how, through the efforts of syndicated press agencies, a series of articles on the tragic humanitarian situation in Somalia popped up as front-page news in city after city and in newspaper after newspaper. The campaign was well orchestrated. But there were several other considerations which contributed to this momentous decision. Firstly, with the end of the Cold War, large spending cuts were unavoidable in a now oversized military-industrial establishment. President Clinton, who had just been elected to succeed Bush, was rumoured to be preparing a new social security plan, which he was likely to try to finance out of spending cuts in the Pentagon budget. For supporters of a large defence budget, the Somalia operation seemed attractive.

Secondly, there was an image component. The Iraq Desert Storm Operation, although very successful militarily, had drawn a great deal of political criticism. By contrast a large military intervention in order to save starving children in an underdeveloped African country would be a very good image-building device in a predominantly Muslim area where the US and the

West in general were far from being liked. Thirdly, the US Army, after some initial reluctance, was finally happy to test in real life the efficiency of its Rapid Defence strategy, especially since it involved activating the military base on the island of Diego Garcia, never used for this kind of operation before.

The problem with the way the whole operation was conceived was that, while the technical details were very carefully thought out, its general policy framework was almost completely neglected. The US–UN forces, grouped under the United Nations International Task Force (UNITAF) banner, walked into Somalia almost completely unaware of what awaited them. This naiveté was not exclusive to America. As the US announced its decision to employ its forces in Somalia on the eve of Thanksgiving (25 November 1992), many Western nations jumped on the bandwagon, without any more serious planning than the Americans themselves. Bernard Kouchner, founder of Médecins Sans Frontières (Doctors Without Borders) and subsequently French Secretary of State for Humanitarian Affairs, declared: 'The international intervention will succeed very quickly because we are faced here only with young teenagers with machine guns who are just going to run away.'[15] When this author, who was at the time a government adviser on African affairs, phoned the well-known Africa Unit at the Elysée Palace and asked what was the rationale for French troops to join the intervention, the unit's director, former ambassador Bruno Delaye, answered:

> I don't know. But I phoned the President,[16] and he said if the Americans are going, we have to go too, otherwise we'll look stupid and cowardly. So we are going.' And when I added a question about our planning for the intervention and eventual withdrawal, he answered: 'There is no planning, only logistical arrangements. We don't really know what we are doing. I just hope it doesn't last too long.[17]

This unfounded optimism was, at the time, widely shared and those who seemed to doubt that the mission was actually carefully thought out were not heeded. Henry Kissinger asked: 'Could somebody explain in detail what exactly it is that we are trying to do, for how long and what are the limits to our involvement?'[18] Jane Perlez of the *New York Times*, who was based in East Africa at the time and who was one of the few journalists who had stayed behind in Somalia, monitoring closely the first rather inefficient moments of UN involvement, wrote: 'What many aid and UN officials here in Somalia do not understand is why Washington did not prod the United Nations to sharpen its flailing military operation in Mogadishu before making the quantum leap of committing large numbers of American troops.'[19] In fact, if we think about Bernard Kouchner's remarks, there seems to have been a fair amount of Western arrogance in the attitude which informed the whole thinking about Operation Restore Hope.[20] The idea was that the whole Somali confusion was caused by a bunch of primitive teenage gangsters with automatic weapons, who were going to vanish into thin air as soon as Western troops with strong firepower arrived on the scene. Then food could be peacefully distributed and, hey presto, the state itself would be restored. None less than French Minister of Defence, Roland Dumas, thought along those naive lines:

> The first phase of the action consists in opening up humanitarian access corridors, by force if necessary ... once this is done ... once the bands have been chased away and disarmed ... in a second phase, the Blue Helmets will crisscross the country and prepare the third phase, the national reconciliation and the rebuilding of the state.

The steps he outlines are rather astonishing: first, force 'opens up humanitarian corridors' and somehow this results in 'the bands' being disarmed. This was a dream world because the US had absolutely no intention of being drawn into the dangerous business of disarmament. The UN Security Council Resolution 794 of 3 December 1992, which had created UNITAF, was very clear on that issue. The US government had been adamant that any mention of disarmament would be kept out. The aim of UNITAF's mission was described as 'a return to normal conditions', an expression which could be taken to mean almost anything given the state of disarray during the last few years of the dictatorship. The confrontation between the US Representative to the United Nations and the UN Secretary-General had been rather heated. In a view which was more hopeful than realistic, Boutros Boutros-Ghali was in fact going to try, at least for the first weeks of UNITAF deployment, to get the mission to move towards disarmament. But even had 'the bands' been disarmed,[21] it is difficult to see how this simple disarmament could have brought about the next two successive steps, the national reconciliation—of whom and with whom?—and then the 'rebuilding' of a state, when the root cause of the Somalia problem was that it had never had any cultural, social or political basis for a state. Experts who at the time had the temerity to question the whole non-political approach to an eminently political problem were dismissed as hard-hearted cynics who could not understand the nobility of this 'purely humanitarian' operation.[22]

From the beginning, the UNITAF intervention displayed its main strengths and weaknesses in full view. Its main strength was the speed with which humanitarian aid was deployed throughout the area of intervention.

The UNITAF intervention took place in seven of Somalia's fifteen provinces, representing about 35 per cent of the country's territory and about 60 per cent of its population. Mogadishu was quickly secured, and the provinces of Hiiran, Bakool, Bay, Lower Shebelle and Lower Jubba were brought under partial but sufficient control for food distribution. Conflict and starvation quickly receded. From that point of view, after a period of a few months, one could cautiously say that the operation had been a success.[23] But the problem comes when one tries to look at the political framework within which this felicitous change in the humanitarian situation had occurred. As outlined above, the US decision (and that of America's allies) had been made in a very hurried manner. There had been no political planning before the landings and political improvisation was the rule from day one. On top of this, this improvisation took place without any input from knowledgeable persons, Somali, European or American.[24] As a result, the first political steps taken by the intervention forces were highly counterproductive. As we have seen, the main fighting in Somalia had been between the faction led by 'President' Ali Mahdi Mohamed and the other USC branch under the leadership of General Mohamed Farah Aydid. Both had allied themselves in turn with other major provincial warlords (Omar Jess, General Mohamed Said Hersi, Colonel Yusuf Abdullahi, Mohamed Abshir), who themselves had their own local clan alliances. It was the 'inter-clan' violence spurred and used by these men which had destroyed whatever state there had ever been, ruined what was left of the already inadequate infrastructure, and led to the looting of property, especially food, which caused hundreds of thousands of refugees to flee and tens of thousands to starve to death. These men were scourges of God and man, and, if not the real cause, at least the main agents of the catastrophic violence that Operation Restore Hope had come to suppress.

Contrary to what was then often said or written, these men were not 'clan leaders'. As we have noted, Somali clans were leaderless. They functioned according to a system of extreme democracy verging on anarchy, carried out by elders. As we have seen in the sections devoted to the north, the SNM had managed to enlist the help of elders, and at times to accommodate them even when those same elders went against the SNM. But strong leaders could temporarily emerge in times of war, with pragmatic trans-clanic alliances such as *gaashaanbuur* ('pile of shields'). Such were the men UNITAF had to deal with. Their authority owed nothing to tradition. They were just warlords, a pure product of the disintegration of the state since 1978, and an expression of the anomie of a society in which traditional values had disintegrated and modern ones had failed to take hold. The Somali public expected naively that 'the Europeans' would hang them all or at least arrest them and throw them in jail.[25]

Renowned international experts had warned about the danger of dealing with those men. I.M. Lewis, the respected Somalia historian and possibly the best Western expert on Somali society, accurately predicted the shape of things to come when he wrote at the very beginning of UNITAF's deployment:

> America must be aware of the dangers it faces. Peacemaking between Ali Mahdi and Aydeed and any of the other warlords can only be a short-term expedient and cannot in itself lead to the formation of a viable Somali government ... As long as military support is available, the UN could organize clan assemblies and inter-clan meetings ... This of course assumes an enlarged UN Administration. It also presupposes that these developments take place gradually, against an expanding background of peace, and may require years rather than months. Somali elders' deliberations are always protracted and require great patience from those awaiting their outcome ... If however the effect of U.S. intervention is to shore up the power of Aydeed, Ali Mahdi and other dubious figures ... whom many Somalis consider to be war criminals, that will be disastrous and add further misery to the country's long catalogue of man-made calamities.[26]

And, indeed, clan assemblies and inter-clan meetings are time-consuming and rather trying for the limited patience of modern Western man. But the alternative adopted by US Special Envoy Robert Oakley and endorsed by the rest of the international community—to have Ali Mahdi and General Aydid theatrically embrace in front of the CNN cameras two days after the landings—could not and did not lead anywhere. It brought politics and diplomacy down to the level of showmanship. The US government did not seem to have any long-term strategy. Their main preoccupation was to stay out of trouble, ensure the distribution of humanitarian aid, have no contacts with the local population, pack up and go home as soon as possible. The US started to hint that it would like to be out of Somalia when the new President was due to be inaugurated, which meant a matter of a few weeks. This position, reflecting the lack of an overall agenda for Somalia, clashed sharply with the UN position. On the question of an eventual disarmament of the fighting factions, the differences were well apparent. Thus the UN Secretary-General could declare that 'disarmament of the armed factions in Somalia remains an absolutely necessary condition to restore normal security conditions', while on the same day US Forces commander General Robert Johnston could say that 'my aim is not to disarm Somalia'. US Secretary of State Lawrence Eagleburger also reinforced the same message by declaring: 'The purpose of the U.S. military presence in Somalia is to bring in humanitarian aid for those who need it and not to become a permanent police force or a permanent pacification force.'

With such reservations on the part of the US, which was both the main financial backer and troop supplier of the whole operation, things quickly started to go wrong. The UN organised two 'reconciliation conferences' in Addis Ababa, in January and March 1993. Those were vitiated from the start because they did not respect the Somali ways of peacemaking (*shir*) and tried to push through quickly arranged 'solutions' without really considering how representative the participants were or what motivated them. I.M. Lewis's warning had not been heeded, and the UN was struggling to achieve too much, too quickly and by the wrong methods. This reflected a completely unacknowledged cultural gap, which seems to be a recurrent problem in Western diplomacy in trying to deal with 'alien' cultures. Elegant, well-paid and highly educated UN officials were not about to bend to the ways of a bunch of African nomads. The nomads, who ought to be glad that the world community had decided to 'help them', had to adapt to Western ways and make peace in a civilised fashion, i.e. not by reclining for months under trees composing poems and talking about past wars, but by sitting at tables in air-conditioned rooms and putting their signatures at the bottom of small pieces of paper.

The trouble was that the wild nomads had little idea or even understanding of what the 'international community' was so keen on. The lack of what one would call in Western parlance 'due process' invalidated in Somali terms the meaning of the whole process. They collected their per diem for sitting in Addis Ababa, went shopping, met their friends living in exile in the Ethiopian capital, and then went home. As one of the participants in the March 1993 conference was to remark: 'The speeches were nice, the slogans were really good but the whole thing was quite meaningless.'[27] Participants in these conferences had no sense that they had actually pledged anything by putting their signature on the UN-sponsored document they had been asked to sign. Thus, trying to create a network of local administration committees on the basis of these 'agreements' was like building on sand.

In the meantime, the warlords and their associates had developed highly sophisticated techniques for siphoning off large amounts of money from UNITAF. UN personnel were housed and worked in expensively rented premises which belonged to prominent leaders of the various warring factions. The office personnel they employed, the guards who escorted their convoys, the drivers who drove their trucks, were all selected by the local armed factions and had to pay part of their earnings back to their organisations or clans. Thus, on many occasions when fighting did occur during that period, it was because of quarrels over UNITAF spoils. UNITAF unwittingly became the main provider of finance and equipment (through massive theft) for the warlords.

Meanwhile, the US was growing impatient. Special Envoy Robert Oakley had declared as early as January 1993 that late March should be considered the deadline for American withdrawal. On 31 January, the US Military Command announced the first troop reductions. The UN was trying to preserve US involvement and, by early March 1993, relations were getting tense between the US government and the UN. Special Envoy Oakley explicitly reproached the UN for 'dragging its feet'. The Americans started to withdraw unilaterally, and by late March 1993, when Resolution 814 was passed, US troop strength was down to 1,400 from a maximum of 26,000 at the beginning of Operation Restore Hope. UNITAF blended into UNOSOM 2. Whereas US troops had mostly gone home by the time UNOSOM 2 began in early May 1993, America's allies kept their forces on the ground, even if some, like the French, discreetly scaled down their level of participation. UNOSOM 2 entered the scene empowered with authority under Chapter VII of the UN Charter to use force. This was going to cause a great deal of trouble in a context where the UN had started to play politics without really knowing what it was doing.

If the UN had no more notion of how tactically to approach the Somali political conundrum than the US had demonstrated, then, unlike the US, it had a grand strategic view. The UN's basic idea was that it was necessary to restore some sort of a working Somali state and this implied, among other things, a reunification of the country. The various warlords had different views on this UN position. 'President' Ali Mahdi, definitely the better diplomat, understood the advantage he could gain from playing along with this generous UN illusion. As a result, during the UNITAF period, numerous links were forged between Ali Mahdi and his friends, always careful to humour the powerful foreigners, and United Nations personnel. The presence of several well-known figures from the previous regime around Ali Mahdi helped boost this relationship, as they were experienced in dealing with foreigners and were already personally known to many powerful UN figures. Correspondingly, tension grew between the UN and the Aydid camp, whose members came more and more to consider the 'foreigners' as the allies of their enemy, Ali Mahdi.

Tensions came to a head over the question of local councils and local negotiations. General Aydid had started his own round of consultations and negotiations, all the while loudly proclaiming that he should be left in charge of this process and that peace in Somalia would be achieved by Somali and not by foreigners, however well meaning they were. At the end of May, he called a 'peace conference' in Mogadishu without the authorisation of the UN. Three days later, UNOSOM 2 organised a local 'peace conference' in the southern harbour of Kismayo, to which it invited Ali Mahdi and from which it excluded the local Aydid representative, Omar Jess. General Aydid of course saw this move as another hostile act by the UN authorities, even more so when, on the same day, he was told by UNOSOM 2 that the financial support given to his unauthorised peace conference would be withdrawn and that he would have to manage somehow to pay for the delegates' bills.[28] In this tense climate, the pro-Ali Mahdi radio issued a perfectly explosive statement in which it said:

> Since the objective of the organisations [the various factions Ali Mahdi had rallied to his USC branch] and UNOSOM is to establish a Somali Republic, it is necessary that all national assets and state institutions in the hands of individuals, groups and organisations should be handed over to UNOSOM ... These include especially the mass media such as radio, centres of information and national institutions which are the causes of present instability.[29]

The UNOSOM authorities had of course never officially stated that their aim was to 'establish a Somali Republic', even if in fact this policy had by now become common knowledge in Somalia. But in its unabashed support for UNOSOM and this policy, the ventriloquism of Ali Mahdi's radio broadcast and the general anti-Aydid attitude were to have very serious consequences. At the very moment the broadcast was being aired, UNOSOM 2 Pakistani troops were trying to occupy General Aydid's radio station and ammunition store, neither of which the warlord was likely to hand over, as he was called upon to do by his 'enemy'. The operation did not go very well and 24 Pakistani soldiers were killed in the fighting. Within 24 hours, the UN had voted for Resolution 837, authorising military operations against 'those responsible for armed attacks against UN forces'. What the Somali quickly came to call 'the UN War' had started, and UNOSOM 2 had become just another clan, with its allies and its enemies, fighting to impose its supremacy. This war was to last for four months and cause thousands of casualties.

Resolution 837 had been railroaded through the General Assembly by painting a picture of General Mohamed Farah Aydid deliberately attacking UN forces unprovoked and 'murdering' 24 soldiers. An unpublished UN independent inquiry was much more prudent on the matter.[30] Paragraphs

81–93 of the document describe the growing rift between General Aydid's forces and the UN, and, in regard to the 5 June operation, paragraph 94 states: 'Opinions differ, even among UNOSOM officials, on whether the weapons inspection of 5 June 1993 was genuine or was merely a cover-up for reconnaissance and subsequent seizure of Radio Mogadishu.'

A number of other mistakes were also chronicled, such as the refusal to take into account the Pakistani position (paragraph 100), or the failure to notify the Aydid leadership of the intended 'inspection' (paragraph 101–2). But this inquiry occurred months after the events. At the time, the UN plunged into a war at least partly of its own making, which led to such extremes as the US$25,000 price put on General Aydid's head in an embarrassingly ridiculous parody of the Wild West, and the call by the UN Secretary-General for General Aydid's physical elimination. Worse still, the whole confused attempt at full-scale war was to end in military failure in spite of overwhelmingly superior UN firepower. The increase in firepower was due to a return to the scene of US military units, a fact which seems surprising if we recall the hurried withdrawal only three months earlier. But much had changed during these three months, and for President Clinton re-intervention in Somalia could be seen as a way of recovering international standing at small domestic and financial cost. So the US armed forces had come back into the new 'war', even if at lower strength than in December 1992.[31]

But this time, unwittingly, US forces had to take sides even before they arrived. The Aydid camp was solidly set against what it now termed 'imperialism' and 'neo-colonialism', i.e. foreign intervention, while in north Mogadishu, Ali Mahdi's supporters demonstrated in favour of UN military operations which, they hoped, would crush their rival. Without even realising it, the US had now become part of a war between two Hawiye clans, the Habr Gidir and the Abgaal. Throughout the summer of 1993, fighting escalated to more and more violent levels, to the point where, by the autumn, the US Congress was beginning to voice some doubts about the place of the US in the Somalia tragedy. The UN Secretary-General was desperately trying to retain the US forces, conscious that their withdrawal this time would be final and would put an end to the whole UN political project in Somalia.[32]

In spite of the fighting (which was limited to Mogadishu and did not extend to the interior), the UN still sought to push its political agenda. UN Special Representative Leonard Kapungu flew to the breakaway 'Somaliland Republic' and deliberately tried to interfere in the situation by playing groups such as the USP, the SDA and the USF against the SNM. The result was a complete fiasco and Kapungu was expelled from Somaliland after several tragi-comic episodes.[33]

The climax came on 3 October 1993, when a major assault on General Aydid's positions in Mogadishu resulted in the shooting down of a US combat helicopter whose pilot was taken prisoner, while another crew member's dead body was dragged through the streets. The gruesome video of tae event was repeatedly displayed on television screens throughout the US during the next 48 hours. The US government's decision was quickly made: American troops would withdraw.[34]

At the global political level, the situation had become extremely difficult for the United Nations. Already, on 22 September 1993, Resolution 865 had called for a detailed plan, clearly setting out UN priorities and tactics. Resolution 878 (29 October 1993), passed in the aftermath of the 3 October military defeat, prudently extended the UN presence only to 18 November 1993, i.e. for three weeks. On that date, however, the mandate was extended to 31 May 1994, i.e. for another six months. But there was a definite feeling of exasperation among the participants. Most European countries announced plans to scale down their presence. By degrees, all European troops started to withdraw, a situation which was tacitly accepted by Resolution 897 (4 February 1994), which mentioned a scaling down of forces to a figure of 20,000.

At the civilian level, though, the UN administration was still trying very hard to push the district councils system which it had started to implement before the military crisis broke out. This had mixed success. In some areas of the south it worked reasonably well and helped people gain some control over their own local affairs, largely because of the UN's financial help, even if the clan factors remained essential.[35] But further north, in the Benadir and Hiiran areas, the councils were largely taken over by agents of the various militia groups, who used them for their own ends.

This was largely an anticlimactic period. By late March 1994, all European forces had withdrawn, leaving the UNOSOM exclusively manned by contingents from low-income countries whose governments had little or no interest in the Somalia situation.[36] Initially, there were fears that Somali militias would attack these troops for which they had no respect. In fact, these fears proved unfounded. What did happen, however, was that these very poorly paid troops started to sell the expensive stores and equipment over which they had control, thus contributing further to the reinforcement of the various clan militias.[37] This behaviour also progressively turned the UNOSOM presence into an increasingly bizarre factor.

UNOSOM's mandate had been renewed on 31 May 1994 for another four months by Resolution 923. When this period came to a close, the US, which had already withdrawn all its troops and even civilian personnel, insisted on terminating the operation for financial reasons. After a diplomatic struggle the operation, which was now clearly petering out, saw its mandate finally extended until 31 March 1995.

At the political level, the situation had not changed very much. The various faction leaders once more signed a worthless paper agreement, this time in Nairobi (on 24 March 1994), but they had not been either able or willing to reach any kind of real understanding. The clan division of the country remained, roughly as it had been before the international intervention of December 1992. In October 1994, feeling that UN withdrawal was imminent, General Aydid tried to convene a 'national convention' in order to quickly put together some kind of a 'national' executive which could try to inherit UNOSOM's dubious 'legitimacy'. But his faction was so weak internally that he never managed to bring his 'national convention' together and thus failed to produce any sort of government before the final UN withdrawal. By late February 1995, ahead of schedule, international forces had withdrawn from Somalia's soil.

How did the self-proclaimed Republic of Somaliland survive?

As mentioned above, the region covering the former British colony of Somaliland had (re-)proclaimed its independence on 18 May 1991. After an initial period of calm between May and December 1991, there were repeated clashes between the government forces of Abdirahman Ali 'Tuur' and rebels backed mostly by the Habr Ja'alo and some sections of the Habr Awal clans,[38] starting in January 1992. The situation was one of utmost confusion, the main cause of fighting being physical survival. Every group fell back on their lineages even though a government had been formed on 18 May 1991. But this government barely controlled the vicinity of the capital, and the rest of the territory was racked by what critics called 'looting' and observers called 'survival theft'. The situation was further complicated when Colonel Abdullahi Yusuf, head of SSDF, attacked Bosaso, which had become a kind of 'Islamist capital'. The militants of al-Ittihad al-Islami were defeated and fled across the Sanaag border into 'Somaliland', further complicating the disorderly picture.

In December 1991, the confused fighting acquired a new and more sinister dimension, with new battle lines appearing for an organised attempt at controlling the Berbera harbour customs, the main source of financial revenue in the country. The fighting could be described as 'clanic'—Habr Awal versus Habr Yunis—or, raised to a higher political level, rebels versus the 'government', but it was mainly about food, fuel and warehouse control. From there the fighting spread out to Bura'o, the region's main cattle market and supplier of live animals for export to Saudi Arabia, via Berbera. Eventually the fighting was ended in two steps—the *Kulanka Nabadeed* (peace meeting) in October in Berbera followed by the Sheikh *shir* in November 1992—which slowly disentangled the security arrangements from the economic aspects. But it had all taken place over a largely torn clanic tapestry. On this point, it was fascinating to notice how non-Issaq clans, both western Dir (Issa, Gaddabursi) and eastern Darood (Warsangeli, Dhulbahante), acted as umpires and facilitators among the Issaq sub-clans. They knew they had lost the war and they now feared, in seeing the Issaq sub-clans at each other's throats, they might also lose the peace. It was here, in the furnace of those post-civil war conflicts, that a new type of Somali state perhaps began to be born. It was also the time a new female militancy appeared. The SNM was no EPLF and had no women fighters.[39] But it was after 1991, during the post-conflict conflict, that female militants asserted themselves. 'We have had enough of war,' one told me in 1995, 'now we have to impose peace.'

Many politicians in the north, aware of the fissiparous tendencies of Somali clan politics, felt that their 'state' needed to be put on a firmer footing. This led to a long (24 January 8 June 1993) and well-organised *shir* in the town of Borama, during which delegates from all over Somaliland converged on the Gaddabursi capital.[40] There were 150 of them.[41] The first debate was about institutions, with several proposals favouring parliamentary democracy and others a presidential regime. The presidential regime won out but it was accepted with an informal understanding that the presidency should alternate between the various main Issaq clans and the two non-Issaq clan families, Dir and Darood.

After this decision was made, the *shir* moved to electing the first President. Abdirahman 'Tuur', who had been the reluctant President of re-independent Somaliland, did not stand for office. There were several candidates, the best known of whom was Omar Arteh. But the former diplomat (and victim) of Siad Barre bore a handicap in running for the Somaliland presidency: the fact that over the previous two years, he had been based in Djibouti, officially as the Foreign Minister of the Ali Mahdi government, practically as a kind of roving ambassador for Somalia's unity. To switch suddenly from that pro-UN position and from being the favourite of the international community to standing as a candidate for the position of President of an unrecognised, self-proclaimed secessionist state was unexpected. His main rival was Mohamed Ibrahim Egal,[42] his suffering and humiliated doppelgänger, still very recently himself a 'unitarist', a living embodiment of Somalia's contradictions. But that particular *shir* almost self-consciously grew into what in a different political context would have been called a constituent assembly, the mother of all *shirs*, the road finally heading for the light at the end of the tunnel.[43] Even if no constitution came out of the *shirweyne* (big assembly), this was what everybody wanted and time had to be taken later to discuss it. The situation was ripe for action but not yet for long-term legislation.

From June 1993 onwards, President Egal tried to stabilise Somaliland's difficult economic and administrative situation. His election brought back a measure of political calm, and business, especially in the form of livestock exports, started to pick up. In 1993–4, livestock exports through the harbour of Berbera were estimated to be around US$140 million, a figure which compared favourably with pre-war levels. A small tax base was slowly rebuilt through export taxes in Berbera and semi-voluntary contributions from the wealthiest businessmen. At the end of 1994, the 'government' had collected US$13 million and was hoping for US$20 million in 1995. The capital of Hargeisa, entirely destroyed during the 1988 terror bombings and the subsequent fighting of 1988–91, began to be rebuilt. Smaller towns such as Bura'o and Sheikh re-established modest local tax bases in the US$10,000–$20,000 range.

Yet President Egal was a Habr Awal and his election disappointed the previous clan coalition (Habr Garhadjis), which had held power under Abdirahman 'Tuur'. Trouble started brewing in April 1993 when, with the support of UNOSOM 2, the former President declared from his self-imposed exile in London that he was still head of the Somali National Movement[44] and that he had renounced the idea of independence for Somaliland. A UNOSOM 'grant' of US$200,000 and a promise of help from General Mohamed Farah Aydid seems to have greatly helped him change his mind.[45]

This was, in fact, partly the result of a reversal of alliances in the south. General Aydid, the former arch-enemy of UNOSOM, understood that the United Nations still believed in the possibility of bringing together some kind of a 'national government' as a face-saving device before withdrawing. Trying to reposition himself in the good graces of the UN, General Aydid developed the scheme of 'resuscitating' Tuur and using him so as to appear himself as a 'national' leader in UN eyes, one who would oppose the secession of Somaliland, which he had previously accepted. This was meant to take the wind out of the sails of his political rival, 'President' Ali Mahdi, before the departure of UNOSOM forces, since both were competing for the material leftovers of the international operation and for the continuing political support of the international community. But by then UNOSOM had become a war factor rather than a peacemaker in the complex Somalia equation. In June it started an anti-Aydid campaign in the south[46] and, in an internal report,[47] had recommended the 'disaggregation of the self-proclaimed "state of Somaliland" by supporting the hostile populations that border the Bari province'. Lansana Kouyaté, Special Representative of the UN Secretary-General with UNOSOM, had gone to Sool and Sanaag and harangued the local Dhulbahante populations in favour of a unitary state. So when his political officer, Leonard Kapungu, flew to Hargeisa and directly asked President Mohamed Ibrahim Egal to renounce independence, threatening him with invasive military action, Egal answered him: 'In that case, Hargeisa will be the Dien Bien Phu of the United Nations'. When Kapungu protested, Egal told him to leave within 24 hours. He immediately complied.

The UNOSOM support for Abdirahman Ali led to the expulsion of all UN personnel from Somaliland in late August 1994. A few days later, on 30 August 1994, the former Somaliland President arrived in Mogadishu where he met Mohamed Farah Abdullahi, leader of the anti-SNM branch of SDA, and Abd-er-Rahman Dualeh Ali, the USF president. The meeting was sponsored by General Mohamed Farah Aydid and the SNA,[48] and it meant a clear declaration of war against the Egal government.

The situation soon became complicated by a distinct (if not completely unrelated) development in Somaliland itself. A group of Eidagalley fighters had been occupying the Hargeisa airport for the previous year, demanding large landing and take-off fees from aid aircraft and passengers and pocketing the money under the pretext that 'Hargeisa belongs to the Eidagalley'. President Egal asked them to return control of the airport to the government but to no avail. In desperation, he had even gone as far as building a small airstrip 35 km from the capital and asking aid flights to use it instead of the 'national airport'. In late September, he threatened armed action and the climate became very tense.

At the same time the situation in the south was moving towards a widening of political alliances, as both Ali Mahdi and General Aydid tried to establish 'national governments' before UNOSOM left. All political forces in former

Somalia took sides in this race, even those in areas far removed from the authority of the Mogadishu warlords. Given the fact that Aydid had now decided to challenge Somaliland's independent existence for his own tactical reasons, President Egal felt compelled to enter the fray. In October 1994, he refused to recognise the election of Colonel Abdullahi Yusuf by the SSDF congress, simply because he felt that Abdullahi Yusuf was now an ally of Farah Aydid and therefore a danger to him. Thus, tension spread over the whole territory of the former Somalia.

In these circumstances, President Egal could no longer tolerate the occupation of Hargeisa airport by the Eidagalley militia, even if they were not under the orders of former President Abdirahman 'Tuur'. On 16 October 1994, Somaliland government troops stormed the airport, thus starting a new war. The conflict started badly for the government side. On 21 October, rebel troops entered Hargeisa town and started indiscriminate shelling. The Central Bank was looted and thousands of refugees streamed out of the city, where violent fighting raged until early December. Egal and his cabinet fled to Borama. As the battle gradually spread to the countryside around Hargeisa, the refugees fled all the way to Ethiopia, where about 80,000 arrived by Christmas 1994. Fighting at last slowly abated during January 1995.

But to the west of the capital, USF forces, manipulated by Djibouti, took advantage of the battles between the various pro- and anti-government Issaq clans to try to wrench the Issa-populated areas away from Hargeisa's authority. Their attempt ended in failure and their troops were badly mauled by forces loyal to President Egal, as had been the case in the past when similar attempts were made.

Skirmishes went on between government forces and the rebel Eidagalley–Habr Yunis coalition during most of early 1995. But the fighting moved progressively away from the capital, first to Salahley and then to the eastern part of the country. It was there, near the town of Bura'o, the local capital of the Habr Yunis clan, that a major eight-day battle was fought in late March and early April 1995. Both sides used significant force, including heavy artillery and tanks. There were at least 1,000 dead and the rebels suffered a defeat.

Refugees started cautiously to come back to Hargeisa, whose population in July 1995 had returned to 80 per cent of that in November 1994. Economic activity slowly returned to near-normal levels. The rebel leaders (Abdirahman 'Tuur', Ismail 'Buuba', General Jama Qalib) were all in Mogadishu and none had dared come back to the north, even at the height of the fighting, which was carried out partly in their name but also, in a sense, independently of them. This is an important political point: even though President Egal had acted undiplomatically in terms of clan sensibilities and alienated the various Habr Garadjis sub-clans, it did not mean that these same clans sympathised with the reunification platform supported by the 'official' rebel leaders. Those who fought against the Egal government did so in their own name and not in support of the exiled leaders. Even President Egal's opponents supported the secession, a fact Abdirahman 'Tuur' and his friends were so well aware of that they did not dare return to Somaliland for fear of being killed or arrested, possibly even by their own 'supporters'.

In May 1995, the *Guurti* (National Assembly of Somaliland) decided to extend Mohamed Egal's presidential mandate for another year. Even those MPs who were opposed to the President voted for the extension, because of a feeling that the situation, although stabilised, was still too precarious to allow for a major political change just then. Although the war had damaged the economy (the 'new Somali shilling' fell against the US dollar and estimates of government tax revenue had to be downscaled from US$20 million to US$15 million), livestock exports were still strong. The major obstacle to a more healthy stabilisation of the country was its lack of recognition by the international community and, given the UN position, it did not seem that such recognition was at all on the cards for the near future.

But a key point seemed to have been reached: the international community had flunked its Somalia test woefully. In the south, after the 'Black Hawk Down' episode and the progressive evacuation of the ONUSOM troops, the whole 'Restore Hope' construction had come tumbling down, leaving no visible traces except abandoned warehouses and bombed-out buildings. As usual, the humanitarian NGOs were left behind to pick up whatever pieces they could. Politically, the disaster was complete: the former USC duel had ended in a draw and the lack of any visible government had opened what became later known as 'the time of the warlords' (1995–2005).

In that field of disaster, Somaliland, unrecognised, marginalised and abandoned, achieved what the whole rest of Somalia was still blindly looking for: peace. The last 'post-war war' of 1994–5 had taken place on three fronts: an Issa–Gaddabursi low-level conflict for the control of the commercial road from Djibouti; an Eidagalley–Sa'ad Musa fight over the control of the airport; and a Habr Ja'alo–Habr Yunis contest for the control of Bura'o and its surroundings. All eventually died down through a series of local *shir* processes. None of these had been set up by foreigners or financed by them, except for very modest contributions by humanitarian NGOs. The whole organisational and political process was borne by Somaliland, not so much from the central government, whose budget was low and administrative network limited, but from the local clan or sub-clan structures, which provided the essentials. Traditional processes were used and, at times, adapted. For example, the usual way of dealing with blood violence in Somali culture involved the payment of *mag* (blood price) to compensate a lineage for the loss (or even the wounding) of a member. There were no prisons and the death penalty would have simply meant adding one killing to another killing, which seemed like a stupid idea. But what to do in a situation of civil war using modern weapons? The payment of *mag* would have involved impossible amounts of money and huge numbers of camels. So the Somaliland clans generalised the practice of *xaladhaley* (lit. innocence), which was known to some of them, particularly among the Ogadeni. It was a 'total wiping out of blood accounts', whereby, beyond a certain number of *mag*-owing deaths, the slate was wiped clean. It was introduced in Bari to help settle the scores between Habr Yunis/Issaq and Dhulbahante/Darood. It amounted to a form of creative emotional accounting.

Peace had returned to Somaliland. But did Somaliland exist? It depended on the point of view you chose to adopt.

10

ODD MAN OUT

SOMALILAND'S FRAGILE PEACE ON THE EDGE OF SOMALIA'S WAR WITHOUT END

In search of a credible state

(a) Somaliland

The first and most spectacular event which followed the UNOSOM 2 withdrawal was a non-event: Somalia did not in fact blow up and revert to the pattern of wild clanic fighting which had existed during the period from January 1991 to December 1992. But neither did it manage to re-create a unitary state. At first, life went on pretty much in the same way as during the late UNOSOM 2 period, i.e. with a rough sort of peace disturbed by the occasional short bout of fighting between militias and, more frequently, by bandit attacks. This was not peace but it stayed at a low level of violence. Basically this was because the SNM zone needed a state but struggled to re-create one, while in the south those who had power did not want to return to a state. What happened in the south was the emergence of artificial 'neo-clan leaders' who were soon to be called 'warlords'.[1] As two qualified observers, Ken Menkhaus and John Prendergast, noted at the time:

> In the past [i.e. before 1991] the centrifugal tendencies of clan politics were overcome through a combination of foreign aid-fuelled patronage and military coercion. While militia leaders still have the ability to intimidate local com-

munity leadership, they are nowhere near to possessing the kind of well-funded and intrusive security apparatus of the Siad Barre regime ... Politically, there continues to be powerful vested interest in statelessness ... a growing number of Somali entrepreneurs are perceiving that their business interests will now be better served by the creation and recognition of some sort of authority, though one which will co-exist rather than challenge the mafia-based economy on which these merchants profit.[2]

During the heyday of international intervention, clan militia leaders had made a lot of money by renting land and premises to the UN force. Several of them invested this money in trade rather than in weapons, and with the stabilisation of the situation in the north-west (i.e. 'Somaliland') and with the virtual loss of border control by the Ethiopian government in Ethiopia's Region Five (the Ogaden), a truly 'national' trade network began to develop throughout all the Somali-populated areas. By late 1994, this trade network had become profitable. It was fuelled by two factors, livestock exports to the Gulf countries, and remittances from refugees abroad (mostly in Europe and North America), as well as from migrant workers in the petro-monarchies. A new brand of businessmen, warlords-turned-entrepreneurs, started to develop. Although they could not be considered as really 'modern' entrepreneurs, they were in many ways reminiscent of the early European merchants of the 13th–14th century who combined piracy, trade and extortionate money-lending to build the basis of Europe's capitalist economy in the Late Middle Ages.

The question of the state had therefore to be approached from a very different angle. The UN was aiming at 'rebuilding' some kind of a Somali state—which had never existed prior to colonisation—in order to be able to restore Somalia to the system of nation-states, which has been the very basis of the UN idea since 1945. The UN was the only actor in the confused Somali situation of 1992–5 pursuing this goal for its own sake. Somali warlords had nothing against something called 'the state' provided they could control it and use it to plunder the rural areas by force while siphoning off large amounts of 'foreign aid'. But they had no interest in a real 'state', an abstract entity devoted to public administration and especially to socio-economic management. So they fought alongside or against the UN inasmuch as they saw the UN helping them or preventing them from furthering their own business goals. Previously they had fought among themselves in 1991–2, when they still thought that they could re-create and control a 'state' entity as it had existed in the Siad Barre days, i.e. a wealth-pumping machine. But by the end of UNOSOM 2, most of the warlords realised that there would not be any 'state' to conquer and rule in the foreseeable future even if some kind of order was needed to carry out their activities.

With the departure of UNOSOM the strength of the factions, weakened since the UN money which was used as their financial base, had vanished. They were now left with the necessity of establishing a mutually acceptable way of doing business. As Menkhaus and Prendergast aptly wrote: 'It would not be too inaccurate to compare these initiatives to a meeting of the heads of Mafia families in New York City.'[3] These two authors called this 'the radical localization of Somali politics'. The following factors were involved:

- the weakening of the state-conquering factions after UNOSOM 2 left;
- the birth of a new group of pirate entrepreneurs (purely on the southern flank of Puntland);
- an upsurge in trade in Somalia;
- a lack of interest in the re-establishment of a 'normal' state; and
- a multi-lateralisation of local networks of business control, especially in the various coastal harbours. Kismayo was the main prize, since the reopening of the Mogadishu harbour looked like an impossible dream.[4]

This was the 'southern' situation to which Somaliland had to adapt. In Somaliland, on the other hand, the whole effort of civil society was geared at re-establishing a state, meaning of course a Somaliland state and not an overall pan-Somali state. Those with money (usually very little) among the businessmen sought to back their clan in an attempt at achieving control, or at least in supporting its influence in the new state they envisaged. This is a key point: the populations of Somaliland had had their fill of violence from an avowedly pan-Somali state and they did not want that type of authority any more. The Siad Barre dictatorship after 1978 had been a joint venture controlled by a consortium of Darood clans, mostly the Marehan, Ogadeni and Dhulbahante. Somaliland, being a product of the SNM struggle, was mostly an affair run by the Issaq clan family. But the Somaliland regional experience had been so brutal and so destructive that the clanic entrepreneurship system held little attraction. Fighting for control, after the brief period of civil strife in 1992–5, was a non–starter. Apprentice warlords soon found that even their own Issaq sub-clan would be loath to support them. They might gain influence, but any attempt at overall control would produce a reaction.

Somaliland nationalism was based on federating clanic ambitions and setting limits, including for members of the dominant Issaq clan family. This became obvious during the period of the Ahmed Mohamed 'Silanyo' presidency (2010–17), when power escaped from the hands of the ailing President into the control of a palace camarilla. Then, for a brief period in 2016, the danger of illegal action and violence became a possibility. Previously, during the whole 1995–2010 period, I had periodically obtained 'secret reports' from the French Intelligence in Djibouti predicting some imminent uprising. These might have been real, fake or, even more probably, both, i.e. concocted by genuine French sources but unofficially, most likely at the behest of the Djibouti authorities.[5] The uprising was always supposed to take place among the 'Samaron tribe', i.e. the two Somali clans best known to the Djibouti-based French.[6] The tone was vaguely anti-British, with 'Somaliland' being a kind of metonym for perfidious Albion. The uprisings never happened, however much it may have been wished for in Djibouti. Regardless of the tensions between the Issaq clans and the Dir in the west (Gaddabursi) or the Darood in the east (Dhulbahante, Warsangeli), who had all or in part fought against the SNM,[7] there were clashes—especially in the east—but never widespread fighting.[8]

(b) Puntland

The north-east is nearly homogeneously populated by Darood of the Majerteen clan.[9] Of course, the fissiparous tendencies of Somali clan politics were at work there as anywhere else, with the main tensions being between the Omar Mahmood, the Issa Mahmood and the Osman Mahmood, the three main Majerteen sub-clans. The other smaller sub-clans, such as Ali Gibrail, Siwakroon or Ali Suleiman, located in the extreme north of the country, did not have an independent political position. Since the end of the anti-Siad Barre civil war, the north-east had regained a relative peace. The only fighting that took place occurred in early 1992, when the SSDF strongman, Colonel Yusuf Abdullahi,[10] expelled the radical Islamist group linked to al-Ittihad,[11] which had taken over the north-eastern 'capital' and main harbour of Bosaso.

After Yusuf had retaken control of the Bosaso region, he began to extend his influence over the Majerteen areas that he had controlled in his days at the head of the SSDF. The border problem with Somaliland came from the Dhulbahante, who were theoretically part of the former British colony but were in fact quite autonomous from both the Majerteen and the Issaq. During the war the Dhulbahante general Ahmed Suleiman 'Dafle', longtime boss of the National Security Service (NSS), had committed massive atrocities and survived the conflict. He had recruited not only rank-and-file can-non fodder for the war against the SNM but also 'special operative members' of NSS who were Dhulbahante. Because of the usual clanic (and, in this case, sub-clanic) solidarity, a whole segment of the clan was both fearful of, and hostile to, the victorious SNM. Therefore the place of the Dhulbahante within the newly seceding state was far from easy. For Yusuf this provided a useful 'social hinge' with neighbouring Somaliland if only he could restore his control over the Majerteen.

In February 1998 a large *shir* had started in Garowe, assembling all the populations of the north-east. It was in essence very much the equivalent of what had happened in Borama for the north-west and in a similar vein it aimed at state creation. Thus, on 27 July 1998, Puntland was born, with a cabinet named on 18 August and a parliament 'elected' on 16 September.[12] Behind all this was Abdullahi Yusuf managing his old SSDF network. This created a crucial difference with Somaliland, which can still be felt in today's Puntland: the democratic factor was much weaker than at Borama. Of course, Mohamed Egal had also relied on influence networks at Borama but he had had to 'win over' the gathering of a guerrilla movement of which he had never even been a member, or cause people to overlook the fact that he had been very much party to the disastrous 1960 Somalia fusion, whose consequences the SNM had had to fight. In Garowe, on the contrary, Abdullahi Yusuf was a bit of a Frankenstein, trying his best to make the audience look away from the persistent scars of his catastrophic leadership of SSDF. And now that he had created that new entity, he carefully refrained from imitating Somaliland and proclaimed its independence.

Puntland was a country in everything but name, even if its new President pretended to keep it within the 'Somalia' fold, thereby cleverly isolating it from the rigidity of the international system and from pan-Somali national-ism. Thus the birth of Puntland was a double-barrelled threat to Somaliland, which was all too aware of its intentions. Incidentally why could the Somalilanders not accept what had happened? Having been in Somaliland in those days, I tend to think that the cause was emotional. The origins of the SNM rebellion had been so deep-seated, and their eventual consequences so brutal, that in Bura'o in 1991 emotions were stronger than hard-headed politi-cal calculations. Declaring formal independence was, of course, a tactical mistake, which ended up exacting a huge price in the long run. Puntland could sit out the warlord anarchy of the 1990s and the later Ethiopian invasion of 2006, all the while benefiting from a discreet and unquestionable legal status, for what it was worth, till 2009. But bad as the anti-Majerteen repression of 1978–80 had been, it never reached the apocalyptic dead end of 1988 in the north. The Majerteen had been savaged but not destroyed, and there had been an end to it. The Issaq had been in a different situation, at the receiving end of an attempted genocide, and like many genocide survivors, they were haunted by the thought that 'they wanted us all dead'. This may appear to be a fine point unless one has witnessed it at first hand. The impact of the action can be seen in the depth of the scars it has caused. In both cases the perpetrators of the violence had been the very promoters, advocates and defenders of a policy of wilful unity and brotherly reunion. In both cases the effect had been atrocities and mass murder. But it could be said that the Majerteen answer to Mogadishu's violence was a kind of Melvillian 'I would prefer not to' while the Issaq answer was 'not over my dead body'.

Another factor in the different attitudes towards independence was the relationship with the south. In 1991 the main southern warlord was Mohamed Farah Aydid, who was an ally and supporter of SNM (he had even asked SNM for troops to help him conquer the south). As long as he was alive and as long as he was a major player in the south, a door remained half open for some sort of an Issaq return to the notion of a unitary state. But by 1998 he was dead.[13] He had been a pretender to a 'national' position and now, with the progressive growth of Ethiopian influence over what had been 'Somalia', it was Abdullahi Yusuf who inherited his pole position in the race towards a possible restoration of a centralised government. And there had never been any strategic alliance or, even less, sympathy between and him the SNM.

Ethiopia had supported the SNM only because it was part of its anti-Siad Barre strategy. But historically Ethiopia had been a threatening rival ever since it conquered the Ogaden in 1887, a position it reiterated in 1946–7 when it used British acquiescence to annex the Hawd. An Ethiopia-supported neighbour was the last thing a fledgling, unrecognised 'secessionist' state needed, especially as the Somalia cockpit was now overflowing with successors for Aydid's leading role, including his own son Hussein, who had first come to Somalia in a US Marines uniform.[14] This was the beginning of 'the time of the warlords', undoubtedly the lowest point in the history of the Somali since the Second World War. Not only was the south skinned alive by the predators but the explosion of a new conflict between Ethiopia and Eritrea—hitherto apparently good allies since the fall of the communist military regime—soon drew the still bleeding country into a secondary theatre of operations in that foreign conflict.

Secession[15] is a protective word: Failed conferences, foreign war and the warlord anarchy

Meanwhile, various efforts had been made to try to give more flesh to the bare bones of the Somaliland declaration of independence. On 10 April 1995 a 'founding congress' opened in Hargeisa.[16] Half-way between a traditional *shir* and a Western-type congress, it lasted till 6 May and dealt with the essentials: laying down the plans for a (very lean) administration, appointing a cabinet and negotiating local peace agreements to put an end to clan fighting. The first cabinet had been an emergency affair, slapped together at the behest of Mohamed Ibrahim Egal. But he was conscious of its unbalanced clanic composition, and it was reshuffled in September to accommodate non-Issaq (Dhulbahante, Warsangeli, Gaddabursi) and even ministers from Issaq sub-clans which were poorly represented in a Habr Awal-heavy government.[17]

Accommodating the Dhulbahante was probably the most important point. That large Darood clan had been the northern bridgehead for Siad Barre during the war against the Issaq, and now it was a hinge group in respect of neighbouring Puntland. The nomination of Mohamed Salah Nur 'Fagadeh' as Minister of Foreign Affairs went a long way to improving things. This former communist and trade union activist was both a Dhulbahante and a Somaliland patriot. He knew that in Laas Anod he was in a foreign country and he acted accordingly, interpreting 'foreign affairs' in a very broad perspective.

In early 1996 the Somaliland Army retook Bura'o from Habr Yunis militiamen (Issaq) supported by a group of Habr Gidir (Hawiye) from the south.[18] In a typical Somali situation, the southerners were not 'fighting against secession'—they probably could not care less—but they had matrimonial or kinship ties with their Habr Yunis comrades.

Somaliland was slowly extracting itself from the Somali quagmire, but too slowly and without the proper legal tools. Its financial situation was such that the Berbera harbour remained the one cash cow and milking it (improvements at the time were financially unthinkable) only brought in about $30,000 per day, a drop in the ocean, helping to finance only 40 per cent of an already meagre budget.[19] Another Borama was in order but the means (and the time) were not available. So Sheikh Yusuf Ali Sheikh Madar called for a congress of clans to prepare for the constitution;[20] his SNM record and, perhaps more importantly, his belonging to a very respected and prestigious lineage having allowed him to do so.

The death of Aydid had been an ambiguous blessing for Somaliland. The most resolute and capable southern political leader, whom the UN ended up using as an ally after fighting him for years, was no more. The time of the warlords had now begun in earnest, something which deflated the centralist pressure on Somaliland (the warlords had no interest in a purely legalistic construction) but also increased the anarchy in the south. The international community organised a series of conferences which the cynical participants took as a joke and an occasion for a holiday.

> The recent meetings in Cairo for a peace conference have been dashed again ... the discussions were dominated by petty issues such as who should host the next conference. Since the fall of Siad Barre six major conferences have been held in neighbouring countries.[21] The whole essence is to make the international community pay for holiday trips for the Somali warlords. And the cruel irony is that after each conference the warlords agree to meet again in a country with better hotel facilities. Djibouti, Ethiopia, Kenya, Saudi Arabia, Egypt ... What next? America?[22]

But soon the international community had more important matters to address in the Horn of Africa: on 6 May 1998 Eritrea attacked Ethiopia on a pretext.[23] This caused a new and major war to develop, which was not without impact on Somalia.

Since Ethiopia had long been considered by every clan or party in Somalia to be the hereditary enemy, the Eritreans prepared the ground to further their plan.[24] On 13 February both Ali Mahdi and Hussein Aydid declared to the Italian envoy, in a rare show of unanimity, that Ethiopia was Somalia's main enemy. Almost immediately Aydid started to receive large arms shipments by boat through Marca and by plane to Balidogle, which he was supposed to use to support the 'new' United Oromo People Liberation Front (UOPLF), basically a rehash of Siad Barre's old WSLF. In the opposite camp the Ethiopians gave weapons to their old friend Yusuf Abdullahi, to the Rahanweyn Resistance Army (RRA) and to the USC–PM. There were so many weapons on the market that the price of guns dropped.[25] But since there was no central government, the RRA could attack Aydid's forces, bringing the Ethiopian–Eritrean war directly onto Somali soil.

In many ways things were back to 1977. The old rebel leader Wako Gutu arrived in Mogadishu[26] and was soon to head an Oromo column and attack Ethiopia from Gedo, with Eritrean support. The Asmara regime also sent agents to Hargeisa where they tried to convince Egal to join the conflict. But given the history of Ethiopian support for SNM during the anti-Siad Barre campaigns, their delegation's reception was lukewarm. Somaliland was wise to keep away from that hornet's nest. Indeed, things soon got worse when

SNF factions started to fight each other in an attempt to pillage some of the Eritrean shipments. Kenya closed its border and the Ethiopian Army entered.[27] This was the high point of what the Somali on the coast called *mussoqmassuq* (mishmash, or clanic anarchy). Somaliland resolutely headed the other way when its parliament approved (on 12 May 1999) a resolution allowing for multi-party democracy 'provided [parties] are not based on religion or clan politics'. When the UN information service interviewed President Egal a few days later, he answered tongue-in-cheek: 'We have had a different colonial experience than those around us and it has stood us in good stead until now.'[28]

In the south the Ethiopians had taken Lugh with the help of a friendly SNF faction[29] and Garbahaarey from an unfriendly one.[30] In the US, Senator Donald Payne (Democrat, New Jersey) was lobbying for the organisation of yet another 'peace conference', but this time in Hargeisa, in the hope of preventing Somaliland from falling into the Ethiopian–Eritrean war pit. Strangely enough, this effort indirectly helped the Islamists to gain ground. After the withdrawal of the Restore Hope forces, various strands of Islamist-leaning groups began to reorganise and coordinate themselves geographically.[31] In the confusion, they looked for some kind of arrangement between their conflicting political interests and their partially converging business ones. Only God could be the umpire of business conflicts, and so the Islamists—from the mildest to the most radical—started to set up legal courts along Shari'ah lines. Their armed branch was separate from their legal organisation. Ali Mahdi had been the first to introduce Islamic law (Shari'ah courts) in the north Mogadishu area and thereby managed to instil a minimum of law and order in his zone.

The Ifka Halane court organised a face-to-face debate between Hussein Aydid and Ali Mahdi; it then cleared all the roadblocks obstructing access to Mogadishu from the north, at a time when Aydid was importing new Oromo guerrilla fighters as back-up for his troops and when Ethiopian agents were killing isolated Oromo in the streets of Mogadishu.[32] Aydid refused to even contemplate a peace conference in Hargeisa, justifying his position by a commitment to Somalia's unity and arguing that President Egal's trip to Washington had not unblocked things.[33]

Somalia finally gets a government and the situation worsens

In December 1999 an IGAD summit in Djibouti devoted to 'peace in Somalia' came out with a resolution calling for an initiative to establish a government. The result was to trigger a large anti-initiative rally from the Islamic Court Union in Mogadishu. Somaliland, which this time felt a threat closer at hand than usual (Djibouti President Ismail Omar Guelleh was a Somali 'centralist'), immediately closed its border with Djibouti. In Bay province, the Rahanweyn leader 'Shattigudud' proclaimed the 'administrative autonomy' of his region while the European Union disparaged the whole idea, saying: 'The famous Djibouti initiative appears to be an empty playing board onto which the various regional actors are putting their pieces.'[34]

The regional powers moved quickly: the Oromo (Ethiopian) OLF rebels were kicked out of Mogadishu, and Ethiopian troops crossed the border to hit al-Ittihad Islamist rebels in Goldogob (on 4 January 2000). Egal, who had attended the Djibouti meeting, declared upon his return to Hargeisa: 'We will go to war if attempts are made by outside parties to unite Somaliland with the Somali factions.'[35] When Gaddafi, who trusted Egal's secular political approach, sent him a memo suggesting that he should offer to become a reunited Somalia's first President, Egal refused.[36] The Arta conference opened in Djibouti on 2 May 2000 with strong international community support.[37]

> Twelve warlords' conferences failed because their signatories could not implement the measures they had signed. President Omar Guelleh made direct contact with the major clan groups ... he was very harsh with the warlords and this produced an immediate response with the Somali people; there was tremendous enthusiasm inside Somalia; so this is not a Western process of card-carrying party members or anything like that. It is a very Somali process ... the elders have come forward in terms of delegations ... this is where the question of fraction leaders will come up ... the actual formation of the delegations will be a crucial step in the next few weeks ... the idea is to have elections within two years ... it is too early to know what the warlords will do. If the clans bring them into the delegations, they will have a role to play. But this will be a political process, not one based on the force of arms.[38]

This is an interesting document both for what it says and what it doesn't say. It admits that all the conferences held for the previous five years were a waste of time, but this was not because the warlords could not keep their word. The basic reason was that the warlords, the very people asked to rebuild a state, were those who had destroyed it and could expect no benefits from its return. It also seemed to give a wide responsibility to 'elders' without actually understanding how the *shir* system worked. Why would these 'elders' (chosen by whom?) bring in 'warlords' unless it was in their clan interest? In any case, regardless of the warlords' presence, the UN position was that 'this will be a political process, not one based on the force of arms'. Blind faith seemed stronger than past experience. This was a Canada Dry conference: it looked like a *shir*, it cost more than a *shir* (after all, the UN was paying) but it was not a *shir* for the basic reason that all the arrangements were top down rather than bottom up. It was not a way of gathering contradictory evidence and then trying to reach a consensus but rather a way—once more—to jerrybuild a structure and ask public opinion to climb aboard. It was an attempt at aping a traditional process but it was synthetic rather than organic.

So it immediately started to wobble as soon as the Interim Charter (adopted on 17 July) decided to assign the seats of the Transitional National Assembly (TNA): 44 seats for each of the four main clan families—Dir, Hawiye, Darood, Digil-Mirifle—plus 24 for the 'minorities' and 25 for 'women' (as if the 'women' had no clan). The TNA was neither a one-man one-vote parliament nor a clanic Senate like the Somaliland *Guurti*, but a questionable combination supposed to work in lieu of a popular election. The Transitional National Government (TNG) was inaugurated on 14 August (and rejected by the warlords on the 15th).[39] Eleven days later the unperturbed TNG elected Abdiqassim Salad Hassan, who had been the last Interior Minister of Siad Barre and had only left at the fall of the dictator and lived as a refugee in Cairo.[40] In an evaluation of the results of the Arta conference,[41] Somalia specialist Ken Menkhaus coolly listed all the warlords, militias and clan organisations that had joined in the rejection of the TNA. It certainly did not give them an alternative majority but it added up to a mass opposition. Menkhaus also offered several alternative scenarios to the TNA–Salad Hassan 'government'; the only credible one was a government that could stem from a federation of Islamist organisations. Though heads were shaken in doubt, in those pre-9/11 days it did not yet seem like such a threatening idea.

How did Somaliland then react to the Arta process? Basically, it did not. The northern drummer was playing to a different beat, and it had meanwhile passed a law authorising political pluralism.[42] Egal declared: 'This conference has nothing to do with us because it calls for reconciliation and we don't have to reconcile with anyone.'[43] The new TNG President picked a combat cabinet, replete with members of Puntland and Somaliland clans, hoping to undermine the existing separate states. This included the new Prime Minister, Ali Khalif Galaydh, a Dhulbahante, and the Minister of Foreign Affairs, Ismail Mohamed Hurre 'Buuba', a Habr Yunis Issaq. But there was a discrepancy between this resolute attitude and reality. The President went to an Arab League meeting in Cairo[44] and asked for troops, particularly from Egypt and Libya, who had supported Siad Barre since 1977 and the war with Ethiopia. The League did not refuse but did nothing. Egal wrote to the UN Special

Envoy: 'I am following through the Internet your efforts to secure for Abdulqassim and his group international support and credibility ... But if you were to be successful you would only be sowing the seeds of civil war.'[45]

In fact, neither Somaliland nor Puntland did anything to oppose the flimsy 'government' which had issued from the Arta conference. The southern Somalia public had welcomed the 'President' but there were two radical forms of opposition: one was 'federalist'—the Rahanweyn had proclaimed their autonomy and so had Hiiran province—but the other was violent and came from the warlords: several TNA MPs were shot dead during November and there was an attempt on the President's life (on 15 December). Musa Sudi Yalahow attacked the government's 'army' head-on since the warlord had more troops than the government. Egal tried to take advantage of the TNG's poor performance but the UN declared: 'The commitment to the unity and territorial integrity of Somalia was reaffirmed by the Security Council in its Presidential Statement dated 11 January [2001].'

At around the same time civil society associations began opening mass graves dating back to 1988

> but the United Nations flatly refused to provide funds for investigating those ... Why this reluctance? I have come to the conclusion that when this genocide was being carried out here in Hargeisa and all over Somaliland, the international community watched with apathy, nobody moved a finger to even object or condemn, let alone stop it. So I think it is a sort of guilty conscience. If these things were investigated, the guilt of those who stood by would be revealed.

At the same time as Egal was saying those words—to another UN branch[46]—he was organising a referendum on Somaliland's independence, which was held on 31 May 2001 and resulted in a 97.09 per cent 'yes' vote. (The TNG condemned the referendum as 'illegal'.) When assessing the way it was carried out, the UN had to recognise that 'it was conducted without violence and the international observers were impressed by the level of effort the government and the people put forth in seeing that the voting was conducted in a fair and open manner.'[47] Not a shot was fired in Somaliland during or after the independence referendum. During that same month of May, over 300 people were killed in the south as the TNG struggled to assert its existence. This did not cause any change in the international community's stance.

From an Islamist opportunity to the CIA coup

On 6 June the TNG announced that it had 'nationalised' the Union of Islamic Courts (UIC). This was wishful thinking. Apart from the international community, the TNG had limited autonomous support while the UIC had much more. Fighting immediately started between TNG and UIC supporters.[48] But the 9/11 al-Qaida New York attack had an immediate impact on the Somalia situation. On 7 November the US government decided to close down and seize the assets of the financial transfer service al-Barakat Hawala,[49] a measure which was bound to have a catastrophic impact on the precarious lives of the Somali diaspora worldwide since remittances represented a major means of survival for Somali people. Randolph Kent, the UN coordinator who was keenly aware of the problem, declared: 'Somalia is on the verge of an economic collapse unparalleled in modern history'. Following the al-Barakat closure, retail prices in Mogadishu went up 50 per cent. It was at the same time that the UNHCR decided to repatriate most of the Somaliland refugees still in Ethiopia. Around 70,000 still remained, and this was the worst time to send them back.[50] As I was living in Ethiopia at the time, I—as well as other expert colleagues—was repeatedly asked by the US authorities whether Somalia should be bombed in parallel with the attack on Afghanistan. We all argued against such a measure but the arguments—basically those presented in the first ten chapters of this book—were hard to summarise in immediately usable form. The key points were as follows:

- Al-Ittihad was a weak parent of al-Qaida and could not take power anywhere.
- In spite of Abdiqassim Salad Hassan's Islamist-friendly stance, the TNG was far from being an 'Islamist front'.
- In any case, what would you bomb? What were the strategic targets available?

The only person of sufficient political standing in Washington who could answer this question reasonably was Ted Dagne, director of the Africa Division of the Congressional Research Service (CRS),[51] who wrote: 'US officials are yet to present any proof of links between al-Ittihad, the TNG and al-Qaida.'[52] With this US panic as background, the warlords had a field day. Aden Abdullahi 'Gabiyow' bellowed from Addis Ababa, where he was trying to get Ethiopian support: 'Somalia has become a haven for terrorists ... There is no peace, no law and order, no nothing... our people are dying.'[53] Mohamed Said Hersi 'Morgan' took advantage of the atmosphere to attack Bardheere, while Musa Sudi Yalahow attacked Mahmood Mohamed 'Finnish', each assuming the role of an 'anti-terrorist' hero.

A CIA delegation visited Egal in Somaliland, looking for storage sheds to rent. Egal made encouraging noises but said Somaliland's help could only be obtained by diplomatic recognition. The CIA visitors were noncommittal. On 8 March the US Department of Defense held a public information meeting on 'The Terrorist Threat in the Horn of Africa', where 'a senior official' started his presentation by saying: 'for those not familiar, the Somalia we are talking about is in the Horn of Africa'. When asked about an al-Qaida presence in the Horn, he answered: 'I am not just really comfortable going into that level of detail ... Bin Laden has saluted the Somali ... Clearly it would be a place where it would be appropriate for al-Qaida members to go.' When asked why some states recognised the TNG while others didn't, the answer was: 'I can't tell you really. Well, it is a state anyway.' A journalist commented: 'We could have gotten more info reading a magazine.' The US Treasury, the Department of State and the CIA tripped over each other, saying that there were no links between al-Barakat and al-Qaida that the CIA could find (the Treasury still refused to allow al-Barakat to operate again), while Dahabshiil (another Hawala, bigger than al-Barakat) was allowed to operate freely. In early May the TNG was allowed to receive a shipment of arms from Asmara comprising anti-tank weapons, which, in that context, could only be used against the Ethiopians (nobody else in the battle had tanks).[54] The official confusion was splendid.

On 3 May 2002 President Mohamed Ibrahim Egal died of natural causes and was constitutionally succeeded by Vice-President Daher Riyale Kahin. On 8 October the new Somaliland President was ambushed in Laas Anod on orders from the Deputy Interior Minister of Puntland, Ahmed Aden. He was wounded and four of his retinue were killed. Ahmed Aden declared: 'We are fighting for the unity of Somalia.'

The unity of Somalia was, meanwhile, entrusted to the former Kenyan diplomat Bethwel Kiplagat, who announced that he wanted to 'work this out through consensus, persuasion and humour'. He would need that last quality in droves. The TNG was becoming more and more irrelevant and yet another a new conference was convened in the Nairobi suburb of Mbagathi to try once more to come up with a half-legitimate government. Its make-up was still based on the old Arta formula of the four clan families plus a smattering of women and minorities, 275 MPs in all, and once again it lacked legitimacy given the selection process.

Somaliland had just had a new presidential election to confirm Daher Riyale Kahin, who had been an interim President since the death of Egal. This was a difficult election since Riyale Kahin was a Gaddabursi—a clan allied with Siad Barre during the war—and he had even been an army Secret Service operative. That did not make him a very popular candidate and he won by only 80 votes out of an electorate of about 500,000. His opponent was the veteran SNM Issaq politician Ahmed Mohamed 'Silanyo', who was furious and asked for a recount. In the recount, Riyale Kahin's victory was confirmed by a very slim margin (185 votes). This forced the Issaq elders to intervene to make that thin margin good enough for the victory of a double outsider to be accepted. But the public feeling was that, since impeccable democratic credentials were so important for the overall fate of the country, the elders' opinion should prevail. The paper-thin recount was accepted but the Islamists loosed their biggest terrorist attack on what they now perceived as a weak regime. The murder targets were all foreign and all those arrested were linked to al-Qaida. They all came from the south.

This pattern was paradoxical because, as the Islamists resorted to terrorism in Somaliland, they developed an increasingly popular—and mostly peaceful—network of action in the south. The prime *raison d'être* of the Union of Islamic Courts (UIC) was to enforce business contracts in a country which had no more courts, no practising lawyers and no police, and it succeeded fairly well. So, little by little, the UIC encroached on other tasks: protecting money changers, guarding health facilities, enforcing neighbourhood security and even removing garbage; in other words, step by step and in an informal way, the tasks of a state. And this took place at a time when the ghost of a state, supported by the international community, looked more and more irrelevant: the rump assembly had voted to bar members without secondary education from becoming MPs.[55] Moreover, 160 'delegates' trying to devise the new authority were kicked out of the Nairobi Hilton because nobody agreed to pay their bills.[56] Finally, in October 2004, former warlord Abdullahi Yusuf was 'elected' by the 'delegates' as 'President'. He immediately asked for the dispatch of 20,000 Blue Helmets and declared: 'We are not a government in exile.'

At the same time, while the 'new TNG' was painfully trying to exist,[57] Somaliland organised parliamentary elections, still hoping to play the card of democratic institutionalisation. An al-Qaida team came from the south to disrupt the process but they fell into an ambush, and were arrested after a gunfight in which four of them were wounded.[58] The attack had no local impact and changed nothing internationally. In Mogadishu, the reality of power was increasingly passing into the hands of the UIC, which was forcefully trying to present itself as completely distinct from al-Qaida or al-Ittihad.[59] The security situation in the capital had become catastrophic and Yusuf knew he could not go to Mogadishu to establish his government; so he took Baidoa as a shelter capital instead.[60]

This deliquescence of the Somalia 'government' and rise of the UIC caused a growing unease in Washington, where some elements of the Bush administration were still frustrated at not having attacked Somalia after 9/11. They found ready partners among the Somali warlords who wanted to resist any stabilisation of the situation.[61] A group of self-proclaimed 'armed ministers' led by Mohamed Qanyare Afrah wrote to the UN to ask it not to lift the embargo on military equipment because they were afraid that Abdullahi Yusuf and the TFG would then be the only force allowed to obtain 'legal' weapons. On 18 February 2006, once the 'armed ministers' had secured CIA support, they created the Alliance for the Restoration of Peace and Counter-Terrorism (ARPCT). This 'organisation' was basically a band of thugs whose main role was to try to eliminate the UIC. But they enjoyed barely concealed US support. On 20 March they attacked in an action that looked exactly like an illustration of the title of a recent International Crisis Group report.[62] Many in Mogadishu who knew only too well who these 'restorers of peace' were rushed to help the UIC. Most of these volunteers had no special ideological sympathy for the Islamists but they nevertheless picked up their guns to help them. The fighting was heavy (over 200 killed and 344 wounded) and the sole beneficiaries were the UIC forces.[63] US diplomat Michael Zorick, who had dared to criticise the piteous ARPCT attempt, was transferred to Chad,[64] and the State Department refused to answer Somalia Prime Minister Ali Mohamed Gedi when he tried to contact Washington.[65]

By mid-June the UIC was in full control of Mogadishu, to the satisfaction of the public. But it had created the Supreme Islamic Coordination Council (SICC), which was quickly turning into an embryonic government rivalling the TFG. Up to then the UIC courts had mostly been composed of Hawiye of the Habr Gidir sub-clan and Ayr sub-sub-clan and limited to Mogadishu proper. But now the new courts were becoming local, and their composition and ideology changed. The rallying of volunteers to their side caused them to misjudge public opinion and believe they now enjoyed majority support. They spread all over Benadir and migrated north, occupying Harardheere and Obyo. Somaliland was not worried and said so.[66] But the Ethiopians were. Foreign Affairs Minister Seyum Mesfin flew to Baidoa and persuaded Yusuf to reduce his cabinet to 31 ministers while Ethiopian troops entered Somalia through Balambale. There had been 11 courts by early 2006 and by September there were 40. Among those, only three could be considered 'radical', while the others were, in the public's eye, 'the best government we ever had since the fall of Siad Barre'.[67]

But the youth branch—Harakat al-Shabaab al-Mujahideen, led by the young fighter Aden Hashi 'Ayro'—had acquired a growing autonomy from the UIC, and the Supreme Islamic Coordination Council began to turn into a projection of al-Shabaab. In August it managed to reopen both the airport and the harbour, which had been closed for fifteen years, and sent troops as far as Kismayo, which it took without a fight. For a while it seemed that the Islamists had finally managed to do what everybody else had failed to achieve: create a reasonably popular national government where this was feasible. But this was without taking the Ethiopian government into account. For Ethiopia the fundamental problem was not the UIC but rather the support it had begun to receive from Asmara. Eritrean hostility to the EPRDF regime was frontal, and help had begun to arrive for the UIC—and especially for its Shabaab offshoot—ever since Abdullahi Yusuf was 'elected' President of the TFG. The Ethiopians deployed their army around Baidoa (2 October) and the radicals of al-Shabaab proclaimed jihad (9 October 2006), in spite of the opposition of Sheikh Sharif Sheikh Ahmed. The Shabaab attacked on 20 December and Meles Zenawi was pleased to be in a position to 'fight back' rather than invade.[68] A week later the Ethiopian Army, piggybacked by some TFG troops, entered Mogadishu. Ten days before that, the UN had passed Resolution 1724 creating the IGAD Peace Mission in Somalia (IGASOM), providing a universal fig leaf for what had become, in fact, a Western war against Islam.[69]

Was the Ethiopian invasion part of a fantasised clash of civilisations?

With Iraq and Afghanistan also in the picture, the resemblance to a clash of civilisations was strong but misleading. This was because the motivation for the Ethiopian intervention in Somalia was at least as much the support Eritrea gave to the UIC as the UIC itself. In the meantime, the TFG had blown whatever credibility it ever had by allying itself with the hated foreign invaders.[70] Groups of Eritrean soldiers and international mujahideen fleeing the Ethiopian onslaught were caught together at the Kenya border as they fled southwards and secretly detained.[71] Meanwhile, the official US war effort focused on Somalia as its latest field of operations and put its propaganda machine to work:

> the grassroots effort is needed in Somalia. The population ... needs to feel a
> genuine sense of empowerment, a sense of ownership and responsibility ... it can

be achieved for only $27 million per month but no funding has gone directly to the TFG currently trying to stave off the well-funded al-Qaida offensive ... Meanwhile, in Somalia men are grabbing their weapons to fight a vicious al-Qaida on the front lines of the War on Terror without uniforms, without boots and without so much as a canteen. We should be ashamed of ourselves.[72]

In this new alignment of forces, where the weak TFG was supposed to represent the bulwark of civilisation against the Islamist hordes,

the United States is using surrogate nations and financial aid to prevent Somalia from slipping further into chaos ... The U.S. has vowed to support an African Union peacekeeping force and has trained elements of the Ethiopian Army which toppled Somalia's anti-American Islamic government.[73]

Owing to global mismanagement of the situation, Somalia had become 'a failed state that threatens the region',[74] and about 100,000 refugees had fled the capital. The African Union decided to send another 8,000 troops,[75] and Somaliland remained determined to keep away from the organised mayhem:

Unable or unwilling to deal with the countless problems facing them, Somalia's politicians have resorted to creating a fictitious world ... a good example is the oft-delayed 'Somali Reconciliation Conference' that is supposed to take place in Mogadishu in June. Instead of bringing together the real antagonists in Somalia ... President Abdullahi Yusuf, P.M. Ali Gedi and Ali Mahdi, the conference organizer, have opted to bring together carefully selected tribal elders who will rubber-stamp their agenda. Things have gotten so farcical that Ali Mahdi is talking about inviting elders from Somaliland to participate in his Mogadishu jamboree ... Can anyone in his right mind believe that these people are going to do anything for Somaliland when they have failed so miserably in fixing their own problems? .... Their towns and villages are being occupied and bombarded by foreign troops and you would think that their first priority would be how to get their own house in order. But no, they would rather waste their time and poke their noses into Somaliland's affairs.[76]

Doubts began to enter US minds as well: 'Well, it begins to seem like the invasion was all tactics and no strategy; we overthrew Somalia's first working government in fifteen years and replaced it with, hmmm ... nothing.'[77] Jendayi Frazer, US Assistant Secretary of State for African Affairs, had considered in late 2006 that 'the demise of the Somalia TFG would have a major negative impact on the Horn of Africa'; but by mid-2007 she was much less sure, saying, 'it is hard to tell whether the situation is now better or worse than it was when Ethiopian troops, with the full backing of Washington, stormed Mogadishu'.[78] Other US diplomats who knew Somalia better had less hesitation: 'Our attitude has been to consider the confrontation as one between us, the West, and radical Islam. This is not the real Somalia equation. It was a confrontation between a majority Darood government and a Hawiye Habr Gidir opposition that rallied behind the Islamic Courts. But we read it according to our own outlook and [US Ambassador] Ranneberger[79] is not really up on that kind of thing.'[80]

Eritrean President Issayas Afeworqi remained in the shadows since he could not fit neatly into the clash of civilisations. The security situation kept worsening—and masses of refugees kept fleeing the fighting, particularly from Mogadishu and Benadir, from where 173,000 refugees had fled by September, doubling the Dadaab camp population in Kenya. Somaliland feared that the US and Ethiopian forces could push into Puntland and bring the war to eastern Somaliland.[81] It reacted by widening its western perimeter and (re-)occupied Laas Anod in September. In Hargeisa many were conscious that Daher Riyale Kahin was hoping to benefit from the mess in the south and postpone the next elections. New, harsher press laws were passed and mildly disrespectful journalists from the Qaran website were illegally arrested.[82] Ryale Kahin went to Addis Ababa and tried to convince Meles Zenawi that he and his UDUB party were the only true friends of Ethiopia, even asking if he would be ready to send troops to Somaliland in case of a Kulmiye victory.[83] Meles, who did not fear anything from Somaliland, prudently refused and said that Ethiopia's alliance with Somaliland was with a state and not a party.[84] This did not stop Issayas from trying to form the anti-TFG exiles in Eritrea into an anti-Ethiopia alliance. This 'alliance' was born in mid-September in Asmara under the name of the Alliance for the Re-Liberation of Somalia (ARLS). Since there were now two camps, the new ARLS forces—in fact, the old UIC—attacked Ugandan AMISOM troops.[85] ARLS was erratically anti-Ethiopian—mostly in the same way the US was blindly pro-Ethiopian. Though the clash of civilisations was lost in the fog, the clash of regional geopolitics was very much there.

Since the nucleus of the ARLS was just a refurbished UIC, that meant that the ARLS was also, just like the UIC before, divided between radicals and moderates. The Eritreans did not manage to control 'their' Somali, resulting in the ARLS splitting in two. The moderates, led by Sheikh Sharif Sheikh Ahmed, left Asmara and went to Djibouti. The Islamists and their radical leader Mukhtar Robow remained in Asmara and refused to accept the evacuation agreement signed in Addis Ababa in October 2008, seamlessly flowing into a permanent insurgency against the TFG known as Harakat al-Shabaab al-Mujahideen (Movement of the Fighting Youth), which is still violently active at the time of writing.[86]

In Kenya, the Dadaab refugee camp had reached a population of 230,000, half of them new arrivals during the previous eight months. On 29 December 2008 President Abdullahi Yusuf resigned from the TFG and in January 2009 former UIC chairman Sheikh Sharif Sheikh Ahmed was chosen to replace him, belatedly reconciling civilisation and geopolitics. On 19 March, Usama bin Laden, who seemed to have missed the proper distinctions, called for the overthrow of the new 'Islamist' President, considering the former UIC chairman to be a traitor. Even the Islamist camp became in turn prey to the typical Somali *mussoqmassuq* (clanic mishmash). After Aden Hashi 'Ayro' was killed by a US drone, the Harakat al-Shabaab not only survived his death but multiplied its terrorist attacks. The new Shabaab leader, Ahmed Abdi 'Godane', who succeeded Ayro, was an Issaq of the Arap sub-clan who had failed to become a prophet in his native Somaliland. The second most important man in the Islamist insurgency was Mukhtar Robow 'Abu Mansur', a member of the very large and poorly regarded Rahanweyn clan family. Both men engaged in a fight for the control of the insurgency, Godane relying on the foreign jihadi while his rival sought the support of the native Somali fighters. At the time there were an estimated 2,500 Somali fighters in the ranks of the Shabaab plus another estimated 700 foreign jihadi.[87]

Facing them were the soldiers of the Somali Army—between 3,000 and 15,000, depending on how you counted them (their reliability was questionable)—and the much more solid 18,000 AMISOM forces (Ugandans, Burundians, Kenyans and Djiboutians), who made up the bulk of the TFG battle corps. There were also the Ethiopians, who by mid-2008 had 24,000 troops and who were not officially part of AMISOM although they received their budget through the African Union, which used funds from Brussels. But unlike their AMISON comrades, these Ethiopian forces answered only to the orders of their own staff officers. They were a foreign expeditionary corps rather than part of an international force.

The Godane–Robow conflict did more damage to the Shabaab than the clash of civilisations. By late 2007 the Ethiopians began to evacuate while the Transitional Federal Government tried to slowly ease itself into transitioning (it is still trying at the time of writing) and the 'official' Somali reality redefined itself under the new 'Federalist' label. This neither solved the Somalia contradictions nor brought any form of international support for peaceful Somaliland.

11

FROM SURVIVAL TO GLOBALISATION

WHAT IS THE NEED FOR A NATION-STATE
IN SOMALILAND?

The cost of survival: Somaliland, 2007–2020

A snapshot of the situation was given by Somaliland President Daher Riyale Kahin in 2007:

> It is too simple to say the T.F.G. has captured Somalia because ... Abdullahi Yusuf cannot come here. It is a daydream that he can come here and govern Hargeisa ... We cannot be one government any more. We made our final decision in 1991 not to be any longer part of that failed union.[1]

For years, Somaliland had had to face two dangers: a centralist threat from whoever was in control of Mogadishu and internal Islamist subversion. For years it had managed to live rather easily with both: those in control of Mogadishu (when anybody was in control) were short of means and had many other problems besides Somaliland on their list of worries; as for the Islamists, they existed more as an external irritant than as a home-grown problem. Ahmed Abdi 'Godane', the al-Shabaab leader, who was a Somaliland Issaq, was finally killed by a US drone strike in September 2014 without ever having managed to develop a Somaliland branch of his organisation. Getting the UIC out of the way and easing the Ethiopians out of Somalia altogether[2] had finally 're-set' the TFG in a reasonably acceptable position, at least on the international scene. But this did not change the terms of the confrontation with Hargeisa.

Somaliland remained independent even if it had begun to choke on its own independence. In 2015 Somaliland's immigration commissioner, Mohamed Ali Yusuf, declared: 'Each month, around three hundred people—mostly young men—leave Somaliland to migrate illegally to Europe.'[3] Somaliland was slowly losing its breath, losing what had been the vital energy that carried it through all the war years and the post-war restoration of peace. Before being a 'government', Somaliland had been a state of mind, a collective resolve to move together towards a better future. But the future had been too long in coming and it was now slowly going flat. Somalilanders under 20 years of age represented nearly three-quarters of the population and it was getting harder and harder for them to wait for a better future. Contrary to the late colonial years, the Greater Somalia dream had nothing to offer them anymore; it just stood for southern domination. The economy, starved of any foreign investment, was still centred on cattle exports and was running out of steam. Per capita income was estimated at around $430, one of the poorest rates in the world. Formal democracy was still wobbling along but it was on a course of diminishing returns.

The threat did not come from authoritarianism but rather from stagnation and decay. In April 2008 President Daher Riyale Kahin had asked for an extension of his presidential term, which the *Guurti* almost immediately granted. The following month all three political parties permitted by the Constitution agreed to meet within the framework of the Electoral Commission, reaching a consensus on scheduling local elections for 15 December 2008 and presidentials for 15 March 2009. But neither date was kept and the presidential election was delayed for more than a year. The reality was that the *Guurti* had turned into a kind of Somali version of the House of Lords. Members were chosen by clan origin and their seats were practically hereditary. The result was a highly conservative body whose decisions were linked to tightly knit clan and family interest groups. Business as usual meant, in fact, careful stagnation. The only important business which had some kind of a Somaliland 'stamp' was the biggest Hawala, Dahabshiil.[4] But its CEO, Abdirashid Duale, downplayed his Somaliland origin for fear of antagonising his many customers in other parts of the Somali world by appearing to back the 'secessionist' state. It was hardly an ideal for the youth.

Somaliland was alive but knew it looked weak and feared that this might be true. For the hard-line wing of the Alliance for the Re-Liberation of Somalia, which mixed old-style nationalism with Islamism, this political landscape seemed inviting and in late October 2008 it started a campaign of bombings in Hargeisa. As a result, 26 people were killed and several more wounded, but it had no real impact. From his Asmara sanctuary Hassan Dawer Aweys called frantically for 'attacks on the collaborators of the Jews and the Americans',[5] but for the Somaliland public that just made him sound like another Hawiye fanatic attacking them. Five of the six suicide bombers were from the south, so the propaganda war was lost before it had even started. Meanwhile, there were 27,000 refugees from the south living in Somaliland, but they were not a fifth column since they had no sympathy for what was snapping at their heels.

But even if the diplomatic campaign from Mogadishu had weakened and the radical Islamist terror attacks had almost immediately hit a dead end, this was no automatic compensation for the home-grown shortcomings. The economy remained shrunken, the youth frustrated and the *Guurti* partly paralysed. Somaliland lived in the hearts of its citizens and, strangely enough, in the eyes of the international community even if that same community perversely refused to turn attention into action and kept pouring money into the bottomless pit of the 'official South'. In 2012 the UN carried out an assessment and discovered that $130 million had been 'misplaced' since 2009 by Mogadishu.[6] In spite of strong comments from the UN, a similar report the following year noted that 80 per cent of the withdrawals from the Central Bank in Mogadishu were made for private purposes and were never accounted for. Still, this did not mean that the budgetary discipline of Somaliland earned it any favour in the eyes of the international community

Politically, there was much more slack. There had been postponements of the presidential election to the extreme limit permitted: first in April 2008, then in April 2009, and finally in October 2009. There were demonstrations (without repression), attempts at diplomatic blackmail,[7] even a bit of brinkmanship (Daher asked the Army Chief of Staff to bring troops to the capital but he refused, after a 24-hour delay spent in consulting elders). Finally, Daher bit the bullet and went to the polls where he lost, securing only 33 per cent of the vote, while his old opponent, Ahmed Mohamed 'Silanyo', scored a decent 49 per cent.[8] There were 1,080,000 registered voters on the recently updated lists of the Electoral Commission and the 70 international observers gave a clean bill of health to the electoral system. But all this was part of the constitutional aspect of matters, which had finally been safely handled. Politically things were much looser. The series of Daher-induced postponements had been nerve-grating and Silanyo had been the focus of very high expectations. But the man was 80 and he had gone through a lot of wear and tear. In addition, his victory was seen by the Issaq in general, and the Habr Ja'alo in particular, as payback after years of Gaddabursi power.

In reality, things were always going to run into difficulties. The first one was climatic: both 2011 and 2012 were years of massive drought. The price of cattle collapsed, exports plummeted, food was rationed, and the growth of al-Shabaab terrorism in the south drew in more refugees than could be accommodated.[9] The hopes that Silanyo's former diplomatic role would somehow secure Somaliland's recognition were to be disappointed, and new layers of corruption developed, centred around the questionable handling of government funds by private financial institutions. Dahabshiil grew into a shadow Ministry of Finance. In addition, the border problem with Puntland re-emerged and a small sub-clanic group of Dhulbahante proclaimed in 2012 a new 'autonomous administration' they called Khatumo, which took a chunk of eastern Somaliland out of Hargeisa's administration.

This contributed to a rekindling of the old Somaliland disease, postponing elections. The President's entourage, just like that of Daher before, thought that the presidency was a juicy morsel and that letting it go would be a mistake. Silanyo could at best work three hours a day, and then only with limited effectiveness. The elections scheduled for June 2015 were postponed and the Minister in the Presidency, Hersi Ali Haji Hassan, who had been progressively setting himself up as a powerful vizier to the ailing sultan, decided to go one step further. On 26 October 2015 he made his move and attempted a palace coup. Thirteen cabinet members resigned at the same time, and he contacted the Army Chief of Staff to see if he could get military backing. But this was refused and he resigned from the government. Why this refusal when the regime was visibly in shreds? First of all, there was what we could call 'the principle of democratic legitimacy', which had become part of the political currency since the SNM days. Moreover, Hersi's move was seen as an 'Islamist' coup. Hersi had family members who were in contact with al-Shabaab even if his dedication to their cause was unlikely. His main motivation seems to have been financial, though the Islamist tag remained stuck to his move. Within the Somaliland political context, this was a non-starter because the equation in the public mind was 'Islamists = southerners', or at least southern government supporters.

But the failure of the coup did not improve the image of the Silanyo administration, especially as it began postponing elections again. In May 2016 the regime had been seduced (or cornered) into signing a momentous contract with the UAE DP World company,[10] and staying in power meant more money for the entourage. New elections were tentatively rescheduled for March 2017. But in January 2017 the death in jail of Abdullahi Ali Barre caused massive demonstrations.[11] It felt as if the regime was sliding into the illegal behaviours that reminded the public of the Siad Barre years. But the recent vagaries had seriously hurt the prospects of the Kulmiye party at the polls and the main opposition party, Wadani, was hopeful about winning. Still, it had a problem as the former putschist, Hersi Ali Haji Hassan, had joined Wadani, adding an ambiguous message to the campaign. This message was in many ways subliminal and it was one to which Mogadishu was discreetly attuned.

Since the election of Hassan Sheikh Mahmood in 2012, the real power structure had shifted. Of course, the President's clan—Hawiye–Abgaal–Waysle—remained a key factor. But he had been surrounded by a previously unknown crowd of neatly dressed young men in dark suits from London, all members of the association ed-Dam al-Jadid (the New Blood). Ed-Dam al-Jadid was very close to the British Tory Party and, in a way, it could be seen as a nice, clean and politically correct Islamist branch of the Conservatives. They installed themselves in Somalia during the 2012 British attempt at saving Somalia through globalisation (of which more below) and stayed on. I remember trying to talk with some of them in my clumsy Somali. Two of them answered with a smile: 'Sorry, we don't speak Somali; but we are learning.' Both were London-born. When Hassan Sheikh left at the end of his mandate in 2017, they stayed on with President Abdullahi Mohamed 'Farmajo'. Having himself lived for 21 years in the United States, Farmajo appreciated their quickly acquired local knowledge and considered that this type of educated 'globalised' Islamist was the best local antidote to al-Shabaab. In his eyes, Hersi Ali Haji Hassan was their Somaliland equivalent and he tried his best to push Wadani towards victory, even going to the extent of asking the UN to destabilise Kulmiye and support the opposition. UN envoy Michael Keating wrote to the TFG president:

> I have presented your strategic initiative to our international partners and regretfully we have come to a unanimous decision not to support this effort. While stabilizing Somalia is our top priority we failed to grasp the logic of potentially destabilizing peaceful Somaliland by interfering in its local politics and favoring one candidate over the other.[12]

A few days later (on 14 October 2017) al-Shabaab carried out its largest terrorist attack ever in Somalia, causing 520 fatalities and over 1,000 wounded and creating a massive wave of emotion in the whole region. Meanwhile, in an ultimate act of homage to his own past, Silanyo—who decided not to stand for another mandate—had chosen the one candidate that the compromised camarilla surrounding him least wanted, former SNM colonel Musa Bihi Abdi. Everybody knew he would not be soft on the Islamist threat, and on 13 November he won the election by a comfortable margin. But would his resolve and his toughness (which nobody questioned, even his adversaries) be enough?

The best summary of the situation was given by a local journalist with a prestigious name:

> The previous administration has passed to its successor an almost uniformly negative legacy ... we need a complete overhaul of our politics ... Musa Bihi is perceived as a staunch nationalist who is irrevocably committed to Somaliland's independence whereas his predecessor's commitment was called into question because of his pro-federalist positions; secondly, Musa Bihi was not implicated in the corruption that enriched the senior members of previous regime; thirdly, the new president is known as a strong leader unwilling to suffer fools while his predecessor was ill and as result absent from day-to-day management; in foreign policy we compromised the country's strong independence stance by entering into a pointless policy of dialogue with the illegitimate governments in Mogadishu ... We subordinated out efforts to the dictates of whatever the 'government of the day' was in Mogadishu ... The Silanyo government abandoned any attempt at a distinct policy, leaving financial affairs to the whims of major foreign donors or investors in the business community ... the only significant action was to impose sales taxes and increase customs duty ... President Musa Bihi has inherited a toxic brew of subservience to foreign donors and domestic investors. But so far, after one year, the new administration has not made a concerted effort or espoused a new strategy ... The new president's patriotism and patience are not in question but there is an increasing groundswell of domestic frustration as many voices are raised, imploring the government to take corrective steps. Musa Bihi must take the matter to heart since this is nothing less than the independence, not to mention the very existence of Somaliland, which is at stake.[13]

Somaliland was politically shaken, ethnically nibbled at the edges by the Khatumo secession in the east (and the fear of another one among the Dir in the west), economically starved and socially haunted by the magnet of *tahrib* (paperless emigration). Youth unemployment had reached an estimated 70 per cent. The country was becoming a hologram. But it still remained proudly nationalistic, even though it was this nationalistic commitment which had driven it against the traffic in the one-way street. Could a collective soul have a price?

Globalising the Somali porcupine: The sterile British attempt

On 25 January 1991, the global legitimacy of the state of Somalia deserted Mogadishu, and it was not until 2000 that some kind of interim reality was able to reimpose itself there and rule over some parts of the territory. But of what territory? Once the internationally recognised Somali Republic had disappeared, what was 'Somalia' going to be? There had never been a country called 'Somalia' before colonisation, and since colonisation there had been five territories reasonably entitled to claim that name, whether wholly or in part. Two had merged in 1960. Together they had tried to conquer a third piece— the Ethiopian Ogaden—and had failed. In 1991, the entity which failed to conquer one of these target territories had, in the meantime, fallen into a state of collapse and broken into several free-floating pieces. Back in 1960 the international community had endorsed the union of two of the former colonies; but endorsed as what? As an achieved 'state', delimited within its new boundaries, or as a 'state in the making', striving towards the inclusion of all other Greater Somalia lands? But what about the objects of this theoretical expansion? By 1991 one of them had become a fully independent, internationally recognised state (Djibouti) and two others—the Ethiopian Ogaden and the north-eastern province of Kenya—were part of other states which were quite unwilling to let go of their Somali provinces. Would this bring the international community to reconsider the 1960 Act of Union? Or would it insist on recognising the de facto union but not the potential rest?

The collapse of the 'united' Somali state opened a legal gap in the post-colonial logic, a situation where reality and legality no longer coincided. And the international community did not—and still does not—have a coherent attitude towards such problems. In December 1971 it agreed to legalise the insurgent and Indian victory in East Pakistan, which was allowed to secede from West Pakistan as Bangladesh. On the other hand, when the main body of the Spanish Sahara population—in Saguia el-Hamra and Rio de Oro— tried to attain independence, this was denied even though other 'Moroccan' Spanish territories—Ifni, Ceuta, Melilla—were never decolonised and left as 'pride-healing' Spanish possessions. Meanwhile, Morocco had been allowed to absorb the former Spanish Sahara. In that same year, 1991, the former Ethiopian province of Eritrea freed itself militarily from Ethiopia, and was recognised as an independent state two years later; while the Soviet Union was 'dissolved' by Boris Yeltsin on 8 December and all its former 'colonies'— i.e. territories that were not culturally 'Russian'—were recognised as full-fledged states. But the case of Somalia was not going to be so clear-cut.

On 25 January 1991, Siad Barre fled from Mogadishu, leaving behind physical fighting and confusion wrapped up in a legally ambiguous package. Twenty-nine years later, while the physical struggle had largely—but not completely—ebbed, the legal situation remained highly problematic. Did 'Somaliland' exist as an organised political entity, did it live according to its own laws, and did it govern itself independently? Clearly yes. But did it exist as such in the eyes of the United Nations, that final court of appeal for international existence? The answer was clearly no. Somaliland was a reality in limbo, a functioning country without recognised validity, an existence whose essence was denied. The Somali national paradox has carried its logical contradictions from the 19th into the 21st century. In a basic way, all Somali are still 'colonised', with their ultimate fate decided by well-meaning strangers thousands of miles away; so in all logic, any possible improvement in their situation is more likely to come from outside the Somali perimeter than from inside the Somali lands themselves. For the last two centuries the Somali have been independent, imperialised, imperialist, defeated, victorious, dissolved, saved, abandoned, hologrammed and resilient. Now, in line with the zeitgeist of our times, they have entered a process of becoming globalised.

In 1991 Somalia was dismantled by war but not yet handled by peace. Twenty years later, in the course of 2011, advisers to the Tory Prime Minister David Cameron brought his attention to a deficit in his 'international statesman' image. He was seen as young, dynamic, clever, but too 'British', too 'provincial'.[14] Nobody had any clear idea of what he could do to remedy this deficit, but the team got to work and the answer was Somalia. This was not unanimous. Several of the advisers, particularly those in close contact with their American colleagues, were aware of the underlying complexity of the problem and tried to oppose that choice. But they were overruled because the Somali option had many advantages:[15] it would be cheap, there were no collateral diplomatic dangers to be feared, it would have humanitarian support, and it would fit with the Western (and particularly US) War on Terror policy. Once more, the Somali world would be a test bed for policy.

But in order to fit the bill of Tory benevolent interventionism, it had to move away from any lingering colonialist flavour. Therefore, the British intervention had to focus on Mogadishu and display no soft spot for Somaliland.[16] An observer wrote:

After 25 years of getting Somalia wrong, there is no easy way out of the imbroglio today. There have been six fully-fledged international peace conferences, fourteen major peace initiatives as well as four foreign military interventions, and Somalia is no better off. As designed, the coming meeting in London is fated to be just another one of these failures. Instead of gathering Somalia's discredited politicians and promising them more help, Cameron should support what already works well in Somalia: the vibrant middle class and Somaliland.[17]

He did neither. The new Somaliland President, Ahmed Mohamed 'Silanyo', who had been democratically elected, was physically refused access to the conference premises and Barclays Bank threatened to close its Hawala accounts even though Hawala were shining examples of Somali adaptability and resourcefulness. Everything was choreographed precisely and the UK Ambassador to Somalia, Matt Baugh, guided the delegates—including President Sheikh Sharif Sheikh Ahmed—with a firm hand. Sheikh Sharif, as we saw, was a former Islamist who had muscled his way into the presidency of 'legitimate' Somalia. The 25-point final communiqué was studded with 'we recognize the need', 'we condemn terrorism', 'we emphasize the urgency', 'we acknowledge the good work', 'we reiterate our determination' and assorted buckets of verbal porridge. The only concrete measure announced in the communiqué was the creation of a Joint Financial Management Board, i.e. an international committee to oversee the accounts of the Somali 'government'. The problem was that such a body had already been created in 2009 and disbanded in 2011 by President Abdullahi Mohamed 'Farmajo' when it reported that most of the public money had been stolen.[18]

The complaints of many Somali observers were interesting and were summed up for me by a man who had come from Mogadishu at his own cost and who said: 'If you want to help us, at least listen to us.' This was a useful lesson in the general Somali attitude towards politics. What we were witnessing in London was the exact opposite of a *shir* process, because in a *shir* anybody can talk even if he has nothing to say. The process is long and, for a European, exhausting. But, at great length, it moves somewhere. It creates bonds, an immaterial track is left, a verbal signpost is erected. So the London conference, in spite of its great presentation, had very limited impact on the situation even if it tried to introduce a new, more 'modern' approach. After the conferences,[19] a whole array of British actors, ranging from detached Foreign Office, Department of International Development and European Union officials to well-assigned UN and private company personnel,[20] descended on Somalia. Even the head of the UN New Integrated Mission for Somalia (UNSOM), Nicholas Kay, was British. His deputy was Algerian. When I met her, she told me with a wry smile: 'But I am British-educated and I live in

England.' It is difficult to assess what the benefits were for David Cameron's embrace of Somalia but they do not seem to have been overwhelming. And—unsurprisingly—the main problem the British-boosted Somali government had to deal with was clanic and territorial. Ironically, Brexit was soon to give this amateurish approach a massive boomerang dimension.

What London was trying was the soft approach, in a bid to attract Somalia into a virtuous partnership with the international community to counterbalance the destructive influence of the Shabaab and their fantasised Islamist caliphate.[21] Then what was the Somalia that London hoped to rally? Basically, it was the old Somalia Italiana of 1960. But in what geopolitical shape? We have already seen that since 1998 the Majerteen clan family had set up the quasi-state of Puntland, which had been careful not to declare its independence, periodically used its army in support of the 'Somali government' when the latter had military problems (all the time), and kept a low profile internationally. The government was chosen by closed-door bargaining between the various clans of the big Majerteen clan family; there were no elections and no democratic bravado in the Somaliland style. In exchange for this low-profile discretion, Chinese oil exploratory teams were allowed to roam freely (they found no oil), and pirates in the harbours of Eyl and Hobyo were supplied and protected, and later brought under (partial) control. Later, the United Arab Emirates began developing the port installations in Bosaso while Puntland supported the Khatumo secession in order to annoy Somaliland and to extend some influence over that Dhulbahante zone, just in case the Chinese finally found oil there. South of that, around Galkayo, where Majerteen and Hawiye met, there was a zone the UN maps labelled 'disputed'.

If we go further south, the two old provinces of Galguduud and Mudug, both inhabited by a variety of Hawiye clans, had fused under the unclear name of 'Galmudug'. At times 'Galmudug' presented itself as a federated state of the Somalia ensemble; at other times the assembly in the 'capital' Dusamareb made declarations that seemed to come from an autonomous entity. Further south, the two provinces of Hiiran and Middle Shebelle had fused to create still another administrative entity which fitted within 'Somalia'. Mogadishu sits practically on the border of Hiiran–Shebelle and the whole region Bay–Bakool–Benadir had become the 'south-west Somalia' where the capital had more or less direct control. There the main problem was the cohabitation of those called the Guri and the Galti. These are not clans; they are the 'natives' and the 'newcomers', the labels indicating who was living there before the massive displacements of the warlord years as opposed to those who had come during the war years. Basically, the 'natives' are Rahanweyn and most of the newcomers are Hawiye refugees who have fled the intense fighting in Mogadishu. Their coexistence is the demographic product of those long years of violent conflict. The Galti are those who have passed through many painful refugee stations, regardless of their clan origin. They have finally dropped down in a place where something—food, shelter, social protection—allowed them to stop their panicked exile. Now they talk in terms of votes, representation and administrative rights.

Finally, in the far south there is Jubbaland, which is a clanic nightmare where Hawiye and Rahanweyn confront each other without any one managing to dominate, while many small clans make claims for ethnic fairness but without the capacity to build anything solid. Faced with the incapacity of the government in Mogadishu to steer this mosaic along a constructive course, both the Ethiopians and the Kenyans—who, through AMISOM, are part of the military-administrative game—have tried to rig local structures without much success.

It is that mass of contradictions that British aid and diplomacy tried to glue together to achieve a number of objectives:

- to arrive at a minimum of peace and stability;
- to promote the British government in the nostalgic role of non-imperialist builder of influence;
- to prop up regionally a number of British businesses ranging from BP and Shell to PricewaterhouseCoopers and Deloitte & Touche (both were already involved in the finances of AMISOM); and
- to stop the regular Turkish encroachment on the Somali zone and prevent Ankara from reconquering this margin of its pre-1914 empire. As we'll discuss further on, that 'margin' would soon become central to a major cleavage in the Muslim world.

Basically, the British plan did not work. It was a daring promotion, half trying to use the traditional tools of cooperation such as the Department of International Development or the UN, and half expecting to heave an economic world into a dimension not yet its own. Conceptually, it was a small-scale, unexpected rehearsal for Brexit, betting that ultra-modernity could promote a back-to-the-future scenario. Somaliland, the old colony still regarded by its citizens with unrequited love, was carefully kept aside. But further globalisation of an even more radical nature was just around the corner, approaching from an unexpected angle.

*Shifting the focus: The Great Quarrel (fitna al-kabira) splitting the
Muslim world and its impact on the Somali*

Globalising Somalia from London did not work. In fact, soon London
seemed to be de-globalising itself. But far away from the English capital, the
long-rumbling contradictions of the Middle East suddenly burst into near-
open conflict. The root cause went back to the 1920s spread of the Muslim
Brotherhood ideology of a return to the fundamentals of Islam. In a way it
was a phenomenon comparable to the Reformation in Europe, even if the
cultural context gave it a very different tinge.[22] But one thing that was similar was the variety of answers to the problem. In 16th-century Europe,
Zwingli, Luther, Calvin and Henry VIII all strongly challenged the religious
and political dispositions of the Roman Catholic Church. But this did not
mean that they agreed with each other or formed a coherent movement.
Since the late 19th century Islam has been in a similar situation of ferment.
Most of the names of the key players and thinkers—Jamal ad-Din al-
Afghani, Mohamed Abduh, Rashid Rida, Hassan al-Banna, Muhamad
Iqbal, Sayid Qutb, Abu l'Ala Maududi and several others—are little known
outside the Muslim world even if their impact has indeed been massive.
Among all those, one man and his movement, Hassan al-Banna and his
Ikhwan al-Muslimin (Muslim Brotherhood), in view of their broad recruitment and good organisation, have had lasting influence, political, social and
economic at the same time. Long before Saudi attackers crashed their
hijacked planes into the Twin Towers, the deep reassessments of Islam had
had practical and political impact, one aspect of which lies at the heart of
what we witness today in the early 21st century.

It all started in the early 1960s when Egyptian President Gamal Abdel
Nasser broke with the Muslim Brothers, who had initially supported his
takeover of the country. One of their key leaders, Yusuf al-Qaradawi, took
refuge in the small Sultanate of Qatar where he acquired citizenship. He and
his Libyan-born associate, Ali al-Sallabi, developed a network of radical
Islamic reformers and organisers. Their political choices were radical but
their tactical adaptations were often more pragmatic. Nevertheless, they
developed, under Qatari protection, a particular 'school' or 'trend'. And
given the massive natural gas reserves controlled by Qatar, they had the
means of financing their strategy.

Facing them was another geographically minimalist but financially maximalist small power, the United Arab Emirates (UAE). 'If Qatar's strategy was

to promote political change by supporting legitimate opposition forces, the UAE's was to help engineer coups that would put in power men who were more to their liking.'[23] In 1973, when the far-sighted Sheikh Zayed Al Nahyan ascended the throne of what was then called the Trucial States, a string of discontinuous post-imperial leftovers, the only danger, communism, was mostly theoretical in the regional environment. But at the end of his long reign in 2004, communism had died before him and been replaced by radical Islam. This was a much more real threat for the *bedawi* (Bedouin) family dynasties reigning over a widely spread-out territory with much oil and hardly any population.[24] When Sheikh Zayed died, the UAE was the sixteenth-largest importer of military equipment in the world. Today it is the fourth, and in relationship to the size of its population, the UAE is now the most militarised country in the world. Its soldiers are well trained and the general capacity of its army is of high quality.[25] The UAE has rapidly engaged in projecting its military forces in a series of foreign endeavours ranging from local to the establishment of permanent military installations, the largest of which is in Assab, Eritrea. The result has been to develop a string of colonial harbours, amounting to an informal empire. Its interventions have been essential and generally opposed to those of Qatar. In Libya, Qatar backs the UN-supported regime of Prime Minister Fayez al-Sarraj, while the UAE helps Benghazi strongman Khalifa Haftar; in Palestine, the UAE is anti-Hamas and supports a tolerant attitude towards Israel;[26] in Yemen, the UAE, which is supposed to support the 'legitimate' government of Abd-Rabbu Mansour Hadi, is in fact discreetly behind the secessionist movement of Aidarus al-Zubaidi, the former Governor of Aden, who hopes to manage a return to an independent pre-1990 South Yemen. The reason why has to do with the association between a man and a strategy. The heir (today's Crown Prince) of Abu Dhabi, Mohamed bin Zayed—colloquially known as MBZ—was the primus inter pares of the confederation and he too had a view of how Islam (and politics, since there is little separation between both) should evolve. MBZ came to power by chance—the state of his brother's blood vessels—but he has kept power in line with a deep form of strategic thinking. Islamism is an ideological construct on top of Islam and, like any ideology, has the capacity to mobilise large masses when they are structurally susceptible to its message. MBZ's country is rich, built on an artificial basis, and operates in a high-risk environment; its fast movements tend to surprise both its foes and its allies.[27]

To try labelling the two approaches we could say: ideologically, Qatar has been politically open—its favorite ideologues support multi-partyism and free elections (provided all contenders operate in an Islamic context and Shari'ah is the law of the land)[28]—but religiously highly conservative. The UAE has had the opposite attitude: to be religiously tolerant but politically authoritarian. If we look at some contemporary conflicts in the Muslim world, Qatar and the UAE have systematically been on opposite sides. All Emirati choices are presented in the Western media as 'moderate' while the Qatari ones are pictured as 'radical'. But this is a gross simplification. 'The point is not that Qatar is innocent of supporting extremists. The point is that these coordinated attacks on Qatar ... are simply a weapon used by the Emirates, Israel and the Saudi to advance their agendas ... What is misleading is not the claim that Qatar funds extremists but that they do so more than US allies in the region.'[29] The division between Qatar and the UAE (now followed by its clumsy Saudi Arabian ally) is more one of geopolitical differences than of 'religious' divergences.

These splits had slowly developed over time since the 1970s but the 2011 explosion of the Muslim world, misleadingly known as 'the Arab Spring', flashed them into full view. And it also represented a change of geopolitical weight for the hitherto diplomatically discreet UAE. The divergent approaches diverged even more. And this is how it connected with the Somali scene.

Quite suddenly,[30] on 9 May 2016, the giant Emirati trading and handling firm, Dubai Port World (DPW), signed a development and management contract with the Somaliland government, announcing a $445 million investment programme. The amount announced was much larger than the budget of the Somaliland Republic. So the problem was set in paradoxical terms from the beginning: was it the Somaliland Republic signing a commercial agreement with a foreign shipping and handling company, or was it a state-shaped financial shark swallowing the minnow of a virtual country? With the signing, the UAE, and all the trappings of its newly developed globalised modern imperialism, had, at the stroke of a pen, become part and parcel of the complex Somali reality, and would soon lead it from behind.

The UAE's capacity for intelligent tactical application of strategic thinking has been displayed time and again in the region: the recovery of lingering South Yemenite sub-nationalism in Aden, the instrumentalisation of the Ethiopian–Eritrean rivalry and, since 2016, the picking apart of the usable remnants of the Somali dream.[31] The question was: what would Dubai do with Berbera?[32] For the UAE, this is a secondary proposition, given the fact that the Emirates structure is built on five pillars: oil; mythical real estate;[33] hard soft Islam;[34] commerce; and resolute military presence. None of the first three elements are transferable to Berbera, at least for the time being. But the fourth and the fifth are where the imprint of MBZ is most visible—and probably why he has kept carefully away from negotiations.

Commerce in the context of UAE strategic thinking has to be understood in a very broad sense, where the tools range from armed militias at one end to international courts at the other. The 2016 Berbera contract was somewhere in the middle. In October 2008 the IMF had coddled the world's states into accepting the so-called Santiago Principles, which asked governments not to use their sovereign wealth funds as tools to carry out the strategic policies their regimes were seeking to achieve. But compliance with these Santiago Principles was voluntary and the UAE paid lip service to them. This meant that their partners also tended to take liberties with the application of these principles. At first Abu Dhabi announced that the Berbera contract would be signed by the P&O company,[35] but then it changed its mind at the last minute and played on the ambiguity of DP World. As a private company P&O could not recognise an unrecognised government, but DP World was closer to 'being' the UAE and could act diplomatically. Mogadishu did not miss what this implied and called the contract null and void. Another regional power reacted nervously to the Berbera contract: Ethiopia. Ethiopia had long considered Somaliland as both an ally and a client.

But on 5 June 2017 the whole geopolitical balance of the region was transformed when Saudi Arabia and the UAE coerced the Gulf Cooperation Council (GCC) into a condemnation and blockade of the Sultanate of Qatar. The GCC presented an ultimatum to Qatar whereby it was supposed to carry out a series of extravagant political and social changes, from shutting down its emblematic TV station, Al Jazeera, to expelling 59 radical politicians and accepting a complete embargo. For a few days it looked as if Saudi Arabia and the UAE might even invade Qatar.[36]

This started a scramble for alliances and alignments according to criteria that were often quite far from the direct causes of the break. Thus Ethiopia had been close to Qatar since the death of Meles Zenawi simply because of tension around the building of the Grand Ethiopian Renaissance Dam (GERD) on the Nile. So when Abiy Ahmed became Prime Minister in Addis Ababa, he had some quick adjustments to make. Given the catastrophic financial situation of Ethiopia, he travelled quickly to Saudi Arabia and Abu Dhabi and revised his order of priorities. But he also had to deal with Ethiopia's own geopolitical contradictions: the presence of the large UAE military base in Eritrea since 2015; and the fact that the Berbera contract was not limited to the improvement of a commercial port but also mentioned the building of a military base. Given Ethiopia's long, problematic relation with Islam,[37] there was a need to reassert priorities. It was quickly done and Addis Ababa quietly joined the Saudi–UAE side of what Muslims were calling *al-Fitna al-Qabira* (the Great Quarrel).[38]

Locally, there were two main consequences. Firstly, the Emirates entered into a structural conflict with Djibouti. Here too this had very little to do with 'the Great Quarrel', even if it came in its wake: the main cause of the tension between Djibouti and the Emirates was the role played by a dual citizen of both countries, Abdourahman Boreh. Boreh had brought DP World into the management of the new Doraleh container terminal in the port of Djibouti. He was half Arab and half Somali. He carried both a UAE and a Djiboutian passport. He was a close associate of Djiboutian President Ismail Omar Guelleh and his very prosperous business partner. In a way he was too prosperous and too much of a partner. He accompanied the head of state on all occasions and began to be known as 'Djibouti's Vice-President'. He basked in the limelight but crossed the red line when he let it be known that he would like to be Ismail Omar Guelleh's successor. He was soon accused of mismanagement and corruption by the Djiboutian government and all his properties in Djibouti were seized. When he decided to sue the Djiboutian government in the Commercial Court in London, the Djiboutian regime upped the accusation to one of terrorism. The only proof of terrorist activity Djibouti could bring to the trial was a video showing an old car being blown up on a disused parking lot. On 3 March 2016 the court, unimpressed, exonerated Abdourahman Boreh from the charges and called them 'politically motivated'. But through the agency of *al-Fitna al-Qabira*, the fight had escalated from a personal and political rivalry to a Djibouti fight against DP World and against the United Arab Emirates. The commercial rivalry between the two harbours was now embedded into a global geopolitical conflict and—willy-nilly—Somaliland had been drawn into it. Ethiopia wanted to ensure its own security in the conflict and negotiated directly with Abu Dhabi, pushing itself into the bilateral arrangements by buying 19 per cent of the proposed port authority (1 March 2018), and moving the deal into a trilateral contract, whereby DP World kept the majority interest of 51 per cent while Somaliland was reduced to a mere 30 per cent.

The UAE tried to play both sides of the Great Quarrel by keeping various stakes in south Somalia—small outposts near Kismayo and Baidoa, a training programme for the Somali Army, a bid for the extension of Mogadishu

International Airport—and dealing directly with Russia and the US over the head of the Somaliland regime. Paradoxically, the foreign partners were seen as more promising than the southern 'brothers', even if the former were far from generous. Abu Dhabi agreed to pay an extra $80 million for the military base, which it forced Hargeisa to accept. Keenly aware that accepting a military base within the context of the Great Quarrel in the Muslim world was a momentous choice, the Somaliland authorities tried to uncouple the non-commercial part of the contract from the commercial one, but the Emirati had been adamant.

This was especially so when their relationship with the south took a turn for the worse in April 2018 after the regime of President Abdullahi Mohamed 'Farmajo', still aligned with the Qatari, hijacked an Emirati plane carrying $8.5 million earmarked for the salaries of the Somali soldiers whom the UAE was in the process of training. The Emirati immediately broke their relations with Mogadishu and abandoned the barracks where they had run their programme. The Somali soldiers in training fought among themselves for the opportunity of looting the installations they had used, and those who won dismantled everything and sold their equipment and weapons in the streets.[39]

For Abu Dhabi, what they had lost was a control point facing the Turks, who had started developing a military training programme in the southern 'Federal states' of Somalia even before the Great Quarrel. The rift became wider by the day. Mogadishu President Farmajo went to Doha where he met the Emir of Qatar and denounced 'the suspicious relationship between the United Arab Emirates and such secessionist entities as Somaliland and Puntland'. There was no immediate military consequence but the Emirati archipelago seethed with anger. In February the Djibouti government suddenly threw DP World out of the Doraleh container terminal, using unsupported accusations of corruption and mismanagement together with even more bizarre claims of 'investing in rival facilities'[40] and violating Djiboutian sovereignty, a transparently false accusation of DP World activities in Berbera. Mogadishu's Prime Minister went to Riyadh and asked the Saudi King to intervene with the UAE and stop the process. The King did not refuse directly but offered money to his visitor to keep the TFG from complaining. His son Mohamed bin Salman did not condescend to meet what he probably saw as the vassal of his fickle ally.

The Berbera contract was a lifeline for Somaliland while for the UAE it was just a link in the chain of a coastal empire in the making. And since that emerging empire was in turn only one element in the struggle for control of an *Umma*-wide international confrontation, one can say that Somaliland had been finally globalised.

To what kind of reality can a virtual Somaliland aspire?

The courage and perseverance of the Somalilanders is remarkable, but these qualities are rooted in their pain and feeling of betrayal at the hands of their 'brothers'. Nobody in Somaliland can forget the horrors of 1988 in Hargeisa, and the memory of the ruthless killing of civilians has been transferred to their children. This is why, after the 1991 victory, those who had fought for this victory wanted to 'be a state'.[41] In the age of imperialism, 'being a state' was the opposite of being a colony, and having a state meant being 'civilised', being part of the world's top club, and later having the right to sit in the UN Assembly in New York, having the right to exist. 'A state' was the only way to be 'officially alive', especially since your life had been subsumed by another structure, another nation, which had seduced you into cultural fraternity before disposing of you when you did not like the way it treated you. This was also the only way to open your rights to a multiplicity of international programmes and procedures that made you participate and allowed you to reap benefits.

Mohamed Ibrahim Egal, Somaliland's first President, was a remarkable man who clearly understood the horns of the dilemma he was impaled upon when he discussed the reasons why the international community refused to investigate the mass graves found after the events of 1988.

> The international community is ambivalent over the affairs of Somaliland ... when the mass graves were discovered, international instances were reluctant to follow it up ... the forensic experts visited them and testified that the atrocities had been committed there. From their report a major investigation should have taken place to establish what had happened ... to establish facts and figures ... but they would have to start with the admission of an error. The people of the south think we are telling a tall tale. They have no guilt about it. The pilots who were piloting the planes ... didn't think they were doing anything wrong ... The closest they came to an admission of error was to say they were following orders. The whole population of the south regards Somaliland as a bonus that was given to them with their independence. They don't regard it as an equal partner. That's why the unification of the Somali people has failed, because of that superior attitude: 'We are the Somali people, and you, you are just splinter groups that are coming back home after the imperialists took you away for a period of time.' But the history of the Somali people is that there has never been a central authority. We were independent tribes and we lived together in equality. We fought over water or grazing now and then. But nobody ruled over anybody else.[42]

This is the initial 'admission of sin' most Somali refuse, for it is as if the 'pastoral democracy' described by I.M. Lewis had been shameful or that at least it excluded the Somali from the concert of nations. So the quarrel was now: who are the Somalis, and which ones have a right to claim this identity as the basis for a nation-state? Mohamed Ibrahim Egal was right. The southern clans had monopolised the claim to be the central stem while the others were just branches. A nation has a state, in a state there is a government, and its territory is its 'homeland'. This was the post-Westphalian creed, confirmed through the Treaty of Versailles after the First World War and reconfirmed—extended to the colonies—when the United Nations was created after the Second World War. All the same, in the case of the Somali, as Mohamed Ibrahim Egal said, 'nobody ruled over anybody else', and the whole system of Russian dolls on which the Westphalian creed rested was inapplicable. If these principles were true, Switzerland could not exist, Hitler's Anschluss should have been confirmed by the Allies in 1945, Bangladesh should be illegal, and the Russian Empire should still stand. In Africa, let's not even mention South Sudan and Eritrea.

But today, what to do? Should the choice be to either deny Somaliland its evident national existence or give it a seat in the UN? Strangely enough, having now become a satellite of the United Arab Emirates might provide a way out of this quandary.[43] This is an old idea that I first heard Mohamed Ibrahim Egal mention towards the end of his life: 'They don't want us to have a country. So we have to design something more or less like the Palestinian authority. Except on what basis?' The fact that there could be such a basis has perhaps now become possible after having floated on an ocean of blood and tears. The emotional power of the blood and tears has begun to recede in time; not to 'disappear' but to become lesser, to fade away. The triumphant age of the nation-state has begun receding, firstly through international treaties—now hegemonic world-wide—and then by division or separation. The combination of the two, underpinned by economic interdependence, has led to globalisation, neither a curse nor a paradise but simply another template which is filled according to different rules. So far—for how long?—it is the equivalent of Mrs Thatcher's TINA—There Is No Alternative. But, as unfortunately often happens in history, the present world is playing according to the rules of a previous one. The United Nations was created in 1945 to prevent nation-state cannibalism. But today, while there is hardly any appetite for such grisly territory-snatching, the lands of conquest are no longer coveted for economic reasons—there are stock exchanges for that—or strategic ones—treaties can be negotiated.

This is exactly where the Emirati and the Saudi approaches have diverged. Under the leadership of Mohamed bin Salman, the Saudi *aggiornamento* was placed under the banner of caprice and flamboyance. The MBZ approach was radically different. Both (uncrowned) monarchs realised during the Arab Spring that the basic principles of governance in their region of the world were obsolete. The secular 'socialist' regimes were bankrupt and radical Islam was in heated competition with Western-style democracy to provide alternatives. Paradoxically, it was the monarchies (Morocco, Jordan, Saudi Arabia, the Sultanate of Oman, Kuwait, the Emirates) which were, for now, surviving better the global storm. They neither wanted the Islamists to be the front-line competitors nor did they want a genuine (and culturally strange) Western democratic revolution. Over and above, there were two medium-sized Muslim powers, Turkey and Iran, which, although not Arab, could not but be counted for geographical and historical reasons. The only two Muslim countries that had a margin of manoeuvre left were Saudi Arabia and the Emirates. Both were in a position to step in during the great confusion that followed the failure of the Arab *aggiornamento*, and their different approaches became evident in the way they engaged in the Yemen conflict. Their way of weighing in was radically different, hovering between alliance and rivalry.[44]

Saudi and the UAE started their attempt to roll back the post-2011 upheaval from different vantage points. Ibn Saud had been a despotic giant of a man, unifying several Arab sheikhdoms, not only by overcoming their fissiparous tendencies but also by avoiding the deadly embrace of both the Ottoman and British empires. With his 25 wives, countless concubines, and 95 children, including those who were to become the next six kings, the throne of Saudi Arabia was the epitome of centralised, family-centred absolute power. One can see that Crown Prince Mohamed bin Salman, grandson of Ibn Saud, lives and behaves perfectly in step with the political attitude of his famous grandfather. The UAE is quite a different proposition. It is a surprising and even more recent construction. Sheikh Zayed Al Nayhan was the exact opposite of Ibn Saud. Quiet, peaceful, he was a builder, an economist and a diplomat. His achievement was to build a structure in which the disparate and somewhat contradictory elements could be combined in a coherent whole. His approach was radically different from the Saudi one: it was founded—and grew wider—on a 'state' he had built out of seven statelets, being conceived along the lines of several sets of non-centralised commercial empires that, before the onset of the nation-state, offered a different reality: the ancient Greek colonies;[45] the ancient Phoenicians colonies;[46] the Hanseatic League in

12th-century Baltic Europe;[47] the Venetian diaspora;[48] and what French historian François Gipouloux called 'the Asian Mediterranean'.[49] The UAE is definitely in that line of non-state powers. And at present the question is whether they will keep trying to be what they are not—an empire—or whether they will try to offer an alternative to the permanent crisis into which 'the Muslim states' have entered. Can the UAE become the opposite—an alternative, not an adversary—of what the whole Islamist movement represents: viz a non-prophetic pragmatist which could deal with these extensions of the UAE (Socotra, South Yemen, Somaliland, Puntland) not as colonies or 'protectorates' but rather as associated subordinates?

This world-wide tradition of multiple belonging could be an appropriate solution, creating a halfway house for Somaliland. 'Going back' to where it has never been—a unified Somalia—is a pipe dream, which is only a forceful projection of the Westphalian abstraction. At the time the two Somali territories joined up, the world was at the height of the era of the nation-state. The Somali themselves had been clamouring for unification, and the international community was broadly supportive of a move that seemed like a popular choice—and, for the colonisers, an atonement for past sins, particularly in the case of the Italians. No criteria can ensure the coherence and loyalty of any social body outside the popular will. Socialism, force, religion, language, have all in one form or another been tried to create a coherent state structure and make it last. In the region we have three examples—Eritrea, South Sudan and South Yemen—which have turned into tragedies because of the violence of their 'imperial overlord', which forced them into nation-states they did not want.[50] The Westphalian-oriented international community has dealt arbitrarily with these exceptions to the world order. In the case of Somaliland, the rejection has been both drastic and immature. The Somalilanders did what could be done at the time of the triumphant nation-state: secede from what they had agreed to join. It was refused for totally arbitrary reasons. Marriage without divorce will obviously not last. Reinsertion within the mythical 'Somalia' ensemble is an impossibility, even if it were carried out through a war of aggression. This was amply demonstrated on 4 October 1993, during the Black Hawk Down incident, when US forces had to kill a massive number of civilians to recover the bodies of their dead soldiers.[51] When the Somali are convinced of the righteousness of what they are fighting for, death in combat is not a problem. And the international community knows this. Somaliland is denounced but not militarily attacked.

For the time being, the UAE has 'globalised' the problem without solving it. The fact that this 'embryonic solution' came from an Arab country has been perceived strangely in Somaliland. 'In fact, we expected it from the British—or the United Nations—or perhaps even from the European Union. But coming from the Arab world, it was like a kind of cultural shock.'[52] This uncertainty is perched on the edge of potential miserly generosity. Because, if we keep in mind the pattern of the 'colonial string confederation' we referred to earlier, it was never 'an alliance of equals'. Such commercial empires or networks had a head and hired members. Venice, Lübeck or Srivijaya were 'on top' of their globalised networks. The opportunity Dubai (and, behind it obliquely, Abu Dhabi) provides is one of hierarchical cooperation. The advantage for Somaliland is that it opens a door. During the late Silanyo years, Somaliland was rotting from the top down. Signing an agreement with DP World and Dubai was not a panacea, just a nudge in the right direction. But, even speaking relatively, this represents immense progress if compared to the bare looting that was the reward of the deluded Somalilanders after 1978, when they retired defeated from the Ogaden battlefield which they had shared with their southern cousins. The Siad Barre 'system', as we saw it, had all the tender mercies Tamerlane visited on Baghdad. Calling for the Somalilanders to reconcile with the debris of that system, which shows daily that the only reason it does not behave more violently is that it is too weak to do so, is not really a winning proposal. Hargeisa is far from being a political ideal, but it is a working proposition. What its satellisation in the UAE network offers is a chance to have a go at it, commercially and, perhaps later, economically. That is, if Hargeisa manages to retain a measure of independence within the Emirati system.

In any case, it is better than begging from the World Bank. The international community betrayed Somaliland first during the Cold War, when the SNM was considered to be a stupid front for the Russians and not even capable of being 'Marxist'. Then it betrayed it a second time when the Somalilanders successfully ticked all the boxes of the democratisation form printed in New York but were not allowed to turn their good performance into any kind of reward. It betrayed it a third time by supporting a grotesque cardboard regime in Mogadishu, asking Hargeisa to bow to that idol. Of course, today the generation that fought the war of independence represents only a minority of Somaliland's population. But the memories keeping the perception alive are still there, existing in a floating way in many different countries, from Poland to Vietnam. Any analysis of the Somaliland case is bound to end up, as here, assuming the tones of a pamphlet because the rhetoric of understatement is horribly incapable of finding a reasonable path to a clean exit. Abu Dhabi is not

Mecca, but it is perhaps a staging post on the way to it. The Somalilanders live, but only de facto. They would love to live in a world where they could breathe legitimately. But in the meantime, woe be to those who must remain trapped in the algorithms of international virtuous fiction.

The Taiwan "full recognition": Way out of the labyrinth or tactical side-stepping?[53]

On 1 July 2020, Somaliland formally recognised the Republic of China (RoC, Taiwan) as 'a representative of China', while the island state issued a decision 'to build closer ties with Somaliland'. The difference was significant: Taiwan, while diplomatically contentious, is an economic powerhouse. And while it has full diplomatic relations with only 14 official UN member countries, for practical reasons this doubles up with 57 others with whom it has para-diplomatic, commercial and a whole array of legal ties. But given the loneliness of the long-distance diplomatic run for Somaliland since 1991, this breakthrough in a relationship with a 'major' country was almost immediately seen as being a 'recognition'. So far the only African country with which Taiwan had full diplomatic relations was Eswatini.[54] Compared to the archaic and poverty-stricken former Swazi kingdom, Somaliland looked like a miracle of democratic and progressive society, qualifiers seldom applied to a Muslim republic. And there was also a kind of immediate kinship felt by those few Taiwanese who had become familiar with Somaliland during its stabilisation period: 'these fellows are like us, small fishes trying to survive in a fish tank full of sharks'.[55] Does that mean that Taipei was actually contemplating entering the Red Sea geopolitical free-for-all at eye level? Of course not. But in terms of the Two-China rivalry, this was a significant move. Taiwan was stepping on territory barely 200 km away from Beijing's one and only military base abroad, Djibouti. This was a place which, since the French (partial) withdrawal after 2000, had become a crossroad of multinational armies.[56] In many ways an open space, especially since China was the top financial aid giver to Djibouti.[57] This was not missed in Beijing. On 7 August 2020, Ambassador Zhou Yuxiao, Special Representative of the Forum on Africa-China Cooperation (FOCAC) rushed to Hargeisa to meet Musa Bihi. Out of the window flew the 'one Somalia' which had ruled the relations of China with the Somalis and the Chinese representative asked in rather rough terms for the total cut-off of relations with Taipei. President Musa Bihi immediately refused the Chinese demand, an attitude which has long been typical of Somaliland in dealing with 'big power' dictates.[58] Washington sent a congratulatory note to Hargeisa and Taiwanese lobbyists started to work on what to do when Beijing would unavoidably block any attempt at recognition at the Security Council level.

So what now? Eventually becoming recognised as a 'full state' by Taiwan might, unfortunately for Somaliland, be a decoy akin to Biafra's reconnaissance by Nyerere's Tanzania and Kaunda's Zambia in 1968. Musa Bihi's refusal to bend to the Chinese dictate was typical of Somaliland's defiant attitude which has been a part of its micro culture since the birth of the SNM. Defiance is more necessary, morally and psychologically, to the 'non-state' survival, of the 'state that does not exist' than clever diplomatic arrangements.

The Somalilanders live, but only de facto. They would love to live in a world where they could breathe legitimately. But in the meantime, woe to those who must remain trapped in the algorithms of internationally virtuous fiction.

NOTES

PREFACE TO THE HARDBACK EDITION

1. *The Economist*, 10 September 2016.
2. Gerard Prunier, 'Somaliland: The Country That Does Not Exist', *Le Monde Diplomatique*, October 1997.

PREFACE TO THE PAPERBACK EDITION

1. This figure is uncertain and depends on whether one accepts the Federal State of Somalia (with a seat at the UN in New York) as *the real Somalia* and on the status you are willing to attribute to the de facto sub-parts of this large soft entity. And then on the degree of legitimacy you give to the various regional administrations it encompasses geographicallly. General agreements are difficult to reach.
2. If we look at the significant native leaders of other Italian colonies—Gaddafi, Issayas Afeworqi, Siad Barre—the succession of Ethiopian heads of state betrays a particular adherence to the Cesarian model.
3. The various colonial masters—Ethiopian, French and Italian—were all authoritarian and provided no attractive models.
4. SSC stands for Sool, Sanaag, Ayn (written with a 'C' in the Somali alphabet, it is pronounced ', like the Arabic glottal stop). Sool, Sanaag and Ayn are provinces of the old United Somalia, strongly populated by Dolbahante.
5. 'The youth', the popular name given to the radical Islamists.

1. A NATION IN SEARCH OF A STATE: THE SOMALI MYSTIQUE OF UNITY

1. I borrow the felicitous title of this chapter from David Laitin and Said Samatar, *Somalia: Nation in Search of a State* (Boulder: Westview Press, 1987).
2. I prefer that word to 'independence', as the latter expression presupposes a type of freedom at all levels, from the economic to the cultural, which is often much more theoretical than the political separation which has given birth to the new states.

3. It is still popularly remembered as the Thirty Years War. The Treaty of Westphalia which ended it was a primitive version of the United Nations Charter, which later ended another bout of European conflict upgraded to the level of a world war. As for the Somali, who had fought on both sides of the Second World War, they jumped on the nation-state bandwagon with a vengeance when they realised that the concept of an independent nation-state might get them what had always been a great ideal of Somali life and culture: freedom.

4. The basic foundational work is an out of print brochure called *The Somali Lineage System and Total Genealogy: A General Introduction to Basic Principles of Somali Political Institutions* (Hargeisa, 1957), 139 pp. (mimeographed). This was written by I.M. Lewis, then a colonial government anthropologist (this position was official) who had just arrived in British Somaliland and who was still under the shock of discovering how deep and all-encompassing the clan system was. This work was later enlarged, generalised, made less technical and published as *A Pastoral Democracy* (Oxford University Press, 1961), a most felicitous title, even if some critics read it as 'a pastoral anarchy'. It was reprinted several times.

5. Following the male line of ancestry.

6. There are exceptions. Some Somali are irritated by this aspect of their culture and deny its native origin (I had once a heated argument with a Somali scholar who insisted the Europeans had invented the system), pretend that it is not as overwhelming as many see it or, as a last resort, refuse absolutely to tell you from what clan they are issued. But they only make up a small minority. Most Somali agree about the omnipresence of the clan system and its pregnant influence on everything from marriage to business and from politics to gossip. The only thing they insist on is that it is easily transcended by friendship.

7. Clan relationships (both internal and external) were governed by a series of codes called *Heer* (*Xeer* in modern Somali spelling). *Xeer* enforcement depended on clan loyalty and expertise. Even after the advent of Islam, when Somali became Muslims, *Xeer* remained more strongly embedded and respected than Islamic Shari'ah. See Michael van Notten, *The Law of the Somali* (Trenton: Red Sea Press, 2005) for an overview.

8. See Virginia Luling, *Somali Sultanate: The Geledi City-State over 150 Years* (London: Haan, 2002).

9. The Somali language was not written down till 1973.

10. To understand its creation following the French evacuation of 1801, see Afaf Lutfi al-Sayyid Marsot, *Egypt in the Reign of Muhammad Ali* (Cambridge: Cambridge University Press, 1984). And to grasp its progressive undoing, see David Landes, *Bankers and Pashas: International Finance and Economic Imperialism in Egypt* (London: Heinemann, 1958).

11. *Maps* is set against the background of the Ogaden War (1977–8), when the then recently independent Somalia state tried to forcibly annex this Somali-populated region of 'Ethiopia'.

12. Saadia Touval, *Somali Nationalism: International Politics and the Drive for Unity in the Horn of Africa* (Cambridge, MA: Harvard University Press, 1963). The author (unintentionally perhaps) took a very 'Somali-oriented' view of the word 'unity' in the Horn context.

13. This in turn posed the question of the identity of 'Ethiopia'. The old Christian 'Abyssinia' had a strong consciousness of its existence. But post-Menelik 'Ethiopia' had tried to extend that *habash* (Abyssinian) consciousness to what had turned into a multinational empire. The Somali of the Ogaden remained Somali first and Ethiopian second.

14. Ali Jimale Ahmed (ed.), *The Invention of Somalia* (Lawrenceville: Red Sea Press, 1995). That title caused a small furore in the limited world of Somalia experts. The Somali themselves barely noticed it.

15. Lest these words (and the vocabulary used) be misunderstood, Jimale quotes representative examples. My own frequent contact with Somali over many years has provided me with numerous examples that confirm Jimale's courageous maverick position.

16. But he drew the line at *adoon* (nigger), which he did not dare mention.

17. He was in fact a rabid 'clanist' (Darood) ideologue who hated rival clanic groups. His early biographers tended to gloss over this unsavoury aspect of his ideology but later ones were more honest. See Abdi Sheikh Abdi, *Divine Madnes: Mohamed Abdulle Hassan (1856–1920)* (London: Zed Books, 1993).

18. There was indeed; but its clanic content was expunged by both Somali and foreign scholars, particularly when it was derogatory, leading to what Jimale calls 'a textual attitude of artificial unanimity'.

19. Basil Davidson, *The Black Man's Burden: Africa and the Curse of the Nation-State* (New York: Time Books, 1992).

20. See Henri Brunschwig, 'Une colonie inutile: Obock (1862–1888)', *Cahiers d'Etudes Africaines* 8, 29 (1968), pp. 32–47. The Côte Française des Somalis slowly grew out of the Obock colony.

21. See Jean-Pierre Diehl, *Le regard colonial* (Paris: Régine Desforges, 1986).

22. Due to a complex system of bonuses, French Army salaries in Djibouti were 20% to 40% higher that their same-rank metropolitan equivalent; in addition, the bonuses were tax-free.

23. Ali Coubba, *Mahmoud Harbi (1921–1960): Un nationaliste djiboutien?* (Paris: L'Harmattan, 2014).

24. Since the pioneering but dated work of Oberlé and Hugo (*Histoire de Djibouti, des origines à la république* (Paris: Présence Africaine, 1985)) and Thompson and Adloff (*Djibouti and the Horn of Africa* (Stanford: Stanford University Press, 1968)), there has been very little material published on Djibouti since decolonisation apart from the work of Ali Coubba, which cleverly hovers between 'serious' history and pamphleteering. This small but fascinating territory—it is hard

to call it a 'country'—remains one of the most understudied parts of the African continent, in spite of its massive relevance in modern strategic terms.

25. The best biography of that remarkable man is by Abdi Sheik Abdi, *Divine Madness*.

26. Brock Millman, *British Somaliland: An Administrative History (1920–1960)* (New York: Routledge, 2014).

27. Gerald Hanley: *Warriors* (London: Eland, 1993 [1971]).

28. See Gianluigi Rossi, *L'Africa italiana verso l'independenza (1941–1949)* (Rome: Giuffre Editore, 1980).

29. For a view of this peculiar existential struggle, see Giuseppe Maria Finaldi, *Italian National Identity in the Scramble for Africa: Italy's African Wars in the Era of Nation Building* (Bern: Peter Lang, 2009).

30. Robert Hess, *Italian Colonialism in Somalia* (Chicago: University of Chicago Press, 1966), ch. 6.

31. His Memoirs—Cesare Maria de Vecchi, *Orizzonti d'impero: Cinque anni in Somalia* (Milan: Mondadori, 1935)—are an explicit testimony of his brutality.

32. This is a point I develop at greater length in 'Benign Neglect versus La Grande Somalia: The Colonial Legacy and the Post-Colonial Somali State' in Markus Hoehne and Virginia Luling (eds.), *Milk and Peace, Drought and War: Somali Culture, Society and Politics. Essays in Honour of I.M. Lewis* (London: Hurst, 2010).

33. This had been a policy first announced by the Labour Foreign Secretary Ernest Bevin in 1946 at the Paris Peace Conference. This made him overnight a hero for the Somali, who still remember his name to this day, as part of their oral history.

34. Kenyan independence was formally proclaimed on 12 December 1963.

35. *Shifta* means 'bandit' in Amharic. Calling the rebels *shifta* gave them a foreign and criminal flavour, in any case not Somali.

36. Lord Lytton, *The Stolen Desert* (London: Macdonald, 1966). Lord Lytton was the grandson of the famous Victorian eccentric and anti-imperialist Wilfred Scawen Blunt, who had opposed the occupation of Egypt. Nonconformist political opinions, particularly on colonial matters, were a family tradition.

37. Of which the Suez Canal was a part.

38. As soon as Emperor Yohannes had been killed in battle against the Mahdists, King Menelik of Shoa proclaimed himself Emperor of Ethiopia (March 1889).

39. Between 1897 and 1917 they built the first railway in the Horn of Africa between Djibouti and Addis Ababa.

40. See Tibebe Eshete, 'The British Administration in the Ogaden and Its Legacy', in *Proceedings of the Eleventh International Conference of Ethiopian Studies*, pp. 323–38 (Addis Ababa: Addis Ababa University, 1994).

41. 'Independent Somalia, a Five-Pointed Star', *Africa 1960 (Confidential)* 8 (6 May 1960).

2. UNITED WE FALL: SOMALIA FROM INDEPENDENCE TO CIVIL WAR

1. The best global overview of the contradictions implicit in the decolonisation of the many pieces of the Somali territories can be found in John Drysdale, *The Somali Dispute* (London: Pall Mall Press, 1964).

2. The only possible exceptions are the borders of Rwanda and Burundi, long-existing African nation-states which have—roughly—kept their boundaries in the post-colonial map of the continent. This close fit did not ensure peace and stability.

3. The reason was, of course, article 4b of the Charter which stipulated respect for the borders resulting from the colonial carving up of Africa. This was, of course, a reasonably pragmatic decision overall; but in the mind of the Emperor it was an anti-Somalia Trojan horse, designed to protect Ethiopia's Ogaden province against a possible Somali threat.

4. He was also both anti-colonialist and anti-communist, which in the 1940s was a paradoxical ideological stance.

5. This is the title of an impassioned book by Louis Fitzgibbon (London: Rex Collings, 1982). But although this will remain a moot point, there is no certainty, given the intrinsic structural problems of Somali society, that political unity would have fostered political balance, peace and economic stability in the Somali world.

6. The Hawd region is a buffer zone between British Somaliland and the northern part of the Ogaden. Although theoretically part of Ethiopian territory, it is a vital zone for pasturing nomads who move in there from Somaliland for at least five months in the year during the dry season. In 1941, it was occupied by the British Army after the Italian collapse.

7. Haile Selassie's speech delivered in Kebre Dehar on 25 August 1956, quoted in Drysdale, *The Somali Dispute*, p. 83.

8. In the late 1950s socialism in the region was largely identified with the Arab world (particularly with Nasser's Egypt) and mixed with nationalism and pan-Arabism. Somali culture being highly autonomous, the political dimension of its Islam was quite distinct from the same religion as it was then lived in the Arab world. Thus pan-Somalism tended to become a poetic and *völkisch* ideology, bearing limited relation to the practical world of inter-state relations.

9. Digil-Mirifle was the term used during the colonial days for a clan family considered to be racially and culturally 'second-rate Somali'. Its derogatory connotations led to its being later discarded and replaced by the name Rahanweyn.

10. Making the whole 'unification' constitutionally illegal.

11. IRIN interview, October 2001.

12. It is impossible to be more precise than this since no census had ever been carried out, neither in British Somaliland nor in Somalia Italiana.

13. Interview with Ina Omane. Hargeisa, 2015.

14. Ibid.

15. There are no known reasons for this reticence. The only possible explanation is that he had no orders from his party superiors since he was an SYL member and on that day there was still no valid legal 'government' in the south. It is also possible that since the draft memorandum was written in English, he was wary of legalising a document he did not fully understand.

16. The mood of these officers at that time is broached by Hussein Ali Dualeh, who was one of them, in his book *From Barre to Aideed: Somalia, the Agony of a Nation* (Nairobi: Stellagraphics, 1994).

17. This alluded to pan-African unity, then a main decolonisation theme of African independence.

18. Quoted in Drysdale, *The Somali Dispute*, p. 115.

19. Ibid.

20. Five of six districts had voted and the secession tally for those—which accounted for over three-quarters of voters—was between 80% and 86% in favour of separation from Kenya and unity with Mogadishu. The vote was never carried out in the sixth district, leaving the referendum legally inconclusive.

21. Politically correct developments in Djibouti politics prior to independence can be found in Philippe Oberlé and Pierre Hugot, *Histoire de Djibouti, des origines à la république* (Paris: Présence Africaine, 1971) while a more realistic blow-by-blow account is given in Mohamed Aden, *Sombloloho: Djibouti: La chute du Président Aref (1975–1976)* (Paris: L'Harmattan. 1999).

22. Hussein Ali Dualeh notes in his book (*From Barre to Aideed*, p. 19) that in 1975, when the colony was still in French hands, a major Issa leader had told him that looking at the way things were going in Somalia between north and south tended to discourage the Djibouti Somalis from joining up with Mogadishu: 'we are few in numbers,' the man had told him, 'and we would be in an even worse position than the Somaliland Issaq are vis-à-vis the Southerners'.

23. In March 1967 the French had changed the name Côte Française des Somalis and renamed the colony Territoire Français des Afars et des Issas (TFAI) to make the word 'Somali' disappear from the territory's official name. The Mogadishu government was immediately hostile to the change and countered it by opening several lines of bank credit to important Djibouti Somali politicians, including LPAI members.

24. The sympathy for Somalia coming from the Arab world was linked to the lip service it gave to pan-Arabism, with pan-Somalism looking like a supportive younger brother.

25. General Nimeiry had already gone in that direction in May 1969 in the Sudan and Libya's Colonel Gaddafi had followed on the same path in September of that year.

26. Interview with Barre Nux, Hargeisa, 2015. The death penalties were not carried out but many of the detainees languished in jail for many years.

27. Interview with Dr Omar Dihood, Hargeisa, 2015.

28. In the Somali world, folk expressions had always carried more weight that Islamic ones. So, with the lack of a calendar (only educated people went by the Islamic calendar), time was rhythmically marked by collective events (usually negative) such as pestilence, drought or war. Each episode had its own name. The Dabadheer drought was the 'long-lasting one', the one that dragged on endlessly and did not stop for a long time.

29. The east of Somaliland is populated by non-Issaq clans. As Darood, the members of those clans were hoping to get a better welcome from their Darood cousins in the south than the Issaq would have got.

30. Interview with Osman Indhoole, Hargeisa, 2015.

31. It was they who became pirates in the late 1990s, after the collapse of the Somali state, when their new profession was destroyed by predatory Pakistani and Korean industrial fishing boats.

32. Actually, one of the underlying causes of the hurried way in which the 1960 Union had been carried out was the fear that the British, having had no preparation for independence, would reiterate their Hawd policy and retrocede the whole of British Somaliland to Ethiopia.

33. There is a very large bibliography on the Ethiopian revolution, usually of high quality. The best and most balanced overall study is arguably Christopher Clapham, *Transformation and Continuity in Revolutionary Ethiopia* (Cambridge: Cambridge University Press, 1988).

34. The acronym was based on the word 'abo', which means 'hello' among the eastern Oromo and 'father' in Somali. Even though the Oromo are distant cousins of the Somali, the use of a single word was not enough to turn them into Somali. Ethiopia was already facing a secessionist insurrection in Eritrea, and seeing Mogadishu support another rebellion among the large Oromo people (the Oromo make up almost 40% of the Ethiopian population) was an existential challenge.

35. See chapter 1 for some general developments on the question, and for further readings consult I.M. Lewis, *A Pastoral Democracy* (Oxford: Oxford University Press, 1961) (for the scientific anthropological approach) and Gerald Hanley, *Warriors* (London: Eland, 1993) (for the everyday, living, human contact approach).

36. Somali Revolutionary Socialist Party. Modelled on the Russian communist pattern, it was created on 1 July 1976 and warmly greeted by Soviet Communist Party Secretary-General Leonid Brezhnev.

37. Somali became a written language only in 1973. The choice of the Latin alphabet was a major cause of cultural, political and religious dispute. See David Laitin, *Politics, Language and Thought: The Somali Experience* (Chicago: University of Chicago Press, 1977).

38. *Africa Confidential*, 24 October 1969.

39. Later the assessment of the Siad Barre regime veered radically around 1988 due

to its massive brutality in the northern civil war. In media terms we went from the Father Figure to the Devil Incarnate. There is no dispassionate historical evaluation of this period available apart from Daniel Compagnon's *Le régime de Siad Barre (1969–1991)*, University of Pau, 1995, which still remains in unpublished PhD form.

40. *Jane's Strategic Survey* (London: 1977), p. 19.

41. The best picture of this strategic and diplomatic mess can be found in the candid memoirs of Ethiopia's Deputy Foreign Minister Dawit Wolde Giorgis, *Red Tears* (Trenton: Red Sea Press, 1989).

42. The best account of the conflict can be found in Gebru Tareke, *The Ethiopian Revolution: War in the Horn of Africa* (New Haven: Yale University Press, 2008), ch. 6.

43. These lands were taken by the British to give to the Habr Ja'alo sub-clan of their Issaq allies.

44. There the beneficiaries had been the Habr Awal of the Issaq, for the same reason. London had rewarded its supporters. In 1978 Siad Barre was hoping to go back on these land transfers by overturning the old decisions.

45. One of the coup leaders, Abdullahi Yusuf Ahmed, fled to Ethiopia from where he launched a rebel movement, the Somali Salvation Front (SOSAF). He started to harass the regime by a series of cross-border raids carried out from the Ogaden.

46. Author's interviews, Somaliland bush, February 1990 and Hargeisa, May 1996.

47. When I interviewed SNM fighters during the war, I found that a fair number of them had volunteered earlier either in the national army or in some kind of a militia to fight the Ethiopians.

48. Both Lixle and Mohamed Ali later became top commanders of the SNM rebellion and both were killed in combat, in 1984 and 1988 respectively.

49. Interview with Abdullahi Jama Abokor, Hargeisa, 2015.

50. Ibid. By then the WSLF was in such a state of contradiction and infighting that its secretary-general Abdullahi Hassan Mohamed did not dare set foot in the Ogaden because he was afraid of being killed by his own men.

51. Interview with Dr Adan Abokor, Hargeisa, 2015. These car thefts in broad daylight by 'important people' happened repeatedly and drove the public to a state of constant outrage. One well-known Marehan wife of an officer even placed orders for stealing certain models of cars that she would then send to relatives living in the south. She also drove some of her booty cars in Hargeisa in full view of everybody.

52. Its basic functioning and effects are outlined in Jamil Abdallah Mubarak, *From Bad Policy to Chaos in Somalia: How an Economy Fell Apart* (Westport: Praeger, 1996).

53. Interview with Mohamed Hashi, Hargeisa, 2015.

54. Interview with Mohamed Abdisalam Yassin, Hargeisa, 2015. Contrary to what

developed later, the radical Islamic movement did not at the time represent a strong and influential political force.

55. Given the violent relations between the local population and the refugees, this disparity contributed to the worsening of the situation.

56. *Deutsche Notärtze*, a private German organisation also known as 'Cap Anamur', founded in 1979, sent volunteers to Hargeisa. Interview with Yusuf Gaydh, Hargeisa, 2015.

57. Yusuf Gaydh interview.

58. Interview with Mohamed Barud, Hargeisa, 2015 and 2017. Colonel Abdullahi was an Issaq commander who was considered to be too friendly to the civilian population. His execution, for unspecified acts of 'national treason', was illegal and deeply traumatic for the local population.

59. The *mabraz* is the large room in which the men gather to chew *qat*, the amphetamine-laden vegetal which is the omnipresent 'social drug' of the Horn of Africa. *Qat* sessions are the equivalent of drinking at a British pub or a French *bistro*, the heart of social and political life.

60. It would be exaggerating to call them 'members' since there was no membership.

61. In the popular memory of the liberation struggle, most people tend to date the start of their moral engagement in the rebellion from that moment. *Dhagax tur* was the first time in Somalia when an unarmed crowd openly defied an armed authority.

62. Interviews in Hargeisa with Said Ali Salaan, Dr Adan Abokor, Khalif Hargeisa, Mohamed Mo'alim Osman and Hassan Guure, Hargeisa, 2015.

3. FOUNDING AND FOSTERING THE SOMALI NATIONAL MOVEMENT (SNM)

1. This is reflected in the work of the greatest living Somali writer, Nuruddin Farah, who wrote many books that are a direct illustration of this problem: *Maps* (1986), *Links* (2003), *Knots* (2007).

2. Brock Millman, *British Somaliland. An Administrative History (1920–1960)* (New York: Routledge, 2014). The next few pages are borrowed from a review essay of Millman's book I wrote for the *Journal of the Middle East and Africa* 6, 2 (April–June 2015).

3. Millman, *British Somaliland*, p. 33.

4. Gerald Hanley, *Warriors* (London: Eland, 1993). The author had published his Second World War East African campaign memoirs under the title *Warriors and Strangers* in 1971 and later separated the *Strangers* part, which is about Kenya, from the *Warriors* part, which is about the Somali.

5. The modern Somali spelling would be *Xeer*.

6. Here we would like to mention again Michael van Notten, *The Law of the Somalis* (Trenton: Red Sea Press, 2005).

7. The number of expatriate staff reached 376 in 1940, with 144 Indians and 232 British.

8. There was no mining of any sort, hardly any agriculture, and the only resource was animal flocks whose excess production was exported to Aden.

9. Including in such otherwise excellent works as Mark Bradbury, *Becoming Somaliland* (Oxford: James Currey, 2008) or Marleen Renders, *Consider Somaliland* (Leiden: Brill, 2012).

10. Abdi Sheikh Abdi, *Divine Madness: Mohamed Abdulle Hassan (1856–1920)* (London: Zed Books, 1993).

11. See chapter 2 for his complex role in leading the first armed groups issuing from WSLF.

12. The Adari are the native population of the Ethiopian city of Harar, quite distinct from their Oromo neighbours.

13. Interview with Mohamed Dacar, Hargeisa, 2015. Mohamed Dacar, a pure Issaq Somali from Somaliland, was a member of the group and was neither Iraqi, nor Syrian nor even less Eritrean.

14. The so-called 'Mad Mullah'.

15. The Issaq often see Mohamed Abdulle Hassan as a historical enemy while the Darood tend to see him as a 'nationalist hero'.

16. Since his adventures in Yemen, and to hide his undercover 'secret Issaq' work, he kept presenting himself as an Eritrean and a socialist revolutionary. Given his previous chequered career with the PLO and Lebanese fighting groups, this strange cover was accepted by many at face value when he joined the WSLF. He was seen as an internationalist, a kind of 'revolutionary without borders'.

17. Interview with Osman Qurux, Hargeisa, 2015.

18. There was no mention of secession or of creating a new state. It was simply a standard declaration of fighting for democracy.

19. The daily BBC broadcasts in the Somali language were listened to with intense attention. Nobody took the broadcasts of the national Somali radio seriously, even among the government supporters

20. Interview with Abdirahman Aqaadir, Hargeisa, 2015.

21. Interview with Abdisalam Yassin, Hargeisa, 2015.

22. The new name of the former SOSAF.

23. One has to be extremely careful about the type of generalisation I just made. There was never a solid Darood bloc fighting a solid Issaq bloc. There were some Issaq leaders who, through an ideological view of pan-Somalism or because of personal interest, stayed on the side of the Siad Barre regime. The opposite did not happen and clan ethnic identity worked as a filter in defining rebel alignment even if some members of the Darood clan family stayed out of the melee. But statistically the generalisation held a lot of truth. In the north geographical origins at times did trump the clanic ones and the result was that there were Gaddabursi on both the government and the rebel sides.

24. When I mentioned this fact in an article, 'A Candid View of the Somali National Movement', *Horn of Africa* XIV, 1–2 (January–June 1992) after spending some time with the guerrilla force, I was severely criticised by some SNM sympathizers for 'presenting a negative image of the Movement'.

25. The last democratically elected President, Abdirashid Ali Shermarke, assassinated on 15 October 1969, had been a Majerteen.

26. Daniel Compagnon, *Le régime de Siyyad Barre (1969–1991)*, University of Pau, 1995, pp. 201–5.

27. They were the distant heirs of the Soviet 'left opposition' and of the Trotskyists.

28. Colonel Gaddafi was then at the peak of his pro-Moscow engagement and he generously redistributed the vast quantities of weapons the Russians gave him to anti-US regimes or organisations, such as the Sudanese SPLA or the Somali SOSAF, and later its SSDF successor.

29. Addis Ababa in the 1980s was a politically strange place. Many members of the Russian and other Warsaw Pact missions who hung around the place had dark forebodings about the future of Communism. Therefore they tended to idealise their African comrades in whom they saw new blood for the future of the world socialist movement. I remember talking with a Bulgarian Communist Party cadre who waxed rhapsodical about Abdullahi Yusuf because the clever Somali colonel had told him he would erect a statue of Lenin in Mogadishu after taking power. But the Somali revolutionary had also told an Ethiopian friend of mine that he had bought a white horse to head the victory parade in Mogadishu, 'so that I can look like Mussolini'. The Ethiopian did not know what to make of that ambiguous remark.

30. Interview with Abdirahman Dheere, Hargeisa, 2015.

31. It was the last time any such popular enthusiasm was to manifest itself till the anti-American uprising of October 1993.

32. I personally witnessed SSDF members engaging in gunplay in the city of Dire Dawa and ending up being shot by the Ethiopian police.

33. See pp. 00–00.

34. He was to remain in jail till April 1991 when the takeover of Addis Ababa by the TPLF guerrillas allowed him to regain his freedom. He then rebranded himself vis-à-vis the victors as 'a victim of communism' and became Meles Zenawi's right-hand man for Somali affairs. But in the end he finally managed to alienate the Tigrayan leader just as he had alienated Mengistu.

35. Interview with Mohamed Dacar, Hargeisa, 2015.

36. The reason for attacking the Habr Yunis was simply that they represented the largest clanic group among SNM fighters at the time.

37. Siad Barre's mother was Ogadeni. But she was Rer Makahil.

38. During the Derg period people were not allowed to move freely around the country unless they had high-level government clearance. That the SNM delegates were

kept at the rank of ordinary visitors showed their poor level of Ethiopian support in 1981.

39. Interview with Abdirahman Dheere, Hargeisa, 2015.

40. It had started with the organisation calling itself Ragga U Dashaq Magaalada (the people of this city), eventually giving birth to the Uffo movement.

41. For more details on Uffo, see chapter 2.

4. SNM: THE SLOW GROWTH OF AN ODD GUERRILLA FORCE IN THE HARD-EDGED COLD WAR LANDSCAPE

1. Starting in October 1982, SNM had begun to set up some base camps in Ethiopia, close to the Somalia border. These were primitive arrangements, which we will come back to later.

2. Quite a few of the detainees were not Somali. There were also Eritreans, Arabs and even Ethiopians. After the 1978 defeat and its resulting desertions, the Somali regime had taken to arresting young men of any origin in the streets and incorporating them into the army. During the war I personally talked with people of six or seven different nationalities captured and press-ganged in Mogadishu, later to be taken prisoner by the SNM.

3. Lixle was a good Muslim but not particularly religious. He was probably using the word as a generic term for 'fight'.

4. Interview with Barre Nuux, Hargeisa, 2015, who personally witnessed Lixle's speech to the prisoners.

5. The small operational cell which had planned the Mandera operation was purely military and purely Ethiopia-based. The civilian external leadership in London was not even aware that the raid had been planned. Later this negligence became an argument for the promotion of military leadership in November 1983.

6. *Qat* (*Catha edulis*) is a small plant whose leaves contain a high concentration of amphetamines. It is used all over East Africa and in Yemen as an energising drug, its use being social and domestic and not linked to criminality. Most of the large quantities of *qat* consumed in Somalia are imported from Ethiopia or Kenya.

7. These were provided by the Ethiopian Army.

8. See chapter 3.

9. By 21st-century standards such a figure looks puny. But in 1982 it was worth easily ten times its value in 2017.

10. We use this party name as an easy marker. In fact the SRSP was the regime, i.e. the army. Even if the Darood clan family was dominant in that group, it was far from being completely clanic and it even comprised several influent Issaq.

11. *Shir* is the name given to a clanic deliberative council. We use this term here as a Somali equivalent (i.e. one where clan considerations would have to be included) of what could be called in another political environment 'a national conference'.

12. This was an interesting development which shows the practical limits of clanism. The Darood being such a large clan family, their most distant members do not feel much of a mutual empathy, which would be quite normal in the case of smaller clan units.

13. *Mag* is the Somali equivalent of the Arabic *Diya*, i.e. blood price. It is the money that has to be paid to compensate a clan for the loss of some of its members who have been killed in a conflict. Mutilations also have their tariffs, with one lost arm being so much, a severed leg so much, an eye so much, and so on, down to the price of one cut finger.

14. In a way they themselves were sandwiched between the two universes because the Habr Gidir sub-clan of the Hawiye was fighting the Marehan, Siad Barre's clan, who used the 'national' army against them.

15. Following the 1978 defeat and the army retreat, numerous roadblocks, arbitrarily called 'customs', had been installed in former Somaliland.

16. Such as Gal Hussein Kulmiye Afrah or Mohamed Sheikh Osman, the assistant secretary-general of SRSP.

17. 'The Cross' is the name for a well-known road junction near a small village.

18. 'Afweyne' (big mouth) was Siad Barre's nickname.

19. '*Faqhash*' (filth) was the nickname of the government troops.

20. And at that time it meant, by default, practically only the SNM.

21. Angelo Del Boca, *Nostalgia delle colonie*, vol. IV of *Gli Italiani in Africa Orientale* (Rome: Laterza, 1984).

22. The allegations of cattle sickness in Somalia given by the Saudi were bogus. The reality was that several Saudi princes had purchased land in Australia and wanted to flood their home market. But the Saudi population preferred the *berberawi* Somali sheep. So the only way to monopolise sheep imports was to ban those from Somalia.

23. The SSDF Ethiopian minders had declined to take part in the military attempt but had not stopped the Somali rebels from going ahead. Their complete failure, in a thinly populated area where they had no possible civilian support, simply illustrated their state of disarray.

24. 'Pik' would repeat the same operation in 1988 with Denis Sassou Nguesso, the Congo-Brazzaville President who was also in need of a post-Marxist transition. The wily South African even got Angola and Cuba to collaborate with him in a sleight of hand that, in the long run, was much more successful.

25. At the time the Comoros were under the presidency of Ahmed Abdallah, who was only a figurehead fronting for the French mercenary Bob Denard. South Africa was among the supporters of that odd regime.

26. *Africa Economic Digest*, 15 February 1985.

27. *La Reppublica*, 19 January 1985.

28. The key to the global change of Libyan diplomacy in the Horn was the 1985 fall

of Sudanese President Jaafar al-Nimeiry, whom Gaddafi considered a personal enemy. It was Gaddafi's desire to oppose Nimeiry that had driven him into a close alliance with communist Ethiopia and from there into a parallel support for SSDF, which was an Ethiopian protégé. Gaddafi stopped supporting the SPLA rebels in the Sudan, abandoned the Somali SSDF, distanced himself from the Ethiopian Derg and got closer to both Egypt and Saudi Arabia.

5. COLD WAR RECESS: THE MOGADISHU–SNM STAND-OFF IN AN INDIFFERENT WORLD, 1984–1988

1. This lack of Ethiopian enthusiasm had two causes: the SNM was perceived by the Derg as a religious (i.e. Islamist) guerrilla force, even if this was not true; and it had no support from Moscow, Ethiopia's political patron. This lack of Russian sponsorship was a real hindrance because it alienated the SNM from the West without providing it with any communist help.

2. Refugees were cynically manipulated and in April 1985 some were left in camps near Hargeisa that were totally bereft of medical services as a cholera epidemic developed. This 'waiting game', which was supposed to 'soften' the Red Cross and UNHCR, propelled the death rate from around 1,500 to over 3,000 in a few weeks.

3. *Indian Ocean Newsletter*, 31 August 1985.

4. See chapter 4 n. 22.

5. This was somewhat similar to the 'Françafrique' system in Paris. But the French parties had no *lottizzazione* system. The ruling party—the Gaullists between 1958 and 1981, later the Socialists between 1981–1995—were the ones cracking the whip: power meant access to the cash. The Italian system made corruption more democratic, more consensual.

6. 'Peace Camp' was an old Cold War formula referring to the Communist bloc and its 'neutralist' friends; the opposite side was the 'Imperialist Camp'.

7. Paolo Pilliteri, *Somalia '81: Intervista con Siad Barre* (Rome: Edizioni Sugar, 1981). The name of the publisher is not a joke, it is genuine.

8. Another name for the same organisation is Cooperazione Italiana allo Sviluppo (Italian Cooperation for Development). Forte was never FAI director but he was the one actually making the key strategic decisions.

9. They were the best-paid university teachers anywhere in the world. But the Catholic monthly *Nigrizia* called the university 'a place where you would not allow the graduates of the Medical School to take care of your dog' ('Facolta di non imparare' [the university of no learning], *Nigrizia*, February 1989).

10. For a vast and critical overview of the FAI scandal, see Gruppo della Sinistra Indipendente, *FAI: Ovvero quando l'aiuto allo sviluppo diventa spreco ed anche peggio* [FAI: When aid for development turns into complete waste and even worse] (Rome: Camera dei Deputati, November 1986).

11. Almirante did not go.
12. Following a comical emergency debate on where the wounded head of state should be sent, Rome or Riyadh. With death looming in the background, the family preferred proximity to the holy sites of Islam over possibly higher-quality medical care.
13. Ginny Hill, *Yemen Endures* (London: Hurst and Co., 2017), p. 2.
14. It is symptomatic that in this moment of great danger for the regime, the people who made up the top emergency resource team were not government officials but clan elders (Siad Barre was a Marehan).
15. His official position was head of the Army Public Works Service.
16. Officially his position was that of Minister of the Interior. This put him in charge of the police and of political repression and he was one of the most powerful men in the regime. On the contrary, Samantar, who was a Sab (i.e. a member of the clanless minorities traditionally despised in popular culture), was institutionally strong but individually weak. This is why Siad Barre had picked him as head of the armed forces and also why Dafle (the blade) supported him.
17. They were released in Addis Ababa in February.
18. We should never forget that 'the Somali question' was (and remains today) an international one. Djibouti, Ethiopia and Kenya, all with large Somali populations, were all preoccupied, to various degrees, by events in Somalia.
19. Siad had lost control of the main WSLF, which had divorced from Mogadishu over the issue of peace. In January 1986 the WSLF hardliners, who rejected any form of negotiation with Ethiopia, had seceded and created the Ogaden National Liberation Front (ONLF), which still exists today (2018) and theoretically still struggles for secession of the Ogaden from Ethiopia. The birth of ONLF destroyed what was left of the WSLF, leaving the remnants as pure and simple instruments of Siad Barre.
20. Interview with Abdullahi Jama Abokor, Hargeisa, 2015.
21. Interview with Prof. Abdisalan Yassin, Hargeisa, 2015.
22. Interview with Abdirahman Dheere, Hargeisa, 2015.
23. Meaning 'make propaganda'.
24. Interview with Dahir Yare, Hargeisa, 2015.
25. Interview with Rashid Sheikh Abdullahi, Hargeisa, 2015.
26. The Hawiye were resentful and some of their young men had joined SNM. But it was a marginal contribution and they were not involved in frontline operations. They just played a support role. Later they would create their own guerrilla group and attack the government.
27. I talked about this with Professor Lewis in his last few years and he modestly denied any influence. But then Karl Marx is also reputed to have said he was not a Marxist.
28. Silanyo had been Minister of Trade.
29. Interview with Ali Abaanash, Hargeisa, 2015.

30. Separate interview with Ali Abaanash, Hargeisa, 2015.

31. Interview with Raqiya Omar, Hargeisa, 2015. Raqiya became the director of Africa Watch in London and published a key document after the 1988 city fighting called *Somalia: A Government at War with Its Own People* (1989).

32. Interview with Fadumo Abdullahi Ibrahim, Hargeisa, 2015.

33. Interview with Sarah Halgan, Hargeisa, 2015. Sarah joined the SNM and became a famous singer of struggle songs.

34. Gerard Prunier, 'A Candid View of the Somali National Movement', *Horn of Africa* XIV, 1–2 (January–June 1992).

35. In fact, what this witness describes here is what is called *shir* in Somali culture, i.e. the clan assembly which is the basic forum for the 'pastoral democracy'.

36. It still exists in today's Somaliland as a kind of clanic Senate which is chosen by clan elders rather than elected, as the parliament is. Its role has unfortunately been abused in the last few years, the present assembly having succeeded in avoiding its renewal and having extended its mandate way beyond what custom should have allowed.

37. This was quite distinct from the piracy that developed in south Puntland after the fall of Siad Barre. In the SNM operations there was no hostage-taking and no threat to life.

38. Interview with Ibrahim Said Ismail, Hargeisa, 2015.

39. Interview with Farah Yusuf Osman Saxar, Hargeisa, 2015. Many military Calan Cas members accused Silanyo of having ordered the murder of Ali Adan Shine. A more probable story is that Ali Adan had been killed by government agents to avenge the assassination of Ahmed Adan, the Hargeisa NSS boss. Silanyo had no particular quarrel with Adan Shine, but this historical point has never been fully clarified.

40. In a later interview with Daniel Compagnon, Silanyo did not deny ordering the executions but he complained that the figures had been exaggerated.

41. There are strong probabilities that this hit squad had been put together and later trained by the notorious but efficient apartheid secret service BOSS (personal interview, Nairobi, 1993). It could be the same unit that shot Adan Shine that same month and Abdiqadir Kosar in Mustahil later in July.

42. World Bank, *Somalia: Recent Economic Developments and Medium Term Prospects* (Washington, DC, 10 February 1987).

43. His deputy was from Siad Barre's clan, the Marehan.

44. These were Jeeps with 106 mm recoilless guns, very useful for the rapid-movement fighting which the SNA carried out with the SNM guerrillas.

45. He had been to Bucharest, Ankara and Sana'a, shopping around the authoritarian governments' market, but to no avail.

46. The anti-*tuttaley* militants had named themselves *Desturi*, i.e. constitutionalists. They had no ready constitution in their pocket but they stood in opposition to the SRSP–Siad Barre dictatorship and wanted some kind of a constitution.

47. Ever the nationalist, Mengistu was furious at the fact that Ogadeni refugees in Somalia had been forcibly drafted into the Somali Army. These men were certainly his enemies but they were Ethiopians as far as he was concerned (even if they did not agree) and he took their brutal treatment as a national outrage. But the core disagreement had to do with the Somali claims to Ethiopian Ogaden territory.

48. Siad had no hostility towards Samantar, whose loyalty he never questioned. But since Samantar could never be President, given his clan-less Sab status, what Siad feared was the scenario in which the Vice-President could be 'recuperated' by an anti-Meslah group and handled just in the way Ahmed Suleiman Abdille 'Dafle' had done while Siad was in hospital in Saudi Arabia. Any strongman could use an intelligent and 'constitutional' puppet. Siad wanted to pre-empt such a scenario.

49. The communist support was of course that provided by the USSR and its satellites *prior* to the Ethiopian Revolution.

50. This alliance was due to two things: their ethnic proximity (Tigrayan speakers represent half the population of Eritrea) and their common Marxist-Leninist ideology. But many social, personal and cultural differences existed, as their eventual military conflict after their common victory eventually showed.

51. In his excellent military history of the war, *The Ethiopian Revolution: War in the Horn of Africa* (New Haven: Yale University Press, 2009), the Ethiopian historian Gebru Tareke calls it 'the Ethiopian Dien Bien Phu' (ch. 8). The comparison is apt. Few battles put an end to a war in one fell swoop, as this one did.

52. The Ethiopian signatory was Foreign Minister Berhanu Bayeh while the Somali representative was the almost unknown Deputy Prime Minister for Political Affairs, Ahmed Mahmood Farah. For Somalia this agreement, in complete contradiction to the pan-Somali ideal, was political poison and its premises had already scuttled the WSLF.

53. Radio Halgan ('struggle') was the rebel radio.

54. Silanyo actually used the delay in the offensive to fly to London.

55. Interview with Ali Abaanash, Hargeisa, 2015.

56. Interview with Osman Qurux, Hargeisa, 2015.

6. AND SUDDENLY ALL HELL BROKE LOOSE, 1988

1. They were definitely not anti-Marxist freedom fighters but rather dissident Marxists themselves. In the euphoric mood of the early 1990s and of the US-sponsored climate of the 'democratic end of history', the dissident Marxists were hailed as born-again capitalists, i.e. democrats. Time passed and by the early 2000s a more sober assessment began to develop.

2. On 13 October 1977 four Popular Front for the Liberation of Palestine (PFLP) commandos hijacked a Lufthansa commercial flight between Palma de Mallorca and Frankfurt with 86 passengers on board and flew it to Mogadishu. They

demanded freedom for some members of their organisation and for four impris-oned Rote Armee Fraktion (RAF) militants detained in Stammheim. On 18 October Siad Barre gave the green light to German Special Service forces to come and storm the plane, killing three of the four PFLP hijackers and capturing the fourth. Back in Germany the RAF militants conveniently committed suicide. To thank the Somali President for his help, the Bonn Republic provided Mogadishu with limited but regular amounts of light weapons (G-3 rifles) and the necessary ammunition.

3. The plot against Silanyo was a mixture of ideological disagreement ('the chairman is weak, the war should be prosecuted more forcefully and with a socialist out-look'), clanic jealousy ('what is this Habr Ja'alo doing up there?') and simple per-sonal dislike ('we need real military commanders, not a lazy bureaucrat in an office').

4. IGADD meant Intergovernmental Authority against Drought and for Develop-ment, and was created in Djibouti in March 1988, just in time for the Ethiopia–Somalia 'peace'. It was the brainchild of Djibouti President Hassan Gouled, who sought to play a big diplomatic role in spite of ruling a small country. So he chose the role of local go-between to mediate in much larger quarrels, a role the pres-ent-day IGAD (the second 'd' for 'development' has been realistically abandoned) still tries rather unsuccessfully to play.

5. The announcements of these measures (Northern military forces assigned to the North instead of a quasi-southern military occupation of 'Somaliland' by Southern troops, Northern civil servants playing a role in the governance of the South) were supposed to point out to a 'national integration policy' which seemed to go with-out saying since Somaliland and Somalia Italiana had supposedly merged in 1960 but which in fact had never actually taken place.

6. Interview with Ali Abaanash, Hargeisa, 2015. The announced transfers of north-ern civil servants to the north or of Issaq promotions in the south were mostly rumours till (Issaq) General Aden Abdu Dualeh was made head of the police in September 1988. But as a precaution he was flanked with a Marehan deputy, General Osman Ahmed Osman. to keep him under control The whole idea of clanic re-equilibration never got off the ground.

7. We can see here that the SNM high command remained quite amateurish in devel-oping even tactical aims. Targets were switched, and troop reallocation and impro-vised counter-attacks were spontaneously undertaken without prior consultation, all this at a time when radio communications were still extremely limited.

8. Interview Omar Gaabuush, Hargeisa, 2015.

9. For the story of these new M-16s, see below.

10. This was typical of SNM operating procedure. The top officer just gave his opin-ion and he could be outvoted by his subordinates. It was a military disaster but it was also one of the cultural processes which solidified the group and gave the SNM a massive capacity for resilience if we compare it, for example, to the traditional

SSDF top-down military style. But in the short run, it played havoc with discipline.

11. In fact, South African,

12. Interview with Hasan Dayax, Hargeisa, 2015.

13. This was the main force of the SNA defending the north and it was placed under the direct orders of General Aden Abdullahi Nur 'Gabiyow', who had to battle with Siad's son Meslah to (illegally) get that command.

14. Another serious mistake. Adadley had already been taken and SNM was in no need of more fighters there. But abandoning the airport was even worse because within days it was back in SNA hands and able to accommodate both transport planes and the Hawker Hunter fighter bombers which were to cause so much damage later.

15. Later elected President of Somaliland in 2017.

16. Somali Patriotic Movement. As the SNA took more hits from SNM and despite holding its ground against the rebellious forces, it started to disintegrate, though not incoherently. The various groups that would either retreat or resist SNM would recompose themselves and create clanic sub-units that would fight SNM while retreating and also at times start fighting each other. Omar Jess and his SPM coalesced into an Ogadeni force that soon attacked the SNA troops which had remained 'governmental'. The pattern of the next period of Somali history—the time of the warlords—was beginning to take shape.

17. United Somali Congress. Led by General Mohamed Farah Aydid, it was a Hawiye front which began to emerge from the ruins of SNA and attack the government (see the next chapter).

18. These men headed for Awdal province where they rebelled and created the SNF (Somali National Front), which was an ambiguous organization, as we will see in chapter 7. SNF had Issa and Gaddabursi fighters who were at times fighting the government but also more often fighting SNM under the semi-hidden leadership of Ismail Omar Guelleh, then director of the Djibouti Secret Service, who was hoping to extend Djibouti's territory eastwards, towards Loyada and Sheikh, as Somalia disintegrated.

19. Interview with Major Mohamed Kosar, Hargeisa, January 2015.

20. Interview with Abdullahi Farah Abdi, Hargeisa, January 2015. This opens the question whether the systematic killings of Issaq could be called a genocide.

21. Interview with Ali Abaanash, Hargeisa, January 2015.

22. Interview of Mohamed Ali Abdullahi (August 1989), quoted in Africa Watch, *Somalia: A Government at War with Its Own People* (London, 1990).

23. 'Victory Pioneers', a government youth movement increasingly used as an auxiliary armed force as the war developed.

24. Interview with Sarah Ahmed Arteh, June 1989, in Africa Watch, *Somalia*, p. 133.

25. Military Security.

26. Interview with Abdirahman Mohamed Jama, Cardiff, July 1989, in Africa Watch, *Somalia*, p. 148.

27. Interview with Hassan Muhamad Abdullahi, Djibouti, August 1989, in Africa Watch, *Somalia*, p. 148.

28. Borama is not an area of mainly Issaq people. The majority population in and around Borama are Gaddabursi, who were at the time broadly on the government side. The prisoners had therefore been selected on a clan basis.

29. 'The Virgin's Breasts', the popular name of two round mountains that overlook Hargeisa. The SNA had a supply base at the foot of those mountains. Later it was on the Virgin's Breasts that the SNA installed its heavy artillery and randomly lobbed shells down into the city.

30. It was from that very airport that the Hawker Hunter fighter-bombers operated by the South African mercenaries were taking off on the bombing and strafing missions to nearby Hargeisa. The fully loaded flying time to Hargeisa was ten minutes, which allowed the planes a rapid turnaround time. Even in a relaxed mood, they could complete a minimum of five missions a day.

31. Interview with Kayser Ismail Adan, August 1989, in Africa Watch, *Somalia*, p. 155.

32. Many weapons also came by way of Berbera. The non-occupation of both Hargeisa airport and of Berbera were major strategic mistakes of the SNM in the spring of 1988, resulting in a staggering human cost.

33. This opens the question whether the systematic killings of Issaq could be called a genocide. See *The Nation*, 22 October 2018, https://www.thenation.com/article/in-the-valley-of-death-somalilands-forgotten-genocide/, which takes a new look at the topic

34. CAA statement on Somalia, 12 January 1989.

35. Published in translation in the July 1987 issue of *The New African*.

36. 'The rotten ones', derogatory name given to the SNM rebels by the government.

37. They flew too high to risk being hit by SNM fire and, as a result, their own bombing and machine-gunning was hopelessly ineffectual. Moreover, some of the pilots were not enthusiastic about the job and made the attacks even less dangerous by deliberately dropping their loads away from the targets. On 12 July a Mig-17 pilot completely refused to attack a column of refugees, flew to Djibouti and bailed out of his plane over the Gulf of Tadjourah.

38. These were planes that had been in service in the UAE Air Force for nearly ten years and that Abu Dhabi wanted to get rid of.

39. The following year, when parts began to run out and Siad Barre could not get resupplied from either the UK or the UAE, he sent a mission to Chile where President Pinochet had a few leftover Hawker Hunters he was ready to take apart and sell. But the officers in charge (names withheld) stole the $5 million budget, split it among themselves and went into exile.

40. Interview by the author of some anonymous refugees near Hargeisa, February

1990. In spite of a fair amount of research, this author has never managed to identify 'Mr John'. The ground targets (SNM fighters, refugees) had managed to rig a radio on the wavelength used by the Hunter pilots and they listened to the conversations between the pilots and the Berbera air base. A member of the South African team was a certain 'K. Jones' but he was officially a mechanical engineer, not a pilot.

41. US General Accounting Office, *Somalia: Observations Regarding the Northern Conflict*, Report B-225870, May 1989.

42. Meslah and General Aden Abdullahi Nur were still at each other's throats over the control of the 26th Division and Gabiyow was using the services of Omar Jess to handle the President's son, just at the moment when Jess was betraying his government and busy creating the SPM rebel movement to overthrow the regime.

43. Robert Gersony, *Why Somalis Flee* (Washington, DC: Department of State, Bureau for Refugee Programs, August 1989).

44. Africa Watch, *Somalia*. Although researched separately, the Gersony report and the Africa Watch one came out at the same time. The impact on the US Congress was significant.

45. GAO Report, p. 6.

46. Testimony of Karshe Mohamed, Cardiff, July 1989, in Africa Watch, *Somalia*, pp. 172–92.

47. Testimony of Jama Osman Samantar, London, June 1989, in Africa Watch, *Somalia*, pp. 172–92.

48. Testimony of Hassan Ismail Omar, Cardiff, July 1989, in Africa Watch, *Somalia*, pp. 172–92.

49. Testimony of Samia Sheef, London, June 1989, in Africa Watch, *Somalia*, pp. 172–92.

50. An Issaq sub-clan.

51. Interview with Ibrahim Mohamed Abdullahi, Hargeisa, 2015.

52. These were part of the 'old caseload' batch, i.e. soldiers who had been captured during the Ethiopian-Somali war of 1977–8.

53. Paradoxically, victory had had the same effect on the SNM. Given the huge rush of untrained volunteers, the previous partly trans-clanic regiments had exploded and regrouped people of similar sub-clans (practically all new recruits were Issaq, so the divisions followed sub-clanic lines).

54. On 29 September 1988 the shilling fell from 100 to 247 to the US dollar.

7. THE LOCAL WAR IN THE NORTH GOES GLOBAL, 1989–1991

1. Cf. G. Prunier, 'Benign Neglect versus La Grande Somalia: The Colonial Legacy and the Post-Colonial State', in Markus Hoehne and Virginia Luling (eds.), *Milk and Peace, Drought and War: Somali Culture, Society and Politics* (London: Hurst and Co., 2010), especially pp. 43–5.

2. The Dhulbahante are the northernmost Darood, which put them in the first line of combat against the Issaq. By late 1988, their geographical position began to worry them: Darood, indeed, but very far from the others and perilously close to the Issaq.

3. General Service Unit, a paramilitary Kenyan force.

4. *The New African*, November 1988.

5. *Indian Ocean Newsletter*, 25 February 1989.

6. World Bank (1987).

7. Interview with Rashid Sheikh Abdullahi, Hargeisa, 2015.

8. Assembly of the clans, a form of clanic Senate which came out of the war and remained a constitutional part of post-war independent Somaliland.

9. Interview with Abdikadir Hussein, Hargeisa, 2015.

10. Given the track record of 1960–9 in Somalia, multi-partyism was most likely to become another name for multi-clanism.

11. Al-Jazeera is a beach just outside Mogadishu. The prisoners were shot and summarily buried in the sand.

12. The SNM claimed there had been 1,500 casualties. While this claim is probably somewhat exaggerated, it should be kept in mind that summary executions kept happening during the whole third and fourth weeks of July (see Africa Watch, *Somalia: Tien an-Men Revisited*, 21 July 1989 and *Somalia: An Update on Human Rights Developments*, 22 September 1989). The London-based *New African* compiled a detailed list of 1,048 victims, with a majority of Hawiye (696) and 'only' 150 Issaq (November 1989 issue).

13. Another mission had previously been sent to Pinochet's Chile to acquire spare parts for the Hawker Hunters of the Somali Air Force's last flying squadron but the officers in charge had stolen the budget.

14. They included Mervyn Dymally, Howard Volpe and Albert Gore.

15. In June the US announced the assignment of $15.1 million 'budgetary aid' whose avowed purpose was of a purely economic nature. But the actual reason was to help Mogadishu reimburse the $76 million arrears it had piled up at the IMF and to reopen the international credit taps for money to flow into Somalia and help it fight the war. With the Russians next door in Ethiopia, Mogadishu was still perceived as a questionable but potentially real US ally, under Siad Barre or anybody else.

16. *Gaashaanbuur* ('the pile of shields') is the pragmatic military alliance structure that can be developed tactically by different clans which lack the necessary numbers for simple, direct 'clanic survival'.

17. Interview with Haibe Omar Magan, former mechanical officer of 54th Division (Galkayo), November 1992.

18. By February 1990, when the counting was done, the figure was put at 446,000, far from the extravagant numbers previously insisted upon by the government. But

given the situation in Ethiopia, 70% of them asked to stay in Somalia in spite of the much lower incentive package offered by UNHCR.

19. And girls! I witnessed young women fighters dressed not in hijab but in skimpy shorts and sleeveless jackets, sporting the bushy *gofare* hairdo of the Ethiopian fighters.

20. Interview in Djibouti with a former Prime Minister, January 1990. On 15 December 1989 the Djibouti Minister of the Interior, Moumin Farah Badon, said in an interview to the Saudi daily *al-Muslimin* that the fall of Siad Barre was only a question of time.

21. These included the well-known lawyer Ismail Jumaale Ossoble, who had been jailed since July 1989, and Omar Arteh Ghalib, the former Minister of Foreign Affairs, who had put Somalia on the map of the world before being arrested and condemned to death in June 1982. He was released from jail a few years later.

22. Most of the deserters were either Ogadeni or Hawiye, two origins largely represented in the SNA. Many of the Ogadeni soldiers were legally 'Ethiopians'.

23. Patrick Gilkes, *Two Wasted Years: The Republic of Somaliland (1991–1993)* (London: Save the Children Fund, 1993).

24. Mohamed Haji Ingiriis, 'The Making of the 1990 Manifesto: Somalia's Last Chance for State Survival', *Journal of Northeast African Studies* 12, 2 (2012), pp. 63–94.

25. Congressman Howard Volpe, who had ordered the GAO report on the war and later written the letter to James Baker in order to stop the IMF sponsorship for Somalia (see above), moved in to block the lease renewal.

26. Interview of Minister Giovanni Di Michelis. *Corriere della Sera*, 16 July 1990.

27. As part of the agitation around the First Gulf War.

28. It was actually never used.

29. The Manifesto group was hoping to separate the 'moderates' from the 'radicals' and arrange peace talks with the regime in Cairo.

30. Hissène Habré, President of Chad between 1982 and 1990. After eight years of brutal and barbarous rule, he fought to keep his power and lost. At the time Egal was drafting this letter, he had just fled into exile. He was later arrested and condemned to a life sentence in 2007.

31. Hussein Mohamed Arshad was President of Bangladesh from 1983 till 1990. When faced by a popular insurrection, he stepped down and preserved national unity. He remained a politician and an MP.

32. As the disintegration of the SNA was proceeding forthwith, all clan families were trying to acquire added political respectability by creating their own political organisation, as a prelude to future negotiations. The 'state' perspective was still dominant and all clans wanted to have their part in the future post-Siad 'state'. But the very nature of that state, its constitutional lineaments, its functioning, its territorial definition, were all left vague.

33. The Galgalo had a long-standing feud with the dominant sub-sub-clan of the Habr Gidir. This was clan politics at its grossest level.

34. For precise details of what went on in Mogadishu at that time and for a history of the days closely following Siad Barre's fall, refer to Lidwien Kapteijns, *Clan Cleansing in Somalia: The Ruinous Legacy of 1991* (Philadelphia: University of Pennsylvania Press, 2013).

35. Western secret services at the time estimated that the SNA was down to about 10,000 men or fewer. Those SNA soldiers who were Issa by clan started to sport USF armbands.

36. He was a Habr Awal Sa'ad Musa. Before his arrest, he had been short-listed as a potential UN Secretary-General, before Javier Pérez de Cuéllar had been elected.

37. Interview with his son, Hargeisa, June 2010.

38. On 1 March 1991, there were estimated by UNHCR to be 35,000 left in Somalia.

8. NORTH AND SOUTH BREAK UP AND FIGHT AMONG THEMSELVES

1. Benadir is the small coastal region immediately adjacent to the capital.

2. The SPM was recruited among the various Ogaden clans of the Darood clan family while the USC was recruited mostly among the Hawiye clan family.

3. Aydid was an SNM member and after the Baligubadle *shir* he asked Abdirahman 'Tuur' for 600 men to help him take Mogadishu before his USC rivals could. Tuur refused, for security concerns.

4. Galal was a Hawiye Habr Gidir Saleeban. His Habr Gidir identity made him eventually line up with his former adversary Aydid when the Manifesto group withered away (Ali Mahdi was a Sa'ad, clanically more distant). As for being 'moderate', this is to be seen in the 1991 context, where Galal accepted the idea of negotiation with the collapsing dictatorship while Aydid insisted on military victory. But Galal had been a solid Siad Barre henchman and in 1978, after the Ogaden defeat, he shot 85 Issaq officers by firing squad in Hargeisa because Siad Barre feared that, disappointed by the defeat in the Ethiopian war, they could join the recent Majerteen uprising against his regime.

5. See Kapteijns, *Clan Cleansing in Somalia*, particularly ch. 3. The Issaq were anti-Siad Barre in their majority. But several of their leading families had money and owned real estate. For the Hawiye, who considered that Mogadishu 'belonged to them' (in pre-colonial times, this was indeed part of their land base), their presence could not be tolerated. The clan cleansing was such that within two weeks of Siad Barre's flight, over 8,000 non-Hawiye civilians had been killed, Issaq being one of the main group of victims.

6. Kapteijns, *Clan Cleansing in Somalia*, p. 160.

7. Afgooye is a satellite town of Mogadishu, about 70 km away. Green and well-watered, it has a big market and serves as a food supply centre for the capital.

8. It had been formed on 3 February 1991.

9. The USF was remotely controlled by Djibouti security boss Ismail Omar Guelleh

and was, in fact, a trial structure that aimed at grabbing land for the Issa in the case where Somalia would completely dissolve.

10. The future President of Somaliland, Mohamed Ibrahim Egal, who was Issaq but not a member of SNM, joined the call for attending the conference. Like most of the Somali political class, he was still a 'unitarist'. But in 1991 his siding with the Ali Mahdi–Omar Arteh line was not popular in the north, even among those Issaq who balked at secession but were aiming for the creation of a confederacy, not a centralised unitary state.

11. The victims were mostly Rahanweyn, the marginal clan family which had traditionally been despised in the south. Racially mixed with Bantu and Oromo minorities, they had been tactical allies of the Italians during the colonial period. In the colonial literature, they were called Digil-Mirifle.

12. This was after the SPM had used the post office in Liboi (Kenya border) to contact people in Britain and spoke as if it were a government service.

13. Egyptian Undersecretary of State for Foreign Affairs.

14. Always keen on finding clanic justification for any political positioning, the supporters of that solution invented a common parent called 'Irir', a supposed common ancestor of both the Issaq and the Hawiye. Around 1990–1 both Aydid and Silanyo tried to float the notion of an 'Irir' state.

15. Interview with Hassan Musa Jibril, Hargeisa, 2015.

16. This is not a personal opinion but rather the result of a long experience of post-civil war situations in a variety of African environments. The problem of post-conflict retribution I saw varied from very little (Ethiopia, Burundi, Uganda in the south) to massive vengeance (Rwanda). Within Somalia, the attitude ranged from the excesses of ethnic cleansing in the south to limited, controlled executions in Somaliland.

17. Interview with Abdirahman Dhadhan, Hargeisa, 2015.

18. The main problem of clanic compatibility came not from the Ogadeni sub-clans of the north (Yabarre, Jarso, Rer Ali) but with those Ogadeni from south-central Ogaden, who had no history of common relations with the Issaq.

19. Jijiga is an Ethiopian town. But the war largely went beyond the borders. Being myself in Baligubadle at the time of the February 1990 *shir*, I wandered unknowingly into 'Ethiopia' without realising my mistake. I was escorted back into 'Somalia' by some boys who were herding their flocks.

20. Interview with Daud Khayre, Hargeisa, 2015.

21. Interview with Ahmed Adan Gurey, Hargeisa, 2015.

22. Interview with Omer Hassan Awale, Hargeisa, 2015.

23. The Koodbur Force was an old SNM project that did not materialise for a long time. The idea was to have a trans-clanic regiment rather than—as was the case then—a juxtaposition of clanically homogeneous units. The Koodbur Force finally took shape only after the Baligubadle congress, when members of the old Uffo

pre-war association (see chapter 2) became active in SNM organising. Koodbur was neutral in intra-Issaq tensions.

24. The Gaddabursi militia, former ally of the Mogadishu regime.

25. These had come from Ethiopia to escape Mengistu's villagisation policies and gave their allegiance to OLF.

26. Interview with Hassan Halas, Hargeisa, 2015.

27. Interview with Ahmed Adan Gurrey, Hargeisa, 2015.

28. Interview with Fadumo Abdullahi Ibrahim, Hargeisa, 2015.

29. Interview with Ahmed Adan Gurrey, Hargeisa, 2015.

30. The interviewee is Habr Yunis.

31. The Warsangeli are members of the Darood clan family while the Habr Yunis are Issaq. The Warsangeli had therefore sided with Siad Barre while the Habr Yunis were SNM. But no atrocities had been committed on that particular front.

32. Interview with Ahmed Adan Gurrey, Hargeisa, 2015.

33. The last one was the 1997 conference held in Hargeisa after the end of the third Somaliland civil war between the Habr Garhadjis and the government.

34. The interviewee is not talking about the war against the Mogadishu dictatorship but about the three bouts of civil war internal to Somaliland in 1992, 1993 and 1995–7 (see next chapter).

35. Interview with Dr Suleiman Abdi Gouled, Hargeisa, 2015.

36. Interview with Shukri Haji Bandare, Hargeisa, 2015.

37. Interview with Ismail Daher Ahmed, Hargeisa, 2015.

9. INDEPENDENCE, HUMANITARIAN INVASION AND SAILING INTO THE UNKNOWN

1. This was at the heart of the debate on the Koodbur Force (see chapter 8).

2. Interview with Omer Essa Awale, Hargeisa, 2015.

3. It was a partial USC government since it was supported by the Ali Mahdi faction but not by the Aydid group. Roughly the first faction represented the Abgaal Hawiye sub-clan while the second stood for the Habr Gidir sub-clan of the same clan family.

4. Interview with Omer Essa Awale, Hargeisa, 2015.

5. Interview with Omer Essa Awale, Hargeisa, 2015.

6. It was the misinformed rumours concerning those crimes that caused the blind US-led international intervention of 1992–5 known as Operation Restore Hope.

7. Interview with Osman Qurux, Hargeisa, 2015.

8. At Baligubadle in February 1990, when Silanyo was sidelined and Abdirahman 'Tuur' became chairman. But since both were against independence, it was not disagreement on that point that fostered civil war.

9. Interview with Abdi Giire, Hargeisa, 2015.

10. This is a tremendous difference with the south, where no election, clanic or oth-

erwise, could yield a real operational result. This is where the British political culture influenced participants in one way while the absence of applied Italian political culture abroad left the southerners at the mercy of clanic *Xeer*, a form of legal obligation which was designed for statelessness.

11. Interview with Abdi Giire, Hargeisa, 2015.

12. See ACLED Report, *Somalia September 2017 Update*, link does not work. think it might be: https://acleddata.com/2017/09/22/somalia-september-2017-update/, accessed 23 September 2017. Due to a variety of circumstances, this book took a long time to get into print and I did no additional research during the editing period (which might have given a clearer view of the type of violence still in play today). But a geographically diversified form of violence is still an incontrovertible reality in the former Somalia Italiana, apart from Puntland territory.

13. See chapter 10 for post-1997 north–south relations in Somaliland/Somalia.

14. This section is broadly based on a long paper I wrote in July 1995 for the Writenet Network (a subsidiary of Practical Management UK), under the title 'Civil War, Intervention and Withdrawal: The Somali Crucible (1990–1995)'.

15. Agence France Presse, 3 December 1992.

16. François Mitterrand.

17. Telephone conversation, 3 December 1992.

18. *New York Times*, 1 December 1992.

19. *New York Times*, 28 November 1992.

20. This was the US name for what was known internationally as UNITAF (United Nations Intervention Task Force).

21. This view of the armed Somali population, such as presented above, was fantasmatic. And the parallel lack of perspective on the intractable political conundrum completed a picture of complete ignorance

22. I was one of them. After publishing a piece called 'La politique bafouée' (political blindness) in the Paris intellectual monthly *Le Monde des Débats*, I was vilified for 'blatant cynicism' and accused of 'not caring about the death of babies'. With the end of the Cold War, Somalia became one of the key turning points in trying to deal differently with geopolitical problems. The switch tended to trade old rigidity for a new naivety.

23. On the delicate question of human losses and lives saved, the best study is Steven Hansch et al., *Lives Lost, Lives Saved: Excess Mortality and the Impact of Health Interventions in the Somalia Emergency* (Washington, DC: Refugee Policy Group, 1994). Note the carefully neutral vocabulary of the title: here we are not at war, we are evaluating 'an emergency'.

24. From this point of view, the memoirs of Robert Oakley, who was Special Envoy to Somalia for both President Bush and President Clinton, are very revealing. In the chapter devoted to 'Political Consultations on the US Intervention' he mentions some UN personnel, a variety of African envoys at the UN and 'European

Heads of State', none of whom had any particular knowledge about Somalia. There was no consultation with either Somali or real US experts (see John Hirsch and Robert Oakley, *Somalia and Operation Restore Hope: Reflections on Peacemaking and Peacekeeping* (Washington, DC: Institute of Peace, 1995)). The dominant idea seems to have been—and probably remains—that Africa was in itself a 'unit' and that any 'African' or foreign 'Africanist' could provide a valid opinion.

25. Author's interviews with many Somali of all walks of life in 1993–4. Later, in a rather astonishing display of honesty, the former Siad Barre minister turned warlord, General Aden Abdullahi Nur 'Gabiyow' publicly declared that he and his fellow militia leaders 'should be arrested if there is to be any hope for the country' (*Somalia News Update*, 11 July 1994).

26. I.M. Lewis, 'Pacifying the Warlords', *The Times*, 12 December 1992.

27. Interview with General Aden Abdullahi Nur 'Gabiyow', SNF leader, Addis Ababa, April 1993.

28. *Indian Ocean Newsletter*, 5 June 1993.

29. BBC quoting Radio Mogadishu (which was pro-Ali Mahdi), 5 June 1993.

30. *Report of the Commission of Inquiry Established Pursuant to Security Council Resolution 885 (1993) to Investigate Armed Attacks on UNOSOM II Personnel* (New York: United Nations, 24 February 1994).

31. About a maximum of 4,700 men during the second period (*Somalia News Update*, 5 October 1993.

32. 'UN Chief Warning US against Pullout of Force in Somalia', *New York Times*, 30 September 1993.

33. *Indian Ocean Newsletter*, 18 September and 2 October 1993.

34. The event was dramatised by a bestselling book published a few years later: Mark Bowden, *Black Hawk Down: A Story of Modern War* (New York: Grove Press, 1999). The movie made from the book in 2001 by Ridley Scott is for many people the epitome of the Somalia question when in fact it is a most atypical representation of the conflict or the country. The movie was shot in Morocco, there were no Somali actors and no Somali consultants for veracity. It was just another 'action movie'.

35. Bernard Helander and Mohamed Haji Mukhtar, *Building Peace from Below? A Critical Review of the District Councils of Bay and Bakool Regions of Southern Somalia* (Uppsala: Life and Peace Institute, April 1995).

36. The main contingents were from India and Pakistan. The other large ones were from Malaysia, Morocco, Egypt, Nigeria and Zimbabwe.

37. *The Economist*, 24 September 1994.

38. The post-Bura'o government was supported by what was in fact a Habr Garhadjis alliance, i.e. the Eidagalley, Habr Yunis and Arap sub-clans.

39. To be completely honest, I once saw one. She carried an AK-47 and had grenades slung around her waist but was dressed in a feminine ankle-long dress. She had

picked up a gun after she saw her husband killed under her eyes by the Siad Barre army. The men around her treated her with respect but thought she was 'special'.

40. The choice was deliberate. During the war, most of the Gaddabursi had sided with Mogadishu and their commitment to Somaliland independence was at first half-hearted. But their facilitating role in the various post-war *shirs* earned them respect.

41. 90 Issaq, 34 Darood and 26 Dir.

42. Egal was a Habr Awal of the Issa Musa sub-clan. As a former Prime Minister of the original Republic (1960–9), prisoner of Siad Barre (1969–82) and self-exiled 'leader of conscience' of the ailing post-Ethiopian war Somalia, he was a living symbol of the achievements, sufferings and errors of the country. He never publicly recanted anything, not even his adherence to the 1960 unity (which he recognised in private to have been a mistake).

43. The population called the conference 'Alaa mahad leh' (Grace be given to God).

44. The SNM had de facto dissolved itself after the end of the war. Abdirahman 'Tuur' himself had previously admitted that its Central Committee had not met for months, even before the Borama Conference.

45. See *Somalia News Update*, 14 December 1994.

46. This is not to excuse all of Mohamed Farah Aydid's political actions. But by mid-1993 the UN in Somalia had taken sides, culminating in issuing Wild West-type posters reading 'MOHAMED FARAH AYDID: WANTED. $25,000', which seemed to mark a very low level of diplomacy.

47. S/26319 (17 August 1993).

48. The SNA was a new entity set up by Aydid to regroup his supporters under a common banner. By then *all* the former anti-Siad Barre guerrilla groups which had ousted the dictatorship had split into pro-Aydid and pro-Ali Mahdi groups. By attending an SNA-sponsored meeting, Abdirahman 'Tuur' announced his new colours.

10. ODD MAN OUT: SOMALILAND'S FRAGILE PEACE ON THE EDGE OF SOMALIA'S WAR WITHOUT END

1. This was a word borrowed from a period of the Chinese Revolution when in the 1920s the provincial governors became *tuchun*, i.e. 'warlords', practically independent from the impotent government existing in Beijing at the time. The Somali warlords did not even have a ghost 'government' till 2000.

2. Ken Menkhaus and John Prendergast, *Political Economy of Post-intervention Somalia* (Washington, DC: The Center of Concern, April 1995), p. 3.

3. Menkhaus and Prendergast, *Political Economy of Post-intervention Somalia*.

4. Mogadishu being too tempting a target, any attempt at reopening it to international traffic would immediately cause a free-for-all among all the prospective 'armed managers'. Attempts at collective management all failed one after the other when the prospective participants fought each other over the sharing of the resource.

5. In Djibouti the post-colonial habits are so ingrained that the boundary limits between (unofficial) French and (quasi-official) Djiboutian positions are so porous that the difference is often ambiguous.

6. This is an old term used in 19th-century anthropology to designate the members of the Dir clan family, i.e. basically the Issa and the Gaddabursi. The very choice of that name had a dated connotation, as if coming from an old sepia-coloured 1910 daguerreotype.

7. 'Against the SNM' is closer to reality than saying 'for the Mogadishu regime'. Of course the SNM was seen by these clans as the embodiment of Issaq domination of the north. But fighting *against* this threat of clan domination did not mean agreeing with the official pan-Somali ideology, which was locally seen for what it was, i.e. southern domination.

8. For an excellent study on the sub-regional geopolitics see Markus V. Hoehne, *Between Somaliland and Puntland: Marginalization, Militarization and Conflicting Political Visions* (Nairobi: Rift Valley Institute, 2015). It gives a balanced view of the sub-regional clanic relationships and of their global effects.

9. There are a few Warsangeli-related Darood sub-clans in the north-western corner of the country, although they do not make up more than about 5 per cent of the population.

10. Yusuf had parlayed his 1986–91 imprisonment at the hands of Mengistu into a badge of pro-freedom-in-Ethiopia status. Never mind that his imprisonment at the hands of the dictatorship was not due to any embryonic yearning for democracy but for murdering his own subordinates. After being freed, he had become the champion of Addis Ababa in the Somalia melee.

11. This was the largest of the four or five Islamist groupings which were competing to reorganise Somali politics along radical Muslim lines. See Mohamed Abdi Mohamed, 'De l'Islam traditionnel à l'Islam intégriste en Somalie' (Unpublished paper, Besançon, February 1995) and Roland Marchal, 'Mapping Political Islam in Somalia' (European Union paper, October 2013). After their defeat, the al-Ittihad fighters fled first to Laas Qoray in Somaliland where they were not welcomed; they later went all the way down south to Gedo.

12. In fact it was chosen on a clanic basis.

13. He had been shot in a skirmish in August 1996.

14. He was an interpreter and never in a combat role. Further in the text, 'Aydid' will refer to his son Hussein, who attempted to fill his father's position after his demise.

15. In fact the Somalilanders never use the word 'secession (*kala go*) but rather 're-establishment' (*dib ula soo noqosho*), meaning back to the four days during which Somaliland was independent from Great Britain before joining Somalia Italiana.

16. Radio Hargeisa broadcast, 10 April 1995.

17. *Africa Confidential* 36, 19 (22 September 1996).

18. Radio Hargeisa, 15 January 1996.

19. The gap was financed by printing inflationary shillings, by diaspora remittances and by customs: nothing with much of a future. See 'Somaliland: Shrinking Horizons', *Africa Confidential*, 16 February 1996.
20. Radio Hargeisa, 6 July 1996.
21. The number ultimately rose to over thirty.
22. Abdel Nasir Jama Barre, *The New African*, January 1998.
23. A dispute about border delimitation in Badme, an area without either economic or strategic interest. Issayas Afeworqi was persuaded that the new Ethiopian regime, which he had helped set up in 1991, was so unpopular that it would collapse under the slightest impact. But he failed to factor in his own unpopularity with Ethiopian public opinion, only managing to raise support for Meles Zenawi, who became a symbol of Ethiopian nationalism and resistance.
24. Ethiopia had multiplied armed interventions in Somalia to support useless 'peace agreements' and hosted still another international conference in Addis Ababa on 21 October 1998.
25. An AK-47, which cost $225 in Karan market in Mogadishu in January, had dropped to $137 in March 1999.
26. Wako Gutu (1924–2006) was the grandfather of all Oromo rebellions in Bale, who had fought the central Ethiopian domination since the days of Haile Selassie.
27. AFP dispatch, 9 April 1999.
28. IRIN interview, 18 May 1999.
29. AFP dispatch, 6 June 1999.
30. AFP dispatch, 28 June 1999.
31. At first the phenomenon was limited to Mogadishu itself.
32. AFP dispatches, 28 June and 10 July 1999.
33. *Indian Ocean Newsletter*, 9 October 1999.
34. EU confidential memo, Brussels, 15 December 1999.
35. Reuters dispatch, 19 February 2000.
36. Reuters dispatch, 12 March 2000.
37. Arta is a high-altitude small town above Djibouti. The atmosphere there is a bit cooler. The delegates were 500 at first and 2,500 after a few weeks. The food budget went from a planned $1.8m to an actual $7m and nobody even dared to publish the telephone bill.
38. David Stephen, UN Secretary-General Kofi Annan's Special Representative, IRIN, 8 May 2000.
39. *Financial Times*, 15 August 2000.
40. 60% of the TNA members were former MPs in the so-called parliament of the Siad Barre regime.
41. Ken Menkhaus, *Somalia: Situation Analysis* (Geneva: UNHCR, October 2000).
42. *Jamhuuriya*, 21 June 2000.
43. IRIN interview, 11 July 2000.

44. Somalia had been an Arab League member since 1978.
45. Mohamed Ibrahim Egal, Letter to Randolph Kent, 4 November 2000.
46. IRIN interview of Mohamed Ibrahim Egal, 28 May 2001.
47. IRIN, 20 June 2001. The only part of Somaliland where there was a lower pro-independence vote was in Sool province (54.73%) where the Dhulbahante vote was more divided.
48. This was fierce and domestic since in both cases the organisations had a majority Hawiye support. So the fighting often involved Hawiye sub-clans, with whatever majority they could mobilise locally.
49. The Hawala are money transfer networks in the Muslim world that operate very efficiently. The US authorities decided, after a quick perusal, that these must have been the financing channels of al-Qaida. Eventually the Commission of Inquiry on the 9/11 attacks concluded that al-Qaida had mostly used US banks to finance the attack and not Hawala. But this clarification took five years.
50. The decision had been taken before the 9/11 attack.
51. He was by birth an Ethiopian.
52. CRS communiqué, 17 January 2002.
53. IRIN interview, 18 January 2002. The gentleman forgot to say that he himself was very much part of the problem.
54. Private interview, Paris, 6 May 2002. The Ethiopian Army was unofficially supporting the TNG.
55. *The Economist*, 1 April 2004. There were several illiterate MPs.
56. *The New Vision*, 26 May 2004.
57. Its name had been changed to Transitional Federal Government (TFG).
58. BBC, 3 October 2005.
59. Declaration of Sheikh Sharif Sheikh Ahmed, UIC chairman to IRIN, 7 February 2005.
60. He had picked a monstrous cabinet of 127 ministers in the hope of satisfying as many clans as possible.
61. To be fair one must remember that when Usama bin Laden was forced to leave Khartoum, he had considered going to Somalia. But his close counsellors advised him against the move, telling him: 'the way things are there, they will simply sell you to the highest bidder' (Private interview, Khartoum, 1997).
62. ICG, *Counter-Terrorism in Somalia: Losing Hearts and Minds* (Brussels: ICG, July 2005).
63. John Prendergast, 'How the War on Terror Is Empowering Islamist Militias', *The East African*, 12 June 2006.
64. Private interview with a State Department official, April 2006.
65. *Sudan Tribune*, 12 April 2006.
66. 'My government does not believe that Somaliland (or Kenya) are under any immediate threat': Fuad Aden Ade, Somaliland Minister of Foreign Affairs, 31 July 2006.

67. Interview, Mogadishu, April 2014.

68. On 8 December 2006, Meles had been visited by US CENTCOM Commander General John Abizaid, whom Meles asked about war in Somalia. Abizaid had answered, 'You'll be on your own if you attack' (private interview with an EU civil servant who had attended, Addis Ababa, November 2012).

69. In February 2007, IGASOM was 'Africanised' by getting its name changed into AMISOM (African Mission).

70. In March 2007 crowds in the Barawa neighborhood of Mogadishu took the bodies of five TFG soldiers, shouting 'Ethiopian stooges', 'Down with Somali troops' and 'We will burn you alive'. To help the TFG troops, Ethiopians used tanks in the streets, killing a number of civilians (*The New Vision*, 21 March 2007).

71. Human Rights Watch letter to the Kenyan Ministry of Foreign Affairs, New York, 22 March 2007. HRW writes of over 150 individuals from 18 nationalities detained and held incommunicado in Kenya for interrogation by US secret services. Several later disappeared in Ethiopian jails.

72. Steve Schippert, 'Do or Die in Somalia', Front Page Magazine.com, 3 April 2007.

73. Jim Michaels, 'U.S. Tries New Strategy in Somalia', *USA Today*, 4 April 2007.

74. *The Economist*, 7 April 2007.

75. The first AMISOM troops (about 1,200 Ugandans) had landed on 1 March in Baidoa.

76. *The Somaliland Times*, 2 June 2007.

77. Private interview with US diplomat, Nairobi, June 2007.

78. *The Nation* (Nairobi), 9 July 2007.

79. Michael Ranneberger was then US Ambassador to Kenya and covered Somalia from Nairobi.

80. Private interview with US diplomat, Nairobi, June 2007.

81. In April a US Navy frigate had bombarded the Cal Madow mountains (in Puntland) to dislodge an alleged Islamist group, killing nearly one hundred civilians (estimated). The fear was that Dhulbahante sub-clans hostile to the Issaq would help the 'Islamists' and let them spread into Nugaal.

82. Amnesty International communiqué, 4 September 2007.

83. UDUB was the presidential party and Kulmiye the main opposition. According to the new set of laws recently enacted by Hargeisa, there could only be three political parties allowed to compete in elections. This was designed to prevent the multiplication of micro-clanic parties but it was accompanied by an atmosphere of media control.

84. *Somaliland Times* website, 1 September 2007.

85. Reuters dispatch, 17 November 2007.

86. May 2020. Al-Shabaab had been the name popularly given by the public to the military arm of the UIC.

87. This is my own estimate after talking and asking several researchers who were

'Shabaab observers' (this is not my case). These figures are impressionistic and they are impossible to prove. But they offer a reasonable order of magnitude.

11. FROM SURVIVAL TO GLOBALISATION: WHAT IS THE NEED FOR A NATION-STATE IN SOMALILAND?

1. IRIN interview, 2 May 2007.
2. Sheikh Sharif Sheikh Ahmed, the former UIC chairman, had declared that the only question preventing a reconciliation conference from being convened was the presence of Ethiopian troops on Somali territory (AFP dispatch, 24 May 2007).
3. IRIN interview, 16 July 2015.
4. 'Transfer Window', *The Economist*, 17 October 2015.
5. *Terrorism Monitor* 6, 23 (8 December 2008).
6. UN Monitoring Group for Somalia, *Report* (July 2012).
7. Which posed the question: who deals with an unrecognised state? In that case it was the Ethiopian Foreign Affairs Deputy Minister Tekeda Alemu and the British Deputy Head of Mission in Addis Ababa John Marshall.
8. The 17% balance of the vote had gone to Faysal Ali Warabe, the UCID candidate.
9. 'Drought-displaced families seek shelter in Somaliland' (IRIN communiqué, 29 July 2011); 'Somalia: Security risks overshadow aid delivery' (IRIN communiqué, 1 August 2011).
10. For more details on this essential development, see below.
11. Abdullahi Ali Barre was the president of the money changers' trade union. He had been jailed because he refused to use the official change rate of 6,800 shillings to the US dollar while the actual free market rate had reached 9,000 shillings.
12. Michael Keating, letter to Abdullahi Mohamed 'Farmajo', 3 September 2017.
13. Mohamed Ibrahim Egal, 'The Poisoned Chalice and the Sabotage of Somaliland', *Berbera News*, 21 November 2008.
14. It was the same preoccupation with international authority that later drove him to try reaffirming his position by organizing the dubious 'Brexit' referendum of 2016.
15. Confidential interviews with US State Department and CIA specialists, Washington, October 2012.
16. There was still a small residual 'Somaliland lobby' at the Foreign Office. But this 'decoupling' from Somaliland partly explains the use of ed-Dam al-Jadid.
17. Alex de Waal, 'Getting Somalia Right This Time', *New York Times*, 21 February 2012.
18. Rasna Warah, 'Two Thirds of Donor Aid to Somalia Stolen', *The East African*, 24 July 2012.
19. A second one had taken place a year later (7–8 May 2013).
20. For the names and positions see the *Indian Ocean Newsletter*, 17 May 2013.
21. This word should be taken etymologically, not in contemporary historical per-

spective. Al-Shabaab always remained faithful to the al-Qaida line and fought resolutely against any attempt by Daesh to replace it.

22. One constant in the eschatological approach of Islam is to put the essentials of metaphysics in the past. Happiness is supposed to be a return to the time of 'the well-advised caliphs'.

23. James M. Dorsey, 'The Gulf Crisis: Small States Battle It Out', SSRN blog, 25 July 2017. This fifteen-page presentation is a remarkably detailed introduction to al-Fitna al-Qabira, 'the Great Quarrel', which underpins a very large part of the Muslim world's international relations today.

24. Out of a ten million residential population, only 11% are citizens while 89% are foreigners whose main loyalty is to their pay cheque.

25. Particularly its air force whose combat aircraft (140 French and US fighter-bombers) are in top condition. The navy is not really capable of carrying out large missions while at about 70,000 (including 30% of foreigners) the ground forces are the most efficient for their size in the Middle East apart from those of the Jordanian Army.

26. This eventually led to the so-called 'Abraham Agreement' of 13 August 2020 which paved the way to the recognition of the Israeli State by the U.A.E.

27. The relationship of the UAE with its Saudi 'ally' in the Yemen war is typical of the difference both in strategic thinking (or lack thereof) and practical efficiency.

28. Yusuf al-Qaradawi, 'The Legitimacy of Peaceful Demonstration', Facebook, 27 November 2013, link does not work. think it might be: https://www.facebook.com/alqaradawy/posts/672339929472741?streamref=5.

29. Glen Greenwald, 'How Former Treasury Officials and the UAE Are Manipulating American Journalists', https://firstlook.org/theintercept/2014/09/25/uae-qatar-camstoll-group.

30. There had been a series of prudent preliminary discussions that were kept secret.

31. The UAE landed in Bosaso (Puntland) roughly at the same time as it began to form its Somaliland beachhead.

32. Since May 2016, the UAE have been careful to present only their commercial Dubai face to Hargeisa and never their political Abu Dhabi side. International recognition has been dangled in front of the Somaliland regime but never seriously supported in New York or elsewhere by MBZ.

33. Dubai Mall, Dubai Marina, artificial sea-borne prestige housing, these elements of a tourism public scene resemble the Hilton girls, famous because they are well known. But 80 million visitors a year come anyway, giving reality to this life-size human entertainment park.

34. By this we mean the authoritarian management of a moderate apolitical Islam.

35. In 2006 DP World had bought this grand old British colonial institution for $6.8bn. It was meant to be used for handling the clientele of smaller harbours. In Somalia it was P&O which signed a contract for the handling and development

of Bosaso in Puntland (6 April 2017). Contrary to the Berbera deal, it caused no conflict with the Mogadishu government because of Puntland's non-secessionist precautions.

36. Turkey, which had a military base in Qatar, sent reinforcements.

37. To this one might add the nervousness of the EPRDF regime towards the wave of democratisation threatening authoritarian governments during the Arab Spring.

38. The word *fitna* in Arabic has a multiplicity of connotations linked with both politics and religion. The 5 June 2017 Saudi initiative has opened a major split in the Muslim world—not only in the Arab world—since Turkey and Iran have joined the Qatari camp.

39. Reuters dispatch, 25 April 2018.

40. *The East African*, 23 May 2018.

41. Those who had fought (and the civilians) but not the majority of the SNM leadership including Abdirahman 'Tuur', who proclaimed independence against his will.

42. Mohamed Ibrahim Egal, IRIN interview, 28 May 2001.

43. Becoming recently recognised as a full state by Taiwan (June 2020) unfortunately might be for Somaliland a decoy akin to Biafra's reconnaissance by Nyerere's Tanzania and Kaunda's Zambia in 1968.

44. For a remarkably clear summary of the confused situation, see Kristian C. Ulrichsen, link does not work. think it might be: https://pomeps.org/endgames-for-saudi-arabia-and-the-united-arab-emirates-in-yemen.

45. John Boardman, *The Greek Overseas: Early Colonies and Trade* (London: Thames and Hudson, 1999).

46. Josephine Quinn, *In Search of the Phoenicians* (Princeton: Princeton University Press, 2017).

47. Phillip Dollinger, *The German Hansa* (Stanford: Stanford University Press, 1970).

48. D.S. Chambers, *The Imperial Age of Venice (1380–1580)* (London: Thames and Hudson, 1970).

49. François Gipouloux, *The Asian Mediterranean* (Cheltenham: Elgar, 2011).

50. For a reflection on this topic, see John Agnew, 'The Territorial Trap: The Geographical Assumptions of International Relations Theory', *Review of International Political Economy* 1, 1 (Spring 1994), pp. 53–80.

51. The exact number will never be known. But I remember interviewing a man who had fought the Americans on that day and telling him: 'You had to lose a massive number of people to get eighteen "Gal" (Christians).' He grinned and replied: 'About 1,500. But there was a huge difference in firepower.'

52. Interview, Hargeisa, November 2017.

53. Since the issuing of the '1992 Consensus' rather than demanding full recognition as the representative of China, the RoC has settled for a 'dual recognition' system. But Beijing has not reciprocated and keeps insisting on a single and exclusive recognition of the PRC as China's sole representative.

54. The only recent study on Djibouti and its multinational military role can be found in Sonia Le Gouriellec, *Djibouti: la diplomatie de géant d'un petit état* (Lille, Septentrion, 2020).
55. The new name of Swaziland.
56. Conversation with a Taiwanese (Hargeisa, December 2017).
57. Djibouti's debt to China represented 303% of the country's GDP in February 2019.
58. After the 15 July 2016 Gülenist coup attempt in Turkey, Erdogan demanded from the various Somali political entities that they expelled Turkish citizens linked with the putschists. While Mogadishu complied immediately with the demand, Hargeisa answered that since the persons targeted had no criminal record in Somaliland, there was no legal reason for an expulsion.

SELECT BIBLIOGRAPHY

Abdurahman M. Abdullahi (Baadiyow), *The Islamic Movement in Somalia (1950–2000)*. London: Adonis and Abbey, [2010] [A study centred on al-Islah but providing a global description].

Africa Watch, *A Government at War with Its Own People: Testimonies about the Killings and the Conflict in the North*. New York: Human Rights Watch, 1990 [The basic document that chronicled the tearing apart of Somaliland from the rest of Somalia].

Ali Jimal Ahmed (ed.), *The Invention of Somalia*. Lawrenceville: Red Sea Press, 1995 [Relativises the view of Somalia as a fully homogeneous society].

Bradbury, M., *Becoming Somaliland*. Oxford: James Currey, 2008 [An overall study of how Somaliland came into being].

Einashe, I. and M. Kennard, 'In the Valley of Death: Somaliland's Forgotten Genocide', *The Nation*, 22 October 2018 [Deals with the northern massacres of the war years from the angle of forensic medicine and attempted genocide].

Fontrier, M., *Annales de Somalie, vol. 1. L'Etat démantelé (1991–1995)* Paris: L'Harmattan, 2012 [A step-by-step account of the Somali civil war after the collapse of the state].

———, *Annales de Somalie, vol. 2. L'illusion du chaos (1995–2000)* Paris: L'Harmattan, 2015 [A continuation of the above, with the same precision].

Hansen, S.J., *Al-Shabaab in Somalia*. London: Hurst, 2013 [An analytical work by a scholar who worked in close contact with his dangerous subject].

Harun, Maruf and J. Dan, *Inside al-Shabaab*. Bloomington: University of Indiana Press, 2018 [The best informed and factually straight journalism].

Hersi, Mohamed Farah, 'Somaliland's New Cold War Diplomacy', *Ethiopia Insight*, 6 September 2020 [a comprehensive effort at assessing Somaliland's "recognition" by the Republic of China]

Hoehne, M.V., *Between Somaliland and Puntland: Marginalization, Militarization and Conflicting Political Visions*. Nairobi: The Rift Valley Institute, 2015 [A focused study of political ethnology].

Hoehne, M.V. and V. Luling (eds.), *Milk and Peace, Drought and War: Somali Culture, Society and Politics*. London: Hurst, 2010 [Essays in homage to the great historian and analyst of Somali culture, I.M. Lewis].

Ingiriis, M.H., 'The Making of the 1990 Manifesto: Somalia's Last Chance for State Survival', *Journal of Northeast African Studies* 12, 2 (2012), pp. 63–94 [How contingent factors can turn into historical consequences].

International Crisis Group, *Averting War in Northern Somalia*. Brussels: ICG, June 2018.

———, *Somaliland: Democratisation and Its Discontents*. Brussels: ICG, July 2003.

———, *Somaliland: The Strains of Success*. Brussels: ICG, October 2015.

Kapteijns, L., *Clan Cleansing in Somalia: The Ruinous Legacy of 1991*. Philadelphia: University of Pennsylvania Press, 2013 [An analysis of the crucial moment when Somalia turned into a completely unmanageable polity].

Keating, M. and M. Waldman (eds.), *War and Peace in Somalia: National Grievances, Local Conflict and al-Shabaab*. London: Hurst, 2018 [A massive compendium of the contemporary Somali world; useful as a reference book].

Laitin, D.L., *Politics, Language and Thought: The Somali Experience*. Chicago: University of Chicago, 1977 [On the interrelationship between culture and politics in Somali society].

Lewis, I.M., *A Pastoral Democracy*. London: Oxford University Press, 1982 [1961] [A model of the traditional Somali world by a colonial anthropologist; time-frozen but absolutely fundamental].

———, *Blood and Bone: The Call of Kinship in Somali Society*. Lawrenceville: Red Sea Press, 1994 [Concrete structural examples illustrating the essential role of kinship in Somali society].

———, *Understanding Somalia and Somaliland*. London: Hurst, 2008 [A slim pocket-sized encyclopedia of the essentials of the Somali world].

Michailof, S., *Africanistan: Development or Jihad*. Oxford: Oxford University Press, 2018 [Centred on the Western Sahel, this book's analysis is highly relevant to Somaliland].

Millman, B., *British Somaliland: An Administrative History (1920–1960)*. London: Routledge, 2014 [The only published account of the colonial history of Somaliland].

Notten, M. van, *The Law of the Somalis*. Trenton: Red Sea Press, 2005 [On how clanic *Xeer* is more powerful than Shari'ah in the Somali world].

Reenders, M., *Consider Somaliland: State Building with Traditional Leaders and Institutions*. Leiden: Brill, 2012 [A description of contemporary Somaliland which puts a special emphasis on how the society used its traditional traits to stabilise its functioning].